RSAC

D1553643

RIGHTS FOR VICTIMS OF CRIME

RIGHTS FOR VICTIMS OF CRIME

Rebalancing Justice

Irvin Waller

ROWMAN & LITTLEFIELD PUBLISHERS, INC.
Lanham • Boulder • New York • Toronto • Plymouth, UK

Published by Rowman & Littlefield Publishers, Inc.
A wholly owned subsidiary of
The Rowman & Littlefield Publishing Group, Inc.
4501 Forbes Boulevard, Suite 200, Lanham, Maryland 20706
http://www.rowmanlittlefield.com

Estover Road, Plymouth PL6 7PY, United Kingdom

Copyright © 2011 by Rowman & Littlefield Publishers, Inc.

All rights reserved. No part of this book may be reproduced in any form or by
any electronic or mechanical means, including information storage and retrieval
systems, without written permission from the publisher, except by a reviewer
who may quote passages in a review.

British Library Cataloguing in Publication Information Available

Library of Congress Cataloging-in-Publication Data

Waller, Irvin.
  Rights for victims of crime : rebalancing justice / Irvin Waller.
    p. cm.
  Includes index.
  ISBN 978-1-4422-0705-9 (cloth : alk. paper)—ISBN 978-1-4422-0707-3
(electronic)
  1. Victims of crimes—Civil rights. 2. Victims of crimes—Government policy.
I. Title.
  HV6250.25.W35 2011
  362.88—dc22

                                              2010022080

∞™ The paper used in this publication meets the minimum requirements of
American National Standard for Information Sciences—Permanence of Paper
for Printed Library Materials, ANSI/NISO Z39.48-1992.

Printed in the United States of America.

CONTENTS

FIGURES

ABBREVIATIONS

BJS: Bureau of Justice Statistics, the agency responsible for producing and disseminating statistics on victimization and other criminal justice issues in the Office of Justice Programs, U.S. Department of Justice.

CDCP: Centers for Disease Control and Prevention, a component of the U.S. Department of Health and Human Services, located in Atlanta, Georgia. Here it refers mainly to the Division of Violence Prevention, which is part of the National Center for Injury Prevention and Control.

DWI: Driving while intoxicated—refers to crimes committed when the driver of a vehicle is impaired.

FBI: The Federal Bureau of Investigation, an agency of the U.S. Department of Justice. Its main function is to do skilled detective work on major offenses. It publishes the UCR (see below).

GAO: Government Accountability Office, mandated to assess implementation of the Justice for All Act.

IACP: International Association of Chiefs of Police, the world's largest nonprofit association of police executives with 20,000 members from the United States, Canada, and other countries. Its headquarters are located near Washington, DC.

IBCR: International Bureau for Children's Rights, based in Montreal, Canada.

ICVS: The International Crime Victim Survey, which focuses on a representative national sample of 2,000 respondents in most major developed countries. It is completed every five years and asks a number of questions important to this book that are not included in NCVS (see below).

INTERVICT: The International Victimology Institute Tilburg was established to use knowledge about victims of crime and remedies to their problems to better implement rights for victims of crime.

IOVA: International Organization for Victim Assistance, based in Newberg, Oregon. It was established to make a difference to victims and survivors across the world. Its founders combine many decades of experience working with victims of crime.

MADD: Mothers Against Drunk Driving, an organization that leads legislative battles to reform U.S. state and national laws on drinking and driving.

Magna Carta: An abbreviation for the Declaration on Basic Principles of Justice for Victims of Crime and Abuse of Power (1985)

NCVS: The Bureau of Justice Statistics undertakes the National Crime Victimization Survey every year to provide national statistics on the victimization of adults (including whether they reported the crime to the police).

NIJ: National Institute of Justice, the agency that funds research on victimization and criminal justice issues. It is part of the Office of Justice Programs, U.S. Department of Justice.

NOVA: National Organization for Victim Assistance, a network of persons working to provide assistance to victims of crime. It promotes rights and services for victims who have suffered from crime and other crises.

NRC (U.S.): National Research Council, part of the United States' National Academies, which enlists the foremost scientists in the United States to provide policy advice under a congressional charter. The Institute of Medicine is a component.

NVCAP: National Victims Crime Amendment Passage, a group that came together to promote a victims' rights amendment to the U.S. Constitution.

OVC: Office for Victims of Crime, established by the Victims of Crime Act in 1984 and a component of the U.S. Department of Justice.

PTSD: Post-traumatic stress disorder (see the American Psychiatric Association Diagnostic Standards Manuals IV and V) is a set of psychological symptoms that victims of crime may experience. Common symptoms include sleeplessness, inability to return to work, and frequent reliving of the trauma.

UCR: Uniform Crime Report, issued every year by the FBI to provide statistics on crime in the United States. It is limited to crime recorded by police departments.

VAWA: Violence Against Women Act, first passed in 1993, revised and reauthorized in 2000 and 2005, and slated for reauthorization in 2010.

VOCA: Victims of Crime Act, passed in 1984.

VSE: Victim Support Europe, a network of the national victim assistance organizations in Europe, has played a key role in recommending improvements in the delivery of services for victims of crime as well as equity between victims and offenders in courtrooms.

WHO: World Health Organization, headquartered in Geneva, Switzerland. The WHO's section on Violence, Injuries, and Disability has done landmark work to advance the prevention of violence, traffic injuries, child maltreatment, and gender-based violence.

WSV: World Society of Victimology, a non-profit nongovernmental organization that aims to advance victimological research and practices around the world.

FOREWORD

In January of 1987, after my brother was murdered, I encountered the criminal justice system with new eyes. My viewpoint suddenly shifted from that of a very successful criminal defense attorney to that of a victim of crime and a victims' advocate. I realized firsthand how problematic the criminal justice process was for crime victims and their families. As a defense attorney I had known the concerns of criminal defendants and had supported their need for balance and fairness in a justice process that often diminished their lives. But suddenly I became aware of how often the lives of victims and surviving family members were likewise diminished by the lack of access to, and standing in, the criminal justice system.

At the age of forty, I was appointed a chief justice of the Texas Court of Appeals in El Paso. One of the first things I did—without fully appreciating the national consequences of my actions—was to stop the traditional protocol found in appellate opinions of calling a victim an "alleged victim" or a "complainant." By the time cases reached my chambers, years after the initial victimizations, the grass may have grown over the graves but the hurt was not forgotten. The victims stood before me not as "alleged victims," but as true memorials to a criminal justice system out of balance.

Rights for Victims of Crime: Rebalancing Justice embraces critical issues that I embrace. It calls upon everyone to recognize the fact that, for all the progress that has been made, there is a new need for leadership.

More Offices for Victims of Crime, clear professional standards for victim assistance providers, and ombudspersons for victims. It also calls for the establishment of institutes for victim services and rights. Whether or not these are limited to research and development and based in a university setting, the very proposal reflects the vision of Benjamin Mendelssohn when he first proposed such institutes in the late 1940s. And although this idea has been late in coming, I firmly believe that now is the time to bring it to fruition in North America and that such institutes should include all levels of educational and training opportunities including those that might exist at high schools, community colleges, and vocational schools across North America.

Rights for Victims of Crime: Rebalancing Justice focuses on the next steps forward for victims: comprehensive laws, permanent funding, and rights. Professor Waller's analysis of how funding and resources could be allocated to bring about real solutions is enlightening and is sure to inspire my colleagues in the victims' movement as they continue their pursuit of a proper balance of the constitutional rights of criminal defendants with those of victims of crime.

I encourage anyone who has been a victim of crime in any sense of the word, or anyone who knows someone who has been touched by the criminal element, to read and embrace this book. It is a work that people must hold up to their legislators to demand that victims' issues be urgently addressed through legislation that will change our national agendas. Only then will we see a proper balance of justice in our society.

Chief Justice Richard Barajas (ret.)
Texas Court of Appeals, El Paso

ACKNOWLEDGMENTS

This short book prepares its readers to advocate for the rights of victims of crime. It shares what I have learned from the leading advocates across the world over four decades. I have been inspired by many exceptional and dedicated individuals, but none more than Marlene Young, through her speeches, her vision, her academic knowledge and her ability to put it all together so that victims of crime could have a better life.

My active engagement in shifting public policy to respect the rights and needs of victims of crime started in 1982 as we moved mountains in just three years to get the General Assembly of the United Nations to adopt the *magna carta* for victims of crime. Elias Carranza, Yael Danieli, Matti Joutsen, Irene Melup, Leroy Lamborn, and Claudio Stampalija were my partners, friends, and teachers. It continues today in the International Organization for Victim Assistance with the brilliance, vision, and commitment of John Stein, Karen McLauglin, and Sherry Young. You are the unsung heroes, whose outrage at the lack of justice and caring for victims of crime has fired our lifelong pursuit of justice and caring where it is still needed most. You have taught me many things, but more than anything that we *can* and *will* make a difference.

From the 1980s forward, I was lucky to be inspired by the pioneers on the board of the National Organization for Victim Assistance. I am grateful for the bravery of so many of the leaders of the World Society of Victimology who knew that academic debate without practical outcomes is not fighting for justice. To mention but a few—K. Chockalingam, Sarah Ben David, John Dussich, Paul Friday, Ester Kosowski, Marc Groenhuijsen, Maria de la Luz Lima, Hidemichi Morozawa, Helen Reeves, Chris Sumner, Paul Separovic, Jan van Dijk, and Ray Whitrod.

In Canada, I am grateful for the guidance, encouragement, and inspiration from so many, including Micheline Baril, Ruth Campbell, Arlene Gaudreault, Ross Hastings, Heidi Illingworth, Holly Johnson, Sharon and Gary Rosenfeld, Steve Sullivan, Claude Vézina, and Priscilla de Villiers. In Washington, I appreciate the support and trust of new friends as we fight on the front lines for victims' rights, particularly Steve Derene and Anne Seymour.

We have made progress, but as this book shows, there is much more progress for the next generation to make. Elmar Weitekamp, Dick Andzenge, Marian Hilft, Gerd Kirchhoff, and Robert Peacock and their network from the Dubrovnik course are inspiring a growing number of young people from across the world with their teaching and commitment to social justice. We are lucky to have the brilliance and commitment of so many—Maria Josefina Ferrer, Veronica Martinez, Emilio Jose Garcia, Sam Garkawe, Michael O'Connell, JoAnne Wemmers, and Xin Ren.

I acknowledge the editorial skills and support of Elizabeth Bond in completing this manuscript.

And last but not least, I'd like to dedicate this book to Susan and our growing family, whose patience and support is immeasurable.

INTRODUCTION

Reinvigorating the Victim Rights Movement

Despite a decrease in rates of crime by 40 percent or more in the 1990s, more than 20 million Americans will still be victims of crime this year. That's more than one in ten Americans over the age of twelve. Although the majority of victims of violence will be male, nearly a million women will be victims of sexual assault this year alone. Another million women will be victims of violence at the hands of an intimate partner at least once over the next twelve months. What's more, three-quarters of a million children are reported as being victims of abuse—and sadly, the real number of young victims is likely much, much higher.

Economists have added up the costs of medical care, mental health counseling, property damage and loss, and work days lost for victims in the United States and have found that these exceed $100 billion a year. And if they factor in the pain and suffering lived by victims—assuming that a monetary value could ever be put on such a thing—the total damage and losses exceed $450 billion. Proportionate to population, the picture is similar in Canada and in England and Wales.

Many victims will not report the crime to the police. Those who do will experience the disillusionment of being a witness rather than a client—that is, they will be treated as a disenfranchised bystander to their own experience rather than being a first among equals with a voice. Initially lost to the aggression of the accused, victims have difficulty regaining their personal power. Not surprisingly, this leaves a lot of victims (who are taxpayers and voters, don't forget) disillusioned, indignant, and angry. All victims in the United States are now entitled by law to a variety of basic services, but many of these people will still find law enforcement officers and judges who do not have the time or inclination to respect those laws because they are preoccupied with enforcing the laws that affect the perpetrators.

Today, victims aren't the only ones who know about the pain, shock, humiliation, loss of control, and powerlessness that victims of crime experience at the hands of their offenders. A growing number of advocates and social scientists know only too well how feelings of anger, depression, worthlessness, and fear oscillate and reverberate over the weeks, months, years, and even decades following a victimizing incident. While law enforcement agents and judges may not be inclined to transfer their focus to the victim, many of these advocates and social scientists are experts in how to respond to victims in caring and just ways, and in some cases they even have solutions to stop victimization from happening in the future.

More often than not, we know how to provide emotional support and counseling to victims. We know how to protect the victim from the accused and how to give the victim a voice and power in the criminal justice system. We know how to inform victims of services that will help them and how to get them access to those services. We even know how to pay their mounting bills and how to stop much of the violence. In sum, we have the solutions as to how to put victims back in the center of our support, reparation, and justice systems. It is baffling, then, why governments are still not doing enough to apply this knowledge.

If you are robbed while walking down the street, it should be your right to expect other citizens to come to your aid. If you call the police, it should be your right to expect the responding officer to listen to you, to protect you, and to tell you about what he or she will do next. It should be your right to have law enforcement help you to access social or medical assistance and inform you of what services are available to support you. Unfortunately, these obvious, inalienable rights are a reality only in some places, and only some of the time.

If you are a victim of sexual assault, it should be your right to speak to an officer or counselor of the same gender if you so wish. It should be your right to get medical attention and counseling to help you recover. It should be your right to get reliable information on how to avoid being attacked again. It should be your right to have reparation ordered from the offender and have assistance getting that reparation. If you are injured and the offender cannot pay reparation, it should be your right to be afforded compensation from the state. It should be your right to participate in the criminal court process with legal representation to protect your safety, your search for the truth, and your need for reparation and justice. Again, these obvious, inalienable rights do not yet apply in many areas across the United States and around the world.

This book aims to demand that these obvious, inalienable rights for victims of crime be met and that justice be rebalanced with victims in mind. It makes the case for action and identifies what precise and measured responses are needed. Most importantly, it shows how these actions can be funded and implemented.

SEEDS OF HOPE: PROGRESS IN THE PAST TWENTY-FIVE YEARS

In the 1960s, policy makers listened to the rallying cry of Margery Fry, a British magistrate and penal reformer. She was outraged that victims of crime were not able to get the same compensation for their injuries as persons hurt in car crashes or industrial accidents. Governments in New Zealand, England, Wales, and California responded by establishing the first state-run compensation programs for victims of violent crimes.

In the 1970s, a number of new and important social movements came together in response to the urgent need to provide services and rights for victims of crime. One such movement was the feminist movement, which fought tirelessly for change. Not only did they point out the patriarchal nature of rape and domestic abuse, but they also started the first rape crisis centers and transition houses for battered women—usually investing their own time and resources rather than being able to draw on government funds.

Prosecutors in the United States who needed to get convictions or who were facing election turned to showing a sympathetic face to victims, and initiated new offices to work with victims as *witnesses*—not as injured parties with a voice. These offices were intended to make the criminal justice and corrections processes shine (not to ensure that the victims who paid their public office salaries with their tax dollars were satisfied clients).

As criminal justice initiatives were expanded throughout communities in the United States, social workers were recruited to work as probation and parole officers. These officers argued that keeping the offender within the community to work and pay restitution to victims of crime was better than placing the offender in prison.

Academic researchers and government statisticians started victimization surveys to better measure crime. Their discovery of the unexpected numbers of victims led to other insights about the nature of crime, its devastating impacts, and the lack of confidence in law enforcement and criminal justice. The emotions and injustices faced by those victims had their own impact on mobilizing some professional researchers to contribute toward rebalancing justice.

From these movements came victim services pioneers who not only championed their own causes, but also came together to form organizations like the National Organization for Victim Assistance (NOVA) in the United States and the National Association of Victim Support Schemes (NAVSS) in the United Kingdom to fight for victims' rights and promote paradigm shifts. The same recurring issues were being brought up in different countries. Academics, practitioners, and legislators began to meet internationally to discuss the plight of victims and to strategize about what could be done. In 1979, these diverse experts formed the World Society of Victimology (WSV) to advance research, services, and awareness for victims.

The actions of these practitioners and professionals were spurred on by a group of victims who turned their outrage into inspiration to fight for change. Marlene Young, who became the executive director of NOVA and acted as the lightning rod for much of this change, recalls four names in particular from the hundreds of victims' advocates who dedicated their lives to the empowerment and service of victims: Betty Jane Spencer, Robert and Charlotte Hullinger, and Candy Lightner.

Spencer, whose four sons were murdered in a bloody massacre in her home near Indianapolis in 1977, became the focal point of Protect the Innocent. The Hullingers, whose teenaged daughter was murdered by her high school ex-boyfriend in Indiana, reached out to others through Parents of Murdered Children, an organization that remains active in several different countries. Lightner, who lost her daughter in a drunk driving crash in California, formed Mothers Against Drunk Driving (MADD), an advocacy group that leads legislative battles to reform state and national laws on drinking and driving.[1] MADD has become one of the most successful voluntary organizations in U.S. history, not to mention a leading advocate

for a victims' rights amendment to the U.S. Constitution. I   ₀   ·
one family's tragedy became the seed for a successful o
advocates for change with a victim-centered approach.

These voices were calling for much more than more la   ꞏ.ꞏꞏꞏꞏꞏꞏꞏement
and criminal justice. They were insisting that justice be rebalanced to ensure that victims of crime are treated with dignity, compassion, and justice.
By the early 1980s, such advocacy had achieved two landmark accomplish-
ments that set the stage for progress over the next twenty-five years.

The first landmark accomplishment of the 1980s was the establishment
of the President's Task Force on Victims of Crime in the United States.
This task force made victims the focus of its mandate and recommended
actions to be taken by the criminal justice system, the health care system,
and other related government divisions. It called for an amendment to
the U.S. Constitution that would give victims a voice in criminal justice
processes. In response, the U.S. Congress adopted the Victims of Crime
Act (VOCA), which precipitated the establishment of a federal Office for
Victims of Crime (OVC). This office was set up with a funding mechanism
that used fines levied against offenders rather than stable local and state
revenues to subsidize its victim assistance and compensation programs.

In 1994, with the persistence of then-senator and now–vice president
Joe Biden, the U.S. Congress adopted the Violence Against Women Act
(VAWA). This act instituted a special office to subsidize programs aimed
at preventing violence against women, improving criminal justice responses, and assisting victims. The most recent renewal of the act in 2005
continued to maintain the important balance between the prevention of
domestic violence, sexual assault, and stalking, as well as the availability
of follow-up services for victims of these crimes. It added an additional
focus on the prevention of human trafficking and the provision of services for trafficking victims.

The other landmark extended these actions across the world and quickly
became known as the *magna carta* for crime victims. This was the Declaration of Basic Principles of Justice for Victims of Crime and Abuse of Power,
which was adopted by all governments of the world without exception at
the United Nations General Assembly on November 29, 1985. With this
declaration, governments recognized that *crime does harm to victims—*
a stark fact pushed aside for centuries by justice systems focused only
on the criminal. They resolved to make every effort to prevent this harm
by investing in education, health and social services, police, and justice

programs. They put rights and support for victims at center stage—not in the shadows—as persons who needed information, social and medical services, restitution from their offenders, compensation from the state, and a meaningful voice in the justice system.

This *magna carta* for crime victims has justified many legislative shifts in Australia, Canada, Europe, and across the world. Most recently, in 2004, Japan moved beyond any other country when its prime minister led the implementation of a national program to provide support, reparation, and justice to victims of crime by investing in national and universal actions based on this declaration.

While other countries cannot boast the ambition of the United States's VOCA and VAWA, these acts are still only partial solutions. France and Japan are just two of the countries that are giving victims credence and a true voice in their respective criminal justice systems—a voice that goes beyond reading a difficult impact statement in court (a distinction that will be discussed in detail in chapter 6). We can also look to England and Wales, which have established a national professional victim support service and code of national standards. Their system of compensation for victims of violence aspires to what is paid in civil judgments, and on average pays three times what is paid in the United States to proportionately three times as many victims.

The United States could look to other countries around the world to see examples of solutions in action. This book will attempt to identify the best of these solutions as best practices, and also will provide its own solutions for rebalancing justice.

WANTED: CHAMPIONS FOR VICTIMS' RIGHTS

It seems that those persons championing justice for victims of crime were celebrating too quickly in the 1980s. If we look to legislators for cues as to where the issue stands on government agendas today, we might be encouraged by the abundance of political rhetoric about fighting crime and protecting victims. But too often such rhetoric is used self-servingly for the expansion of bureaucratic imperatives such as police forces, legal teams, and industrial prison complexes with inadequate direction to ensure they meet the core needs of victims. Actual services for victims such as transition houses, sexual assault crisis centers, child advocacy clinics, and state compensation may have moved beyond depending on bake sales for funding, but they are still poor cousins often lacking permanent funding from general tax revenues.

What is even more disturbing is that the advocates who fought for those landmark advances are now part of a noble but aging generation. The next generations must be invigorated today before we can move forward. That's what this book is about. There is no shortage of victims of crime. But how can potential advocates—victims who have suffered, taxpayers who are not yet victims, professionals working in the field, academics dedicated to knowledge in service of humanity—be invigorated to ensure that every victim has access to a basic set of rights?

If you are one of those many victims, the chances are that you will have already discovered that few people care about your victimization—and worse, that law enforcement and criminal justice systems still treat many victims as witnesses, as evidence, as objects to be used by the system rather than injured parties who deserve basic services and empowerment to fight for their rights. You're likely disillusioned that victims are treated in this manner even though they are the taxpayers who foot the bills for policing and justice.

If you are not one of those victims of crime, you may be in the future. Social responsibility requires you to ensure that your government's systems of justice are fair to all victims, whether they are male or female, black or white, rich or poor, young or old. Despite the numerous speeches and the adoption of UN norms, governments have left victims without universal services, without fair access to reparation, and without any cogent remedies in court. While it is thankfully true that some victims may be treated well by individual police officers, judges, and compensation boards, the unfortunate reality is that many victims of crime will still not have their core needs met, and most will never experience our systems of justice as being fair or just.

A BOOK FOR EVERYONE WHO SEEKS SOLUTIONS

This is the only book on the shelf with the sole purpose of reaching out to the concerned citizen, the taxpayer, and the (potential) victims who pay for the services and the system of justice. It provides general readers with the knowledge of what victims of crime need and how best to make

1em. It brings the realities of what has been achieved in
ims' rights and services together with what it is *possible*
nately presenting a coherent road map of how to truly
benefit victims of crime and their families.

This book is a clarion call for voters and taxpayers to demand significant
change. Every chapter empowers the reader to know what simple and specific actions they must demand of their legislators. The book is not simply a
critical commentary—although it has every right to be just that. We know
that inalienable rights for victims of crime are guaranteed in at least some
places, at least some of the time, so there's no denying that it can be done.
But for some reason, even though it *is* affordable, it is still not happening.
There is absolutely no reason for this.

This book aims to bring into the public spotlight the research and understanding gained by the closed (and often small) circles of academia, professional associations, and lobby groups. It persuades voters and taxpayers to
call on their legislators for:

- police to balance bringing criminals to justice with bringing safety,
  solidarity, justice, and information to victims;
- sustained funding for victim support programs, sexual crisis centers,
  child safety advocacy, domestic violence shelters, centers for families
  surviving homicide, and other similar initiatives to promote healing
  without any cost to victims;
- adequate ways to ensure that restitution is ordered and paid, and
  (where necessary) governments to supplement by providing fair—not
  token—compensation;
- balanced justice systems that provide participation and representation
  for victims to defend their own safety and respect—not just to show
  their pain while perpetrators have the last word; and
- investment in public safety measures that will prevent victimization
  rather than blindly react with massive expenditures on incarceration.

Chapter 1 brings victims of crime out of the shadows, revealing the statistics and realities of the millions who invisibly suffer each year. It helps
victims, their loved ones, and society to understand the impact of crime on
victims' needs. It identifies seven core needs and how government services
must meet these, including empowering victims within the justice system.
Chapter 2 shows how governments across North America and Europe

agree in their proclamations about what must be done. It uses the work by experts to integrate these into a coherent set of inalienable rights and model legislation.

This book also focuses on what *can* and *must* be done in the future. Chapter 3 looks at how victims should be treated by law enforcement. Actions such as listening to victims and helping them know where to get support and compensation are long overdue. The good news is that leading police organizations want to strive to put victims at the zenith of law enforcement. Chapter 4 looks at how we can care for victims and support their recovery and long-term well-being. It assesses the gaps in and needs for sustainable funding. It looks at the role of family, friends, and the medical professions. It also examines the growing group of victim service providers. Chapter 5 explores the ways in which victims receive (or fail to receive) restitution from the offender, compensation from the state, and reparation from others. It looks at how victims might use civil justice processes because they are more empowering to victims than imbalanced criminal justice processes.

Chapter 6 focuses on how victims can (and should) be able to defend their inalienable rights to safety, reparation, and justice through the criminal courts—probably the most urgent issue facing us. Victims must be able to enforce their legislated rights but also defend their inalienable rights to safety, restitution, and justice (as is the case in a growing number of jurisdictions in Europe and Asia). Chapter 7 outlines good news on ways to reduce and prevent victimization so that there will be significantly fewer victims of crime in the future.

Finally, the last chapter assesses the ways that governments around the world have attempted to rebalance outdated systems of criminal justice that exclude victims of crime. We *can* make victims the center of our criminal justice policies, around which enforcement, justice, and sanctions must revolve (and not the reverse). It demonstrates how our limited tax revenues must be better distributed. It proposes a model law that any jurisdiction could adapt to provide those inalienable rights.

This book and its demands for legislators would not be complete without a renewal of the call to amend constitutions and charters of rights and freedoms to give victims equality with perpetrators in defending their own interests in safety, reparation, and justice. And why should it not be so?

$$\textcircled{1}$$

FORGOTTEN BUT STILL HERE

What about Victims of Crime?

When new acquaintances ask me what I do for a living, I say that I collect knowledge to reduce crime and protect victims. Their inevitable response is to talk about the latest arrest or sensational court case dominating the news that week. All too often, they fail to even mention the victim. And they're not the only ones. A massive industry has grown up focused around justice for the *criminal*. It often justifies its actions as fighting for the victims, too, but somehow overlooks their core needs and their right to justice. It's rare that this new industry asks, *What about the victim?*

Every victim of crime is unique. Nobody, no matter what walk of life they are from, is immune to being victimized. It happens to people in every neighborhood in every city across the United States and around the world. Crime knows no class or age boundaries. The rich and poor alike are victimized by crime. Sadly, crimes happen all too often against the very young and the elderly. Some, particularly women and children and those who are victims of sexual assault, suffer disproportionately. Those who lose a loved one in street violence, domestic violence, or in a drunk driving crash know that finality does not bring closure.

For those who have never been a victim of crime (or haven't yet, at least), you can get an idea of what it is like from a composite sketch drawn from the testimonies of many victims given to the U.S. President's Task Force on Victims of Crime in 1982.[1] While some services and some laws have changed since 1982, they have changed much less than they should have. We can be sure, however, that what has not changed is the shock, the pain, the loss, the fear, the insecurity, the guilt, and the indignity that comes with being victimized by crime. The woman in this composite sketch could be you or someone you know.

> You are a 50-year-old woman living alone. You are asleep one night when suddenly you awaken to find a man standing over you with a knife at your throat. As you start to scream, he beats and cuts you. He then rapes you. While you watch helplessly, he searches the house, taking your jewelry, other valuables, and money. He smashes furniture and windows in a display of senseless violence. His rampage ended, he rips out the telephone line, threatens you again, and disappears into the night. At least you have survived.[2]

This forcible rape makes her a victim of violent crime. Assaults on the street, in our homes, in our schoolyards, and at our places of work make adults and children victims of violent crime. Robberies where a perpetrator takes your property with violence make you yet another victim of violent crime.

Every year in the United States, 1.4 million victims of violent crime are treated in hospital emergency rooms for physical injuries. Some are bruised in a fight. Some are knifed, and others are shot. Some victims are injured in a traffic crash at the hands of a drunk driver. Some are sexually assaulted, which is calamitous enough in and of itself, but becomes even more devastating if it leads to pregnancy or sexually communicated diseases like AIDS. Many victims may be able to return to their homes that same day. Others will have to remain in the hospital for days, weeks, or even months. Sadly, other victims of crime will never leave the hospital alive. Every year, 16,000 will die as victims of homicide and 12,000 will die from injuries sustained in a traffic crash where an impaired driver was behind the wheel.

The effects of victimization are not always so visible. Someone forcibly entering your home to steal makes you a victim of burglary. Someone stealing your car makes you a victim of auto theft. Other forms of theft and fraud make you a victim of property crime. The good news is that, in these cases, victims lose property rather than being injured. Nevertheless, victims of property crime suffer a financial loss, and they may also suffer the loss of an object of sentimental value. A wedding ring or a photo of a deceased loved one may not have much monetary value, but it may have irreplaceable emotional value to the victim.

The effects of victimization from property crime can have damaging emotional and psychological effects on victims as well. Victims of burglary are left frightened in their own homes, and sometimes even forced to leave their communities and move to a new neighborhood. Vandalism in the home or women's underwear thrown around with misogynist messages written on mirrors can exacerbate the fear of what would have happened had the victim been in the home at the time of the crime. Many victims of property crime will have private insurance to recover some financial losses, but nothing can mend their emotional losses or make up for their feelings of fear and insecurity.

The victims of violent or property crimes are left in a state of shock, anger, and frustration. Emotional turmoil and fear can often make it difficult for them to sleep or go to work. For some, these ill-effects will pass in a few days or weeks. For others, residual feelings of fear and preoccupation will stay with them for the rest of their lives.

When the crime experienced is life-threatening, or when it involves sexual assault or inflicts serious injury, the victim may continue to experience intrusive recollections and recurring painful feelings associated with the crime. These flashbacks lead to persistent avoidance of feelings and of situations, as well as sleeping difficulties, outbursts of anger, and an exaggerated startle response.

Many victims of crime who suffer in this way may not even know that there is a clinical term for what they are going through—post-traumatic stress disorder (PTSD). For some, these difficulties sleeping, leaving the house, or taking part in their normal activities may endure for many years following their victimization. For a small but important proportion of victims, the severe and enduring trauma of their victimizations or their resulting physical injuries will never go away. They will never have closure. Their families may also suffer trauma, not only in cases of murder or assault, but also in many less-heinous incidents such as burglary.

Three months ago, Wendy was in a major car accident. She sustained only minor injuries, but two friends riding in her car were killed. At first, the accident seemed like just a bad dream. Then Wendy started having nightmares about it: waking up in a cold sweat to the sound of crunching metal and breaking glass. Now, the sights and sounds of the accident haunt her all the time. She has trouble sleeping at night, and during the day she feels irritable and on edge. She jumps whenever she hears a siren or screeching tires, and she avoids all TV programs that might show a car chase or accident scene.

Wendy also avoids driving whenever possible, and refuses to go anywhere near the site of the crash.[3]

PTSD is now part of our everyday language. It is most familiar to us in terms of soldiers returning home from battle situations in Vietnam, Iraq, or Afghanistan, and its symptoms were formerly referred to as "battle fatigue" or "shell shock." Recognition and formal diagnosis of the disorder was originally advocated by mental health workers who were helping victims of rape. PTSD was first included in the third version of the diagnostic standards manual of the American Psychiatric Association in 1980. The definition is being refined in the upcoming fifth edition of the manual. While diagnosis with PTSD may help a victim to recover insurance or restitution from an offender, its recognition does not make the residual feelings any less painful or difficult to bear.

One of the leading experts on PTSD is Dr. Dean Kilpatrick of the Medical University of South Carolina. In an article he published in 2003, he reviewed what was known in the United States about how many people were victims of violent crime every year. He used data from major crime surveys such as the National Crime Victimization Survey (NCVS) and the National Women's Study (NWS). The NCVS is an annual survey of 76,000 households for the Department of Justice that provides the primary source of data about criminal victimization in the United States. The NWS followed women in 4,000 households over a three-year period and was able to measure not only the rates of victimization, but also incidence of mental health problems such as PTSD, depression, and alcohol use. His findings confirm that for females, close to one-third of assault victims and 50 percent of sexual assault victims experience PTSD.[4] For male victims, PTSD is also common in cases of sexual assault (even though such assaults are much less frequent for males than for females). PTSD is less frequent for male victims of other types of assault.[5]

Scientific surveys do not focus on the range of other emotions that are lived by victims of crime. However, interviews with burglary victims recall their upset, anger, and fear. The feelings of fear are more prevalent and persistent for women than for men. Interviews with rape victims point to their concern about being disbelieved, as well as to the difficulties they face in terms of the reactions of males in their social circles. In many cases, victims of crime have to deal with preoccupations such as organizing repairs, cleaning up, and changing locks. In addition to these unwarranted headaches, victims must cope with stressful responsibilities such as visiting doctors, dealing with insurance companies, and emotionally supporting their children or family members through the crisis.

WHY ARE VICTIMS OF CRIME STILL OVERLOOKED?

For two centuries, legislators have focused on offenders and left victims in the shadows—or worse. Government programs, such as law enforcement, criminal courts, and corrections, focus immense resources on justice for the criminal. In the United States, many states now pay more for the law and order industry than for hospitals and health care. The justice system may lead to long periods of incarceration for the offender, but it also leads to charges being dropped, justice delayed for the benefit of the perpetrator, pleas to significantly less-serious offenses, acquittals, and nonpayment of reparation. These expensive bureaucracies guarantee the rights of every accused and convicted person, but they do little to respect the established constitutional and legal rights—let alone the internationally agreed upon human rights—for victims of crime.

In 2010, Senator Jim Webb of Virginia introduced a bill into the U.S. Senate that talked about a broken justice system and called for a blue-ribbon commission to study criminal justice in America. The original bill focused exclusively on the 2.3 million persons incarcerated in the United States. Amazingly, the bill did not mention the numbers of victims or their losses, shame, guilt, pain, or injury.

Modern Detective Stories: More Titillation Than Truth

The news and film industries romanticize the law and order industry without looking at the often-invisible realities of the emotional helter-skelter for victims. At the time of a murder, robbery, act of abuse against a child, or drunk driving incident, the media capitalize on photographs and descriptions of the individual victims of crime to create interest and intensity. But they do not focus on the victim for long.

Today, these approaches to crime are spurred on by multiple television series that seem to thrive on the battle of wits and might between the detectives and the evil suspects. When I talk to students, their interest in and knowledge of crime comes from the excitement of the *who-dunnit* (the criminal investigation), the climax of the *is he guilty?* (the criminal court proceedings), and the finale of the *how much will he get?* (the sentencing decision). The media may make big profits with these approaches—but it's time we asked ourselves, *at whose expense?*

Everyone has heard of O.J. Simpson. They know that he was acquitted by a criminal court in 1994, but ordered to pay millions of dollars in a civil court. But does the average person know the first name of his wife, whose death he was found to have wrongfully caused? Do they know the name of the friend who also wrongfully died? Do they know that those victims' families will never receive even a basic portion of the $8 million reparation order or the $25 million in punitive damages?

Anyone living in North America in the 1970s will be familiar with New York City's modern-day Jack the Ripper. The Son of Sam case illustrates our fascination with the real-life *whodunnit*. But can you recall the names of any of the victims of Son of Sam, despite a book and a movie on the subject?[6] His case even inspired the state of New York to pass legislation that was named after *him* rather than after his maimed and murdered victims. Were books written about how *their* lives were changed or what *they* lost through their victimization? Did Hollywood think to tell *their* stories? Would the public buy books or watch movies about *them*? Sadly, the answer to questions such as these is a lonely, resounding *no*.

Notable Exceptions: High-Profile Victims Can Turn Tragedy into Triumph

Not all victims are easily forgotten, but those who are remembered are the exceptions and their lasting legacies come at a personal cost to themselves and their families. Some victims of violence have turned their anger and outrage into success. They have won battles and stopped legislators from overlooking victims of crime.

One such example of a victim with a legacy is Marsy, a young university student who was murdered by her boyfriend in 1983. Not long after the murder, Marsy's mother was surprised and shocked to meet the accused murderer in a supermarket without knowing that he had been released on bail. Marsy's family spent the next twenty-five years campaigning for reforms to the California constitution. As we will see in chapter 6, Marsy's family succeeded in their petition in 2008, when 54 percent of California residents voted in favor of Proposition 9.

There are other examples of brave and determined survivors speaking out. Eleven-year-old Jacob Wetterling in 1989 and seven-year-old Megan Kanka in 1994 were murdered by sexual predators. Their cases inspired changes in legislation to protect children from known pedophiles. Young Sarah Payne became a household name in England for similar reasons in 2000. As we will discover in chapter 2, her mother was decorated by the British government for her work to promote rights for victims in England. She spent a year straight-talking to government officials about what was needed for victims of crime, and as a result she is credited with the recent move to establish a nationwide professional victim service in England.

Delaware senator Joe Biden—now vice president of the United States—was one of two senators who insisted that the name of Pamela Lychner—an adult victim of a known sexual predator—be added to legislation to track sex offenders. Similarly, the Justice for All Act of 2004 bears the names of Scott Campbell, Stephanie Roper, Wendy Preston, Louarna Gillis, and Nila Lynn, victims whose families have been longtime crusaders for rights for victims of crime.

Survivors themselves can also inspire hope and change. In 2003, Trisha Meili published her book, *I Am the Central Park Jogger: A Story of Hope and Possibility*.[7] She talks about her own victimization and inspires hope in others because of her miraculous ability to heal her body and spirit.

Mere Numbers: Crime Statistics without Human Faces Are Easy to Overlook

Those activists mentioned above have been able to put a face to a statistic and, by so doing, have inspired legislators to act toward rebalancing justice. We must realize, however, that every statistic represents a human tragedy. Each of these victims suffers in some way—through personal loss, injury, trauma, or worse. And each suffers as the result of the aggression of some other self-serving individual who could have chosen not to inflict the harm.

But the old adage is true—one victimization is a tragedy, while a million is a statistic. Governments, law enforcement representatives, and the justice system act as if many millions of victims are just statistics.

Twelve thousand persons killed due to drinking and driving every year in the United States is a statistic easy to disassociate from the pain and suffering caused by each death. However, when MADD puts a face to each victim by telling the stories of what the victims might have achieved in life had the impaired drivers made different choices, we suddenly get a different reaction.[8] This emphasis on the positive, poignant moments of victims' lives makes the stories human. But even this approach glosses over the suffering that was induced immediately following the crash and the families' frustrations at the endless law enforcement and criminal justice antics in pursuit of the offender.

ALL TOO OFTEN: THE TRUTH ABOUT THE FREQUENCY OF VICTIMIZATION

The next sections of this chapter will focus on the unacceptable number of individuals who are victimized each year, in each community in the United States and around the world. This is the bad news before we turn in the later chapters to the good news that we have the knowledge to reduce the number of persons hurt by crime and improve the way that they are treated after the victimization.

How Is Crime Data Collected?

In the 1800s, trends in crime were measured by the number of persons convicted in criminal courts. Then trends were measured using the number of crimes recorded by the police—in the United States, this was based on the FBI's Uniform Crime Reports. However, neither of those methods focused on the number of *victims* of crime. Today, trends in crime are measured using government surveys, such as the National Crime Victimization Survey (NCVS), of the adult population to estimate numbers of victims.[9] These surveys also provide data on many of the questions discussed later in this book, such as whether victims report to police, if they are helped by support agencies, and their attitudes toward criminal justice.

The information provided by these surveys shows that victimization is a frequent occurrence that often involves loss, injury, and trauma. It shows that data from police and (particularly) court authorities, such as that reported in the media, underestimate the frequency of crime. In cases of forcible rape, fewer than one in six victims report the offense to the police.[10] So, using police data, such as the Uniform Crime Report, alone does not provide even remotely useable estimates if we hope to gauge the problem and seek solutions.

Victimization and You

By using the National Crime Victimization Survey of adults, we can gain a more thorough picture of trends in crime in the United States. In the last fifteen years, these surveys show close to a 50 percent drop in the rates of victimization in the United States. The findings are similar in other countries. While this *is* cause for moderate celebration, it is not cause to forget those who are still the victims of violence.

In 2008, five million Americans aged twelve or older were victims of assault or other acts of violence. If you can imagine a community of 10,000 persons, this is the equivalent of ten rapes or sexual assaults, twenty violent robberies (thefts with violence), thirty aggravated assaults, and 130 simple assaults. That is a combined rate of 190 victims of violent crimes.

In 2008, 16 million Americans were victims of theft and other property crimes.[11] For a community of 10,000 persons, this is the equivalent of 125 household burglaries, 32 motor vehicle thefts, and 490 other thefts. That is a combined rate of 650 victims of property crimes.

If you have not yet been victimized by crime, it's easy to read those figures—190 violent crimes and 650 property crimes a year against every 10,000 Americans—and feel that crimes happen to *other* people, not you. But another way to understand the meaning of these figures is to consider how likely *you* are to be a victim of various crimes in your lifetime. Figure 1.1 uses data from the International Crime Victim Survey, a survey that has been completed periodically over the last twenty years. It is considered a reliable source to compare rates of victimization between different countries.[12]

To put it in personal terms, in the United States you would likely be a victim of assault three times in your lifetime; a victim of a burglary once or twice in your lifetime; and you would have a fair chance of being a victim of an auto theft or violent robbery once. If you are a woman, this survey suggests that, on average, you would also have a fair chance (just as likely as not) of being a victim of a sexual assault. Generally, the chances of being a victim of crime other than sexual assault are higher in England and Wales than they are in Canada or the United States. If you are shocked

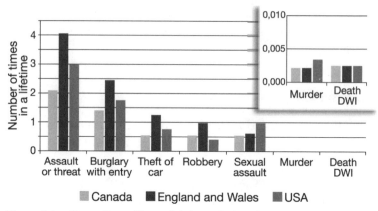

Figure 1.1. How often will an adult be a victim of crime in their lifetime?

by these numbers, then you are not alone. In fact, they fuel victims' rights movements around the world.

As we will see shortly, the human impact of these events can vary from the frequent and mostly benign to the less frequent and more traumatic. Some dismiss the continuing pain to individual victims by pointing out that crime has come down, thereby implying that the problem has gone away. Clearly, these people are not part of the five million individuals who *continue to be* victimized by violent crime each year in the United States alone. We will also see how forgetting about these more traumatic harms exacerbates the anger and outrage that victims themselves feel toward current legislative decisions.

Violence against Women

More sophisticated surveys that ask explicit questions to women show much higher rates of sexual assault and rape than the generic crime surveys do. These specialized surveys focus on the incidence of violence—particularly physical and sexual violence. Unfortunately, they are still not undertaken on a recurring or annual basis. Given the importance of knowing whether or not current programs actually reduce the number of victimizations and effectively serve those who have been victimized, it is vital to begin undertaking these surveys more regularly.

One example of this type of survey is the National Violence Against Women Survey (NVAWS) which was completed in 1996. It suggests that there will be an unacceptable million women physically victimized by their partners in 2010.[13] It is an unacceptable reality and presents an important challenge that cannot be ignored. While statistics show that men are less often injured as victims of domestic violence, that is no reason to abandon efforts to reduce their injuries. However, women tend to be severely injured much more often than men, and women are also more likely to suffer from PTSD as a result of their domestic victimization.

Kilpatrick created one of the most important surveys on sexual violence against adult women and women in universities. It produces the most detailed results of all such surveys. It uses explicit questions about rape that are known to provide more accurate estimates than the questions asked in standard victimization surveys. This specialized survey also confirms much higher frequencies of rape than are suggested by the general national crime victimization survey. While the general national crime surveys find that one million American adult women are victims of forcible rape in their lifetimes, the specialized survey finds that number to be a staggering eighteen million.[14] That is 18 million women who suffered the original pain and indignity of being forcibly raped, and 18 million women whose lives are still marked by that original horror and pain.

These surveys confirm that the number of forcible rapes proportionate to the number of adult women has not significantly risen or fallen in recent decades. Clearly, that should be unacceptable to us today, and we will see in chapter 7 what might work to prevent rape victimizations in the future.

Violence against Children

Studies show that children are victims of violent crimes at heartbreakingly high rates. Follow-ups on more than 3 million cases involving 6 million children led child protection agencies in the United States to identify 770,000 children as victims of abuse or neglect within their families—this is a rate of more than ten children out of every 1,000.[15] In addition to child abuse within the nuclear family, there are many instances of sexual abuse against children committed by relatives, friends, and strangers that go undetected and unknown to authorities and researchers.

The survey on violence against women shows a relatively high frequency of physical violence (close to 50 percent of girls) and of sexual violence (close to 9 percent of girls) that occurred when they were children.[16] Particularly disturbing is the fact that being victimized as a child correlates with being victimized as an adult.

Schools are also spaces where children are victimized at a rate that can no longer be ignored. Violent crimes at school occur at a rate of 26 per 1,000 students, and reports of bullying show that close to one in every three students is victimized.[17] In the United States it is estimated that 160,000 children miss school every day because of bullying, and another 1 million have brought weapons to school because of their fear.[18]

Homicides

Many survivors of violent crime carry their physical and emotional wounds for the rest of their lives. Many other victims of violent crimes do not survive their victimization and their families are left to carry their loss alone. Some 16,000 persons are murdered in the United States each year. Although the chances of being the victim of a homicide are very low, murder rates in the United States are proportionately more than one-and-a-half times higher than they are in Canada (with 600 homicides per year) and England and Wales (with only 850 homicides per year). New York City alone, which has a quarter of the population of Canada and one-seventh the population of England and Wales, has about 400 homicides every year.

While every victim of homicide is unique, some trends are evident. Roughly three out of four homicide victims in the United States are male. Half the victims are between the ages of eighteen and thirty-four years old. A black person is six times more likely to be the victim of a homicide than a white person. In general, blacks are more likely to be the victim of a drug-related homicide and less likely to be the victim in a sex-related homicide.[19]

Criminal Motor Vehicle Crashes

Every year in the United States, close to 12,000 persons lose their lives in motor vehicle crashes that are attributed to alcohol or drugs.[20] An important distinction between alcohol-related car crashes and other types of violent crime is that victims are normally covered by some type of insurance that they or the other driver has paid for. While access to insurance compensation may mitigate victims' financial losses, it does not detract from the injuries and the suffering.

In sum, victimization is a common occurrence. While the most severe and traumatic crimes are the least frequent, this is a relative issue. Clearly these levels of victimization deserve attention. It is not enough for legislators to tinker with penalties and increase punishments without focusing on what really works to reduce these numbers and how we can meet the core needs of victims of crime. This book will show what legislators must do.

NOT AGAIN: HOW OFTEN DOES REPEAT VICTIMIZATION OCCUR?

Although experts know that people are often victimized more than once in a single year, it is difficult to get statistics about repeat victimization in the United States. The British Crime Survey (BCS) provides these data annually. It finds that a staggering 44 percent of all crime is concentrated on only 4 percent of victims.[21] The proportion of victims who will again be victimized through a similar offense within a year is 41 percent for domestic violence, 23 percent for other assaults, 15 percent for burglary, and 13 percent for auto theft, as shown in figure 1.2. The rates are likely similar for the United States.

Clearly, crime is not distributed randomly. Some of the repeat victimization in property offenses is due to the location of the victim's workplace or residence. Those who live in unprotected residences in close proximity to a concentration of potential offenders are particularly at risk of repeat victimization. Unfortunately, initial victimization is a good predictor of later victimization, because the victim's life situations tend to continue. That is to say, their residence continues to be attractive to burglars, their neighborhood continues to be located near potential offenders, and victims

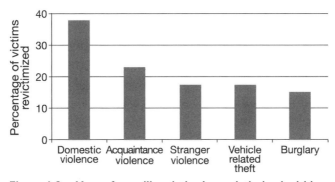

Figure 1.2. How often will a victim be revictimized within a year?

often continue to engage in routine activities that increase their risk of being victimized through no fault of their own.

Repeat victimization is most common—and potentially most dangerous—in domestic violence situations. Violence against women tends to happen more than once to victims who continue to live with the same partner.

Repeat victimization is disillusioning to victims who report their first experience to the police and the criminal justice system but fail to receive the protection of the authorities against the second offense. They feel invisible and forgotten. Being victimized a second time also increases the psychological trauma of the event.

WHAT IS THE COST OF VICTIMIZATION?

The disturbing statistics on the frequency of crime should focus legislators' attention, but they do not. When one looks at the impact of crime on victims and on our society, it creates more urgency for action. Perhaps by putting the cost of crime into a financial framework, legislators will be roused to meet this urgent issue head on.

Although the emotional harm brought to victims and their families by assailants can never be measured, the cumulative monetary costs to the public are immense. In the United States, a seminal report on the total cost of crime was published in 1996 and has received considerable attention since then. The total cost was estimated at $450 billion (or the equivalent of nearly $1,600 per American) per year in 1993 dollars.[22] This price tag consisted of accumulated medical costs ($18 billion); property loss, mental health care bills, and productivity losses ($87 billion); and loss of quality of life for (or pain and suffering lived by) victims ($345 billion).[23]

In order to estimate what the costs of crime in the United States would be today, several factors must be taken into account. For example, in the United States, rates of victimization for most common crimes have come down by about 50 percent from 1994 to 2008. On the other hand, the costs of living have increased by about 50 percent. So, I have recalculated the various expenses using the exact figures from the national crime surveys for 1994 and 2007. I then recalculated the estimates using the real changes in the victimization rates and an increase in costs of living by about 50 percent.

In the end, the final annual cost estimates remain in the same dollar range, with crime-related medical care ringing in at around $16 billion, and the tangible costs of property loss, mental health care bills, emergency services costs, and productivity losses accumulating to $85 billion. Violent crime causes 14 percent of all injury-related medical spending and an estimated 10 percent of mental health care expenditures in the United States.[24] About half of these expenditures go to child abuse victims who are receiving treatment for abuse they experienced years earlier.[25]

But the tangible and medical costs are just a start. The economists have also looked at the pain and suffering that victims of crime experience. They call this the "loss of quality of life." Their main measure was to research the average awards made by juries in U.S. civil courts for similar crimes. So, economists calculated the damages for pain and suffering as being what victims who went to civil court were compensated (as determined by a jury of their peers). This is the $8 million in the O.J. Simpson case (not the $25 million in punitive damages). These estimates for pain and suffering show economists what groups of potential victims (that is, ordinary taxpayers) would have been prepared to pay to avoid the pain and suffering brought on by being victimized. Collectively, they would have paid $345 billion annually in the United States. So the total today is still over $440 billion each year!

In figure 1.3, I have presented estimates for the average costs to victims for medical expenses, mental health care, and loss of income from work for four crime groups.[26] For instance, for assault with injury recorded in the National Crime Victimization Survey, the average medical costs were $2,190, mental health costs were $145, and lost wages were $4,619—for a subtotal of $6,954 in 2007 dollars. The subtotal of these medical and other tangible costs were also around $7,500 for rape and sexual assault and child abuse. However, for homicide and deaths associated with driving while intoxicated, these medical and other tangible costs are over $1.5 million.

Once loss of quality of life or what is more accurately described as pain and suffering is included, the losses are much more significant. In the background of figure 1.3, I have included the estimate in millions of dollars of the total cost annually of these four types of crime. This shows homicide and fatal DWI to cost $113 billion, rape and sexual assault $132 billion, child abuse $69 billion, and assault with injury $32 billion. To put this in perspective, the average price tag for rape goes from $7,300 for medical and tangible costs to over $130,000 when pain and suffering is included. This is greater than the cost of one professional responding to a victim or a professional to run an intensive preventative program to reduce the frequency of sexual assaults. In

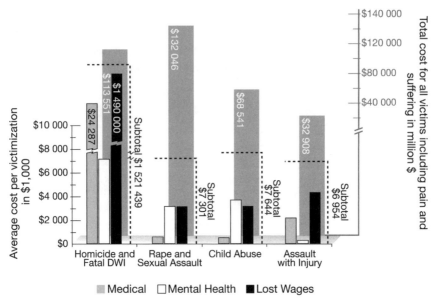

Figure 1.3. Estimates of average costs of selected types of victimization (with total costs for all victims, including pain and suffering)

chapter 7, I will discuss in detail some of the promising practices that would prevent many rapes and sexual assaults and thus save millions of dollars annually in terms of tangible medical costs and quality-of-life savings.[27] For sexual assault on its own, we do not yet have precise figures, but generally every dollar invested in proven prevention programs saves seven dollars in incarceration costs. Likely, the comprehensive programs in chapter 7 would save billions of dollars in pain and suffering. But most importantly, effective prevention programs would allow many more women to go through life without being a victim of a forcible rape.

GET EVEN, NOT JUST ANGRY

These estimates draw attention to the need to invest not only in effective crime reduction strategies (which we are *not* doing yet), but also in what crime victims want and need in the aftermath of being victimized despite more effective crime reduction strategies.

Legislators and many popular movements to change constitutions in the United States have focused on a range of needs of crime victims, such as to have information, protection from the accused, and, as we will see in chapter 6, some participation in the criminal justice process. Unfortunately, legislators have also agreed to massive increases in the budgets for corrections, but have not invested proportionately in other services to help victims recover (which we will discuss in chapter 4). Legislators have also failed to invest in state compensation programs and support for victims to recover their expenses, as we will discuss in chapter 5.

It is a normal part of being victimized to be angry. When Dorothy Morefield's son Nick was shot in 1976 in a robbery, she felt the tremendous physical pain of grief. The pain turned into hatred, pure and simple. But she decided to deal with her anger in a difficult personal journey rather than to allow her feelings of revenge to fester. The criminal justice system had no ability to help her move forward—contrary to what some legislators might believe—and thus services must be in place to recognize the feelings of victims and co-victims and to support them as they strive to assuage their feelings of loss, frustration, and anger.

In North America, victims are not able to get even through the criminal justice system because they do not have a right to participate. Thus, they are left with feelings of anger, often exacerbated by being excluded from a fair justice process. For many years, France has paid for victims of crime to have lawyers in criminal courts so that victims can get even by suing the offender. Germany has recently followed suit. It is important to note that France and Germany have average rates of incarceration, with their numbers of inmates per capita similar to that of Canada (but well below rates in England and Wales), and only one-seventh the rates in the United States. This moderate incarceration rate means that France and Germany have more funds available to pay for legal aid and many other services for victims of crime. Also, granting victims a voice in court is an effective way to increase the use of reparation payment from offenders to victims. In France, as many as half of all criminal cases are considered settled once the offender has paid restitution to the victim.

We also know from much of the research around restorative justice that victims who go through a restorative justice process come out much less angry and vengeful. We will discuss restorative justice more in chapter 5, but in simple terms the victim and the perpetrator are able to communicate their feelings and expectations directly without the frustrating complications of a criminal court.[28]

FINDING BALANCE FOR VICTIMS OF CRIME

This book will be focusing on the needs of the victims of crime—not on the needs of the criminals or the criminal justice system. We will focus on more than just victims' needs for protection from the accused and their expectations of punishment of the offender. We'll also be looking at how to help victims heal and how to prevent victimization in the first place.

Yes, the criminal justice system prosecutes offenders and argues that this is in the interests of victims. But we will see in chapters 6 and 7 that in doing this, law enforcement and prosecutors do not respect the most basic inalienable rights of victims of crime. I will argue that criminal justice is still not working in the best interests of victims because victims do not have power in the systems and because governments are not doing what we know will stop future victimization.

Overall, there is a longstanding confusion between the needs of victims and the needs of law enforcement and criminal justice systems. Too often, legislation's overall purpose is to further the ends of the criminal justice system—not to respect or look out for the needs of victims of crime.

What Do Victims of Crime Want?

From my many years of listening to victims, reading countless studies, and advocating for reforms, it is clear to me that victims have six or seven core needs. In the short term, they are looking for safety and recognition. They want to feel secure that it will not happen again, and they are also looking for someone they can talk to and who can help them sort out the situation. They also want to know the truth about what happened. Victims of rape or sexual assault want to be believed. All victims want help to heal their physical wounds and mental health pain. They are also looking for practical fix-it reparation to get them through the aftermath of their victimization. They want assistance with repairing damage to their home and recovering their possessions.

In the medium term, victims want the offender to repay them for their losses. They want recognition of what happened, and they want the truth to be recorded. They want relief from the anger and pain that they feel perpetrator and the world. However, it is not evident to me want a long, drawn-out, complicated enforcement or a judicial process that excludes them. I don't believe that victims want their role to be limited to a victim impact statement.

Social scientists have often looked at the needs of victims of crime. Some of these studies include my own seminal work with burglary victims in Toronto, Canada, in 1974, as well as other studies undertaken by researchers in England and Wales.[29] This field of research recently received a huge boost after the U.S. National Institute of Justice funded two projects to assess the needs of crime victims. One of those projects was undertaken by Safe Horizon, a comprehensive victim assistance agency in New York City that is one of the largest and oldest in the world. The other project was undertaken by Washington's Urban Institute, known for its policy research on poverty and racial issues. These two studies agreed with the findings of many others that had come before them. They pinpointed the needs of victims of crime and grouped their findings into three categories: needs for emotional and psychological recovery, needs for information or advocacy within systems, and concrete or tangible needs.[30] They included issues of safety and medical care under the tangible needs. Interestingly, the desire to see the perpetrator punished for punishment's sake was not high on victims' list of needs.

Our understanding of victims' needs has been fleshed out even further by other sources and initiatives in recent years. In 1999, the International Association of Chiefs of Police (IACP) held a summit to look at the basic question of what victims want. Victims' advocates, victims, law enforcement, and others were all at the table. Together, they identified seven concerns as the core needs for victims of crime. The needs they identified were safety, support, information, access, continuity, voice, and justice.[31]

Figure 1.4 combines the findings of these studies, as well as those of the IACP summit, into a list of the eight core needs of crime victims. Each of the core needs will be discussed in detail below.

1. Recognition and Emotional Support

Victims of crime need to work through the shock and confusion of their sudden and arbitrary victimization. A good way for them to process some of these jumbled reactions is to have a sympathetic and understanding person listen to them. They want to have what happened to them recognized by others.

	Core Needs for Victims of Crime	Right to legislation and implementation to provide
Support		
1	Recognition and emotional support	Trained informal and professional crisis support and counseling
2	Information on criminal justice, their case, services and personal developments	Timely information on: law enforcement, criminal justice and corrections; case; assistance; and expected developments
3	Assistance to access practical, medical and social services	Advocacy and assistance with repair, practical, social and other services
Justice		
4	Help to pay bills caused by victimization	Emergency funds and restitution from offender, compensation from state, and paid medical and mental health care
5	Personal safety and protection from accused	Prevention of revictimization and protection from accused
6	Choice to voice in justice	Choice to participate and be represented to defend safety, reparation, truth and justice
Good Government		
7	Best public safety	Modern strategies that reduce crime and prevent victimization
8	Implementation	Performance measures and surveys of victims as clients

Figure I.4.   Core needs for victims of crime and possible responses

They want someone to support them through the most frightening and difficult processes of medical care and the criminal justice system. For the most part, victims can find a sympathetic listener in their family members and friends. However, in some cases this support group is not able to provide the support necessary, as they themselves are experiencing feelings of anxiety and victimization. In other cases, it is inappropriate because the perpetrator is part of the group of family and friends.

Professional counseling may be required. As we saw earlier in this chapter, Kilpatrick has demonstrated the high incidence of victims reliving the events, avoiding stimuli associated with event, and exhibiting other symptoms like having difficulties sleeping. These recurring difficulties are common among female victims of assault, female and male xual assault, and female and male victims of crimes that were ing.[32]

2. Information on Criminal Justice, Their Case, S and Recovery

When victims of crime report to the police, they quicl that they do not know much about law enforcement, its where it might lead. They want to gain information and understanding about the wide range of intimidating issues with which they are suddenly faced. They also want to be notified of key events that happen days, weeks, months, and even years after they are victimized. Victims of crime also need to receive specific and up-to-date information on the status of their perpetrators.

Victims of crime want information about how they will process the shock of the crime and to whom they can turn for help. They want to know where and how they can get services from emergency housing to financial compensation. They want this information to be clear, concise, and user-friendly.

3. Assistance to Access Practical, Medical, and Social Services

Victims want help to access and obtain a full range of services. Some of these services relate to practical issues, such as repairs to doors or locks. Others are more complex and less familiar to many of them, involving welfare and security, housing, or compensation. Victims of crime may want an introduction to the civil and family law processes. They also want consistency in approaches and methods across agencies. Victims of violence want to get immediate and sustained health care for their physical, mental, and emotional wounds.

4. Help to Pay Bills Caused by Their Victimization

Many victims of crime encounter out-of-pocket expenses as a direct result of their victimization. One recent U.S. study identified the average costs per victim as $656 for health expenses, $1,307 for property repair, and $1,489 for missed work.[33] Oftentimes, these bills were paid by the victim, who was typically not aware of criminal injuries compensation payable by the state.

5. Personal Safety and Protection from the Accused

Victims want their sense of individual and community safety to be restored so that they can go about their daily lives without fear. In the wake of their victimization, they do not want be reminded that things "could e been worse" for them. Victims also want to avoid revictimization and so are prepared to take reasonable precautions if they are appropriately guided in how to do so.

A victim's individual search for safety will depend on many things, including the crime. But commonalities are evident. All victims want protection from their perpetrators. Women seeking safety from a violent partner can take temporary refuge in a transition house, but they also require an enduring sense of protection and freedom from the stalking that often follows the breakup of a violent relationship. They want this safety for themselves and, importantly, for their children. Victims of other crimes are often concerned about intimidation from an offender who wants to avoid conviction.

6. Choice to Have Their Voice in Justice— Participation and Representation

Victims of crime want standing (or, what the IACP calls "a voice") in the criminal justice system. They want the court to recognize their concerns when making decisions about their cases and their perpetrators. So, victims need to be present, to be heard, and to be represented at critical stages of the judicial process such as bail hearings, postponements, plea negotiations, sentencing, and parole hearings. Victims need to defend their interests in the truth and their personal safety. They also need to know that their concerns about reparation, restoration, and justice have been considered. They need safety in the courtroom and a sense of security when they deal with anything involving their case.

7. Best Public Safety

Many victims call the police because they want future crime prevented. As we will see in chapter 7, there is considerable knowledge about what does—and what does not—reduce crime. Having suffered from crime themselves, victims need to avoid further victimizations in the future. Victims want others to be protected not just from their own accused, but also from other potential perpetrators.

8. Implementation

Victims are not satisfied with unsubstantiated claims about success in preventing victimization. They want performance measures that assess whether crime has been reduced. The victimization surveys that have enabled us to know so much about the numbers of crime victims and the impact of crime on them are essential to measuring performance and assessing the extent to which the harm from crime has been alleviated.

DEMANDS FOR LEGISLATORS

Despite a decrease in rates of crime in the United States of close to 50 percent or more during the 1990s, more than twenty million Americans will still be victims of crime this year. This is more than one in ten Americans over the age of twelve. Surely, we can all imagine the faces of one in ten of our loved ones. Each of these victimizations caused some level of shock, loss, injury, trauma, and mental health problems to the victims and their families.

Victims of crime must become the focus of legislative action and appropriations but in a way that balances the need for support and assistance with transforming justice to better meet the core needs of victims. In hard economic terms, those physical and mental injuries represent more than $18 billion in medical care and $87 billion in property loss and mental health care.

Legislators must take into account that American taxpayers would have paid another $345 billion to *prevent* this pain and suffering and get victims' core needs met to hasten some type of recovery.

Legislators need to invest in repeating the surveys that identify those costs and consequences as well as estimate trends in victimizations.

Legislators must recognize that rights for victims of crime means more than simply building prisons. They must invest in services to meet the full range of core needs for support (recognition, emotional support, information, and assistance) as well as justice issues (reparation, protection from the accused, and a voice in the justice process). They must also invest in effective ways to reduce victimization and to measure whether those goals have been achieved.

(2)

INALIENABLE RIGHTS FOR VICTIMS

Europe and North America Proclaim, Japan Delivers

In the previous chapter, we saw that governments leave victims as the orphans of their criminal justice policies and social service systems. We have identified some of the (eminently surmountable) reasons for them ignoring and forgetting about victims. We've also seen the nature and extent of victimization, and we know that it justifies real actions—*not just words*.

When it comes to words, the United States, the United Nations, and Europe have been good at them. We shall see in this chapter that these governments agree on what must be done—an impressive consensus by any measure. We will look at that consensus here so that we have a basic set of inalienable rights to act as standards against which to measure the demands for legislators in the following chapters.

Many experts on the implementation of victims' services and rights had come to the conclusion that what was needed was much more than proclamations (empty words). In 2005, the group of fourteen experts was brought together at the new International Victimology Institute Tilburg (INTERVICT) in the Netherlands to examine whether governments had reached a consensus on the steps needed to go from proclamation to implementation. The meeting was the brainchild of Marlene Young, president of the World Society of Victimology; Marc Groenhuijsen, director of INTERVICT; and myself. The experts came from every continent, and from every profession that deals with victims of crime, to work with the

INTERVICT team (which itself includes no less than three of the leading international experts on victim assistance, victims' rights, and the psychological aspects of victimization).[1]

The group of fourteen experts was able to identify the elements of the consensus and so outline minimum standards to be met. If governments were to be accountable to each other to meet these standards—to put their money where their mouth is—then they would need to make reforms where they did not already meet the standards. One way to do this is "a UN convention." Governments have done this successfully, if not perfectly, in many other areas such as with the Convention on the Rights of the Child and the UN Charter. The standards must be close to what governments would legislate and implement. In chapter 8, I have transformed the basic principles of the convention into a model law for a nation, state, or province to adopt and have included it in the appendix.

I will now show how the contents of the draft convention developed by the experts are consistent with documents and actions implemented in the United States, at the United Nations, and across Europe.

EIGHT INALIENABLE RIGHTS FOR VICTIMS OF CRIME: THE CONSENSUS

To make it easier to follow, I have organized the content of those standards around the eight inalienable rights that respond to the core needs from chapter 1. Figure 2.1 integrates a list of rights for victims of crime (draft convention), showing key government proclamations. The first column refers to the number of the core need that I identified in chapter 1. In the column labeled "Draft Convention," I have grouped the dozen key elements of that convention into a schematic form organized around my eight core needs (I have included the number of the article in the draft convention for researchers). Then, I have schematically listed a number of key instruments (such as the President's Task Force, the UN *magna carta*, and the European framework decision) to show how each government has made proclamations (and occasionally modest actions) to demonstrate its commitment to the principles.

These are not rocket science. They are obvious inalienable rights that victims of crime would expect, although not necessarily what law enforcement, prosecutors, judges, or other government agencies are providing yet.

Core need	2006 - Draft Convention (Article)	1982 President's Task Force	1984 VOCA 1994 VAWA	1985 UN Declaration	2001 EU Framework Decision	2004 Int. Crim. Court	2004 Japan Human Rights	2005 UN Child Guidelines	2006 UK Code of Practice
Support									
1	Recognition of victims, co-victims, good samaritans (1)	yes	yes	yes	yes	yes	yes	yes	yes
2	Information (7)	yes	yes	yes	yes	yes	yes	yes	yes
	Assistance (8) – referral by police		yes		yes	yes	yes	yes	yes
3	Assistance (8) – short term	yes	yes	yes	yes	yes	yes	yes	yes
	Assistance (8) – medium term	yes	yes	yes	yes	yes	yes	yes	yes
	Special assistance because of age, gender, disability, race (3)		VAWA			yes		yes	
Justice									
4	Restitution from offender (10)	yes	yes	yes	yes	yes	yes	yes	
	Restorative justice (9) – respecting victim rights			yes	yes			yes	
	Compensation from state (11)	yes	yes	yes		yes	yes	yes	yes
5	Protection of victims, witnesses and experts (6)	yes	VAWA	yes	yes	yes	yes	yes	
6	Access to justice and fair treatment (5)	yes	yes	yes	yes	yes	yes	yes	
Good Government									
7	Commitment to reduce victimization (4)		VAWA	yes		yes	yes	yes	
8	Implementation (12)	yes	yes	yes (res)	yes	yes	yes	yes	yes

Figure 2.1. Integrated list of rights for victims of crime (draft convention) showing governments' proclamations

1. Right to Recognition: Victims Are People, Not States

The first inalienable right seems obvious, but law enforcement and criminal justice have overlooked this right for more than two hundred years and, by so doing, have caused much harm and indignation to victims. Obvious as it may sound, crime causes harm, loss, and injury to *people*—to victims of crime—who must be recognized, not overlooked or forgotten or used. This right recognizes that crimes are not just violations of criminal laws, but are violations of individuals. This has already been discussed in chapter 1.

As criminal law practices evolved, governments increasingly took over the prosecution of offenders in order to relieve victims of that responsibility. However, the systems that governments created for this purpose ended up excluding victims from consideration in many different ways. Even today, most systems of criminal justice are still systems of law enforcement for the state rather than protection, justice, and support for victims. Yes, legislators and prosecutors may say that they are prosecuting or punishing in the name of victims, but in reality they are acting on behalf of the state with little regard—and sadly, a lot of *dis*regard—for victims.

The irony of this situation is best understood in the testimony of the wife of a U.S. Navy captain. When testifying in front of the President's Task Force about her rape in 1982, she poignantly exclaimed, "It was *I* who was kidnapped, raped, and robbed—not the state!" In Canada, England, and Wales, the prosecutor is described as acting for the Crown and is called a "Crown attorney," and that is exactly what prosecutors do—they represent the state (in this case, the British Crown), not the victim. A sexual assault is treated as a crime against the queen—not a crime against the victim. Typically, any fine that is ordered is paid to the queen rather than to the victim. Anyone with sense can recognize that the victim is virtually forgotten and suffering a sort of repeat victimization at the hands of the state under such a system.

This right needs also to take into account family members or co-victims who suffer not only when someone is murdered, but also in many other crimes as well, and must ensure that co-victims are not forgotten in the ensuing processes.

2. Right to Information: Victims Need to Know

The second inalienable right is equally obvious. Victims need to be provided with information about a range of issues. They need to know what services are available to help them. They need to know how the law enforcement and criminal justice processes operate so they can decide whether to get involved. If they do get involved, they want to get information about their case. If they experienced a major shock, they want to know how their emotions and ability to cope may evolve. They want to know about services they may need such as medical care, compensation from the state, and so on.

One of the best-established ways to increase the likelihood that victims will pick up on services available to them is directly related to law enforcement. If the victim reports to the police, then the officer and the police service are in a unique position to help victims get information about what to expect next, the services that exist, and the ensuing investigation. If victims get this information, they will be empowered to pursue many positive paths such as compensation from the state. Unfortunately, law enforcement is also in a unique position to contribute to an additional victimization if it does not provide information or attention to the victim as officers go about their enforcement tasks.

3. Right to Assistance: The Right to Counseling and Services

The third inalienable right is that services must be available and accessible everywhere they are needed so victims can access assistance and support. Part of this right involves support and advocacy to have generic services (such as practical, medical, and social services) adapted to the unique needs of victims of crime. Victims' needs evolve from the time of the immediate crisis to the following weeks and months. Some of these services could be made available within existing agencies. Others will require new agencies.

A selection of these services needs to focus on victims of specific crimes. Women will need domestic violence shelters and sexual assault crisis centers. Children will require services geared to their needs, as will the elderly. Services for people of different racial and ethnic backgrounds and language groups will also be required in some instances.

4. Right to Reparation: Reimbursing Victims Fairly

The fourth inalienable right is that victims need to recover the financial losses brought on by their victimization. Some of this can be achieved through restitution from the offender. As we will see in chapter 5, reparation is much more necessary than many judges think. Some victims can obtain reparation through compensation from the state, or through procedures such as restorative justice or third-party suits which will become clearer in chapter 5.

5. Right to Be Protected from the Accused: Essential Safety

The fifth inalienable right is that victims need to be protected from the accused. This is particularly important in cases of domestic violence against one of the partners or the child. But there are many other situations where this is also important. "Protection" must not be confused with many legislators' obsession with increasing incarceration penalties to punish the accused. Yes, there are instances where incarceration provides protection to victims from violent persons who are likely to be violent again, and so is important to meeting victims' needs for this reason. But incarcerating harmless drug users (as so many legislators tirelessly promote) is a different thing entirely.

6. Right to Participation and Representation: A Voice That Is Heard

The sixth inalienable right is that victims of crime must be able to participate and be represented in the legal process to defend their interests. In most of the government proclamations, these personal interests have been left vague and are allowed to be trumped by the rights of accused and convicted offenders. Often victims talk about their desire to be present and to be heard. In response, legislators have provided for victim impact statements—but this provision does not provide the participation necessary. In chapter 6, I will define the interests of victims to have a voice in relation to their safety, reparation, and justice. I will also propose participation and representation for victims so that they can defend these concerns on an equal basis with the accused and convicted and in turn get even, not just angry.

7. Right to Effective Policies to Reduce Victimization: Stopping Future Violence

The seventh inalienable right is that governments must do better at implementing strategies known to prevent victimization by reducing crime.

Many victims call for this so that *other* people will not be victims. This will be discussed in more detail in chapter 7.

8. Right to Implementation—Not Just Rhetoric

The eighth important principle is that the enforcement of the other seven inalienable rights does not happen on its own. We have to take specific measures to ensure that they are implemented. We need to monitor whether victims are really having these rights *realized*—after all, this is an inalienable right all on its own. Proclamations without implementation and independent assessment have happened too often in the last two centuries and more, but today the establishment of victimization surveys and other ways of measuring whether victimization has been prevented or victims assisted provide new and vital tools.

So let's turn to the proclamations and major pieces of legislation. For the United States, I will focus on examples from federal legislation rather than state laws (although the avalanche of laws and amendments to constitutions at the state level are also illustrations of agreement with the first six inalienable rights I have set out above).

PRESIDENT'S TASK FORCE—UNITED STATES OFFERS VISION AND LEADERSHIP

In 1982, the President's Task Force on Victims of Crime described the U.S. system of criminal justice as being appallingly out of balance before making sixty-seven recommendations to remedy the situation.

The task force was about recognizing victims of crime and providing a range of legal and social supports. It understood the importance of providing victims with information and services, and it made recommendations to the judicial, hospital, and school sectors. The first three inalienable rights mentioned above resound throughout its recommendations—as they should. Judges and prosecutors were asked to pay more attention to the impact of crime on victims and to treat victims and witnesses fairly. Victims of rape and sexual assault were not to be liable for the costs of gathering medical evidence. Furthermore, in support of the fourth inalienable right for reparation, judges and prosecutors were asked to order restitution from offenders and states were expected to expand the availability of compensation for victims.

Some of the proposals made by the task force were meant to remedy the porous nature of the criminal justice system—especially in terms of the release of dangerous offenders. About a dozen of the sixty-seven recommendations asked federal and state governments to change legislation to protect victims and the community by keeping such offenders behind bars for longer. Critical issues in bail laws were recommended to be changed, including denying the release of dangerous offenders. Parole boards were also asked to do more to protect victims. Intimidation of victims and witnesses was to be taken seriously. These recommendations may seem obvious, but, as explained in the first chapter, they reflect the frustration of victims with the system (although they are not always the remedies that victims are seeking). These recommendations are consistent with the fifth inalienable right for protection from the accused, and overlap with the sixth inalienable right to participate and to be represented if victims' concerned are to be respected.

In the end, the President's Task Force floated an important amendment to the U.S. Constitution that, if adopted into law, would have given victims a voice in the justice system. Unfortunately, this amendment was not adopted and put into action nationally.[2]

The good news is that in 1984 the Victims of Crime Act, and in 1994 the Violence Against Women Act, were adopted. These acts took some of the recommendations of the President's Task Force and put them into concrete action—at least in some instances, at least some of the time. Undoubtedly, these acts have led to progress in the intervening years, but much more action is needed to ensure that victims of crime receive justice and support when they need it the most, as I will explain in later chapters.

VICTIMS OF CRIME ACT

The main instrument used to implement at least *some* of these recommendations across the United States was the impressive Victims of Crime Act (VOCA), which was first adopted in 1984. VOCA was intended to increase victim assistance services (similar to the third inalienable right for services) and criminal injuries compensation (similar to the fourth inalienable right for reimbursement) from coast to coast. The act established the Office for Victims of Crime (OVC), which was to be the responsibility center for realizing these goals.

It was decided that the necessary funds were to come from special fines levied under the federal criminal code. In the first year alone, close to $70 million in fines was made available for the initiative, and today the amount has grown to approximately $1 billion annually thanks to large fines such as those levied in 1996 against Daiwa Bank ($340 million) and in 2009 against Pfizer ($1.2 billion).[3] While it is undoubtedly impressive to raise $1 billion for victim services without using general tax revenues, this amount is minute when compared to the $225 billion in regular expenditures on policing, lawyers, and corrections. It is also small compared to the federal funding transferred to stimulate prison construction or add additional police personnel, which was measured in the $10 to $20 billion range annually. This issue will be revisited in chapter 8 when we consider implementation of rights for victims of crime.

What is important to note here is that fifteen years after VOCA was launched, the OVC published a report from a group set up to monitor the implementation of the recommendations from the President's Task Force. In the end, after seeing too little movement, this group set forth new recommendations and repeated many of the original recommendations, showing that the original recommendations were as important then as they were when they were first drafted in 1982.[4]

VIOLENCE AGAINST WOMEN ACT

Another recommendation from the President's Task Force was to create a task force on violence against women. Impressive legislation called the Violence Against Women Act (VAWA) was enacted in 1994. It was reauthorized in 2000 and 2005. Like VOCA, the Violence Against Women Act is implemented by a responsibility center called the Office on Violence Against Women, which is part of the U.S. Department of Justice. It focuses on victims of domestic violence, sexual assault, dating violence, and stalking.

VAWA includes funding for programs that are designed to reduce violence against women as well as improve services for victims of violence against women. It focuses on the need for the programs to be tailored to issues of gender, and for victims to be protected from the accused. So, this legislation and program is consistent with the third, fifth, and seventh inalienable rights for assistance, protection, and prevention, respectively.

VAWA's concern with outcomes is very important, and so it is also consistent with the eighth inalienable right for implementation. Issues surrounding the VOCA and VAWA will be discussed in more detail in chapter 4.

GOVERNMENTS OF THE WORLD ADOPT A
MAGNA CARTA FOR VICTIMS OF CRIME

In 1985, every government in the world pledged to commit to meeting the needs of victims of crime. They agreed to make every effort to change laws and programs so that their practices would be consistent with the Declaration on Basic Principles of Justice for Victims of Crime and Abuse of Power (the *magna carta*).[5] This agreement is remarkable but, while governments are still committed to it twenty-five years later, there unfortunately needs to be much more action taken before we can close the gap between those basic principles of justice and the way that victims of crime are actually treated.

This declaration was inspired by the wave of bills of rights in some U.S. states, as well as the findings of the President's Task Force. I was directly involved in developing this *magna carta* with colleagues from the United States and other countries. At the time we started out on our campaign, victims did not generally have access to any justice or support. It was clear to us that ensuring rights for victims of crime was (and still is) common sense, although at that time sense was not (and still isn't) very common. So, it was a welcome surprise to see how quickly governments and non-governmental groups worldwide came to a consensus about the need to provide victims with support, reparation, and balanced justice. We took our campaign to countless meetings with governments and human rights organizations around the world.

The momentum of our campaign was exhilarating. Within only three years, we got consensus on our *magna carta* for victims of crime—which must have been a UN record. On November 29, 1985,[6] every government in the world endorsed the resolution that "affirms the necessity of adopting national and international measures in order to secure the *universal and effective* recognition of, and respect for, the rights of victims of crime and of abuse of power."[7] I have added italics to the quotation above to highlight where the most significant strides of this resolution lay.

The principles set out in this *magna carta* recognize the obvious (but all too often overlooked) reality that victims suffer loss, injury, and trauma from crime, as outlined in the first inalienable right of this chapter. They set the benchmarks for how civil society and governments at all levels should respond to victims and victimization.

We'd like to think that our systems of justice operate on a "do no additional harm" principle. However, at the 1985 UN General Assembly, governments of the world recognized that victims of crime often *do* suffer additional harm through their cooperation with law enforcement and the criminal justice system. Known technically as "secondary victimization," this was a common problem that often went overlooked (and still does). The most basic difficulty was that victims were (and still are) treated principally as a source of evidence. Victims did not (and most still don't) have a right to lawyers to represent them or protect their interests in the criminal justice process. Too often they experienced criminal justice as being callous and uncaring (and many still do). Rape victims may have not been believed (and still might not be); assault victims feared the return of the offender (and still do); theft victims lost the use of their stolen property to the police for longer than the offender had it (and not much has changed). But back in 1985, the *magna carta* ambitiously set out to ensure that our law enforcement and justice systems responded to the needs of victims instead of exacerbating their traumas.

The *magna carta* called for the implementation of measures to ensure respect for the basic principles of justice for victims of crime, which are identical in intent to the first, second, third, fourth, and the sixth inalienable rights mentioned above. However, there are also some notable differences between the *magna carta*'s principles and my eight core needs identified in chapter 1. My needs make support for emotional and psychological recovery much more explicit, and they also stress the importance of reparation that goes beyond financial restitution and compensation. Within the full text of the *magna carta*, some principles specify which agencies must provide certain services. For instance, both police and social agencies are expected to better respond to victims experiencing crisis following their victimization and provide support and respect to victims in the phases that follow. The *magna carta* outlines that both agencies are expected to follow guidelines and to be trained in the application of those guidelines. Unfortunately, governments (with at least the recent exception of England and Wales) have assumed that individual training is sufficient when, in fact, overall guidelines are clearly needed.

Furthermore, in the resolution it called for better prevention of victimization, which is the seventh (and often overlooked) inalienable right of victims. Yes, that's right—it called for programs that would *stop victimization from happening in the first place*. I will talk more about these approaches in chapter 7. It also called for reports on implementation but stopped short of specifying at that time how to assess progress, using independent victimization and other surveys well known to victimologists and indeed many policymakers today.

So, in 1985, it seemed like the world had come to its senses. No lesser group than the General Assembly of the United Nations had taken up the rallying call for victims' rights. The General Assembly, after all, is the forum where the governments of all countries in the world come together to agree on solutions to the world's problems. In effect, countries called on each other to take the necessary steps to guarantee basic human rights for victims of crime and abuse of power, and they determined that they needed to immediately begin implementing the necessary changes. But don't forget that since 1985, unfortunately, many of us have become acutely aware of the obvious steps needed to take these noble words and put them into action, and of the sophisticated tools available from victimology—not more dogmatic criminal law—to assess performance.

FIRST STEPS AROUND THE WORLD TOWARD ENSURING INALIENABLE RIGHTS FOR ALL VICTIMS

Inspired by some U.S. states, the state of South Australia and the province of Manitoba in Canada had moved to implement the provisions as the *magna carta* was being adopted by the United Nations. Other countries and provinces followed suit and began to provide services for victims of crime. Some governments also adopted a list of principles regarding the rights of victims, and some of these even began to incorporate changes into their criminal codes.

In Canada in 1988, the federal and provincial ministers responsible for justice agreed to a Canadian Statement of Principles of Justice in an effort to "Canadianize" the UN declaration. While the intention was good, the principles were not as precise as the bills of rights in the United States or the standards in the *magna carta* and did little to guarantee rights for victims.

In 1998, a Canadian parliamentary committee reviewed the progress that had been made, held public hearings, and made seventeen recommendations to improve the situation for crime victims in a report aptly called *A Voice Not a Veto*. These included the establishment of a fully funded office for victims at the federal level. Instead, in 2000, Justice Canada created the Policy Centre on Victim Issues (PCVI)—which is *not* an independent office for victims—and gave it funding which, even after gradual increases, is today more modest than full and did little to invest in regular victimization surveys or tools to assess progress. This move was clearly inadequate. Although some research in Canada has confirmed partial progress in terms of victims' issues, there are many disturbing indicators that much more is needed. Just one reality that some Canadian jurisdictions face is that in two-thirds of cases, judges continue to waive the fine (victim surcharge) that the law requires judges to order.[8] Clearly, this is in disrespect of the fourth inalienable right for victims' need for reimbursement.

It seems obvious to me that even though there is agreement in principle with the first four inalienable rights in Canada, there is a large gap between the government's proclaimed vision and its actual practices. The good news here is that, in the shadow of its shortcomings, Canadian legislators were able to recognize that they needed to do much more in terms of victims' rights and in 2007 created the Ombudsman for Victims of Crime—a public office to defend the rights of victims—to explore systemic issues at least at the federal level.

The International Bureau for Children's Rights (IBCR) organized a series of investigative tribunals to look into the pressing issue of violence against children in the early 1990s. These tribunals took place in Paris, France; Colombo, Sri Lanka; and Fortaleza, Brazil. One main conclusion reached through those tribunals was that horrendous numbers of children were being sexually and physically abused. Another conclusion was that the offenders were able to continue offending with impunity because their young victims were not able to cooperate with prosecutions and get their rights enforced.[9] In sum, the nonimplementation of the fifth inalienable right for protection left the children scared, intimidated, mistreated by a complex criminal justice process, and much worse. As a result, the IBCR set to work on developing guidelines to protect child victims and witnesses that would be consistent with the victims' inalienable rights and the Convention on the Rights of the Child.

In 2005, with active support of the Canadian government, the United Nation's Economic and Social Council (ECOSOC) adopted the *Guidelines on Justice for Child Victims and Witnesses of Crime*. These guidelines benefited from the cumulative expertise of practitioners and legislators in the United States, Canada, and across the world. They set out good practices based on the consensus of contemporary knowledge and key international norms, such as those outlined in the Convention on the Rights of the Child and the *magna carta* for victims of crime. The IBCR's guidelines covered all the important issues in the first seven inalienable rights.

There are several other examples where governments globally have developed conventions on specific issues (such as human trafficking) and included some elements of the inalienable rights, particularly in terms of information, services, and consideration of restitution. The reality is that these make for great rhetoric but they still have no teeth and no way for independent assessment by victimologists.

TOOLS FOR IMPLEMENTING RIGHTS FOR ALL VICTIMS AROUND THE WORLD

We know that all governments around the world have the information and resources necessary to enforce the rights of victims *if they so choose*. The governments of the United States (through the OVC) and the Netherlands took an important initiative to develop tools to help other governments implement the *magna carta*, which clearly shows their support. For example, in 1999, fourteen years after the *magna carta* for victims of crime was first adopted by the UN General Assembly, the United Nations adopted the *Guide for Policy Makers on the Implementation of the Declaration*.[10] This guide was a short document that went directly to the point. It was designed to be used by legislators in the areas of justice, policing, social welfare, health, and local government. The guide sets out standards against which jurisdictions can assess their own practices and evaluate what changes they further need to implement in order to rebalance justice. It also proposes innovative ways to finance victim services and programs.

In 1999, the United Nations also adopted the *Handbook on Justice for Victims*, a short document that outlines the use and application of the *magna carta.* Like the policy guide discussed above, the handbook was developed in an open discussion with a broad set of academic and practitioner experts.[11] It is designed to help criminal justice and social agencies implement victim-service programs and develop victim-sensitive strategies. It looks at the role of frontline professionals such as police officers, prosecutors, judges, correctional workers, educators, and health care workers. The handbook helps civil society to engage in advocacy, legislative changes, and law reform. It suggests ways for organizations to work internationally, stressing the importance of technical cooperation, education, training, and research, including performance measurement using victimization and other surveys.

THE STATUTE OF ROME TO ESTABLISH THE INTERNATIONAL CRIMINAL COURT

Another important pillar of support for the inalienable rights and their implementation is the Statute of Rome, which was adopted in 1998. In sum, the Statute of Rome is an international agreement that forms the basis of the permanent International Criminal Court, which we will discuss further in chapter 6. The statute endorses every one of the inalienable rights, including many sections that are nearly cut and pasted out of the *magna carta.* Over one hundred governments have not only ratified the statute, but have also contributed funds and personnel to its implementation. Hopefully, the United States will join those countries soon, and the governments that have ratified will bring their domestic criminal justice practices into line with its victim provisions.

COMPREHENSIVE INALIENABLE RIGHTS: JAPAN IMPLEMENTS THE *MAGNA CARTA*

In 2004, Japan adopted a comprehensive government plan to implement the measures outlined in the *magna carta* for crime victims. Led by the prime minister's office, the actions included the monumental step forward of giving victims real standing in Japanese criminal courts—strides beyond simply allowing them to submit a victim impact statement and in accordance with the sixth inalienable right. The measures implemented

by Japan also included improved ways for the police to provide compensation from the government as per the fourth inalienable right. The prime
minister's office is establishing a comprehensive victim service network
which includes involving municipalities. Japan's recent reforms provide an
undeniable example of what a modern, affluent democracy can accomplish
in terms of victims' rights if it truly wants to—and, importantly, if there is
sufficient pressure to do so from taxpayers and voters. It is clear that at
least *some* leading countries are making strides in implementing the measures outlined in the *magna carta* and ensuring the inalienable rights and
standards that were presented in this chapter.

EUROPEAN UNION CALLS FOR VICTIMS TO HAVE THEIR VOICES HEARD

In March 2001, a framework decision on the standing of victims in criminal proceedings was adopted by the Council of the European Union.
The council is the powerful group that runs the common market of the
European Union. A "framework decision" is a fancy name for requiring
all present and future European Union governments to take action on an
issue. In this case, the council required all governments to provide victims of crime with services, information, restitution, mediation, and even
some standing to defend their interests in criminal courts.[12] In short, this
document covers the first five inalienable rights, but is vague on the sixth
inalienable right of giving victims a voice in criminal proceedings, even
though countries like France and Germany already do provide participation and representation. (By the way, most countries in the EU governing
structure have signed the Statute of Rome and set up the International
Criminal Court; see above.)

Unlike the unenforced and unenforceable "bills of rights" in the
United States, the European Union provided a timetable to meet the
standards and a requirement for governments in the union to report
objectively on the implementation of the framework decision. Governments were to comply with most of the provisions by March 2002. They
had until March 2004 to enable victims to fully participate in criminal
proceedings and, if necessary, to have access to legal advice paid for by
the state. Governments had until March 2006 to promote mediation in
appropriate cases.

But despite these goals, enough government reports had been received by 2004 for the European Union to comment on the implementation of the framework decision. The European Union's assessment was extremely negative overall, as governments had changed their legislation very little and did not provide any assessment of whether or not their legislation was leading to the desired changes in practice. With this assessment, the hopes of victim advocates were again dashed. But the game was not over.

Fortunately, the European Union could pay for an independent evaluation on whether victims were indeed receiving the services that were promised. So, it funded Victim Support Europe (VSE) to undertake an assessment. VSE is an umbrella organization of various national victim assistance organizations that now exist throughout Europe. It is similar to what NOVA was in the United States during the 1970 to 2000 period. VSE's assessment was undertaken in collaboration with INTERVICT.

Their recently published assessment looks at three levels of implementation: legislation, practice, and impact.[13] It used a detailed questionnaire that was sent to government agencies, nongovernmental groups, and academics in each country. The overall conclusions were disappointing, as they found little agreement on the extent of implementation. They also encountered many difficulties in knowing whether the standards put forward by the European Union had been met.

VSE and INTERVICT made some critical recommendations regarding how countries of the European Union should increase the standing of victims in criminal courts and ensure that victims' inalienable rights and legitimate interests are recognized in criminal proceedings (as per the sixth inalienable right). Their report recommended that there be equity between the role of the victim and the role of the accused, and also noted that victims must not be subject to undue pressure or secondary victimization. They also called for the state to pay the restitution to the victim and then recover it from the offender in a system similar to California's (in agreement with the fourth inalienable right).

If the countries of the European Union take action on these recommendations, then all of Europe will be brought up to the high standards on this key issue set by France and Germany—and be well ahead of anything enacted in North America to date. Unfortunately, in reality it will take more than a framework decision to get the balanced justice that victims in Europe truly need, but what is most promising here is that the debate is action oriented and well engaged.

ENGLAND AND WALES: CODE OF PRACTICE AND THE LANDMARK VICTIM CHAMPION

In general, England and Wales have been able to take positive action toward rebalancing justice with no task forces, no declarations, and no framework decisions. By the time the *magna carta* for victims of crime was adopted in 1985, the government of England and Wales had already developed a network of victim assistance agencies (referred to as "victim support schemes") as well as a relatively generous criminal injuries program (inalienable rights three and four, respectively). The National Association of Victim Support Schemes (NAVSS) was set up by the British government to establish victims' service standards across England and Wales in 1979. The British government also modified the restitution law so that restitution was to be paid *before* fines—an approach that in principle went a long way in ensuring victims' best interests and the fourth inalienable right.

In 1990, a victim's charter was introduced in England and Wales in order to act as a mechanism to put recommendations into practice and to set performance standards to help victims actually receive what is still only promised in North America—a strong example of the eighth inalienable right in action. The charter first described how the criminal justice system operated, and then gave some examples of best practices concerning how victims should be treated. This charter went to two further iterations in 1996 and 2004 in order to clearly explain what should happen to victims after an offense is reported to the police, and also to outline the standards that victims should expect (as per the second inalienable right for information).

But the British government didn't stop there. In 2006, it adopted the Code of Practice for Victims of Crime, a protocol that governs the services provided to victims. It defines which victims of crime will benefit from which services, as well as which service providers must provide those services. The code starts by outlining the police's responsibility to provide an informative leaflet, online resources, and other appropriate information on local support services to victims. The leaflet then walks the victim through each of the critical stages of the criminal justice process, from prosecution to parole, as well as outlining the criminal injuries compensation procedure. This leaflet is exemplary for ensuring that victims' second inalienable right for information is respected, and it also offers avenues of action for victims of crime who do not receive service at the appropriate standards.[14] This leaflet provides an impressive model for what could—and should—be done across North America to overcome the frequent failures in the implementation of services on the ground.

The minister of justice for England and Wales appointed a victim champion to advocate for victims' issues and advise top levels of government on victim concerns. In 2008, the government appointed Sara Payne—mother of nine-year-old Sarah Payne who was sexually assaulted and murdered by a repeat pedophile in 2000—as victim champion for a year's term. Sara Payne became a popular champion of the fifth inalienable right, changing legislation to better protect victims of crime and advocating to keep known sex offenders from committing further attacks. She also called for more integration between victims, criminal justice, and health agencies, and advocated for improvements to how victims and witnesses are treated by the criminal justice system.

In 2010, England and Wales began to roll out two new initiatives to better serve victims of crime. The first was to launch a National Victim Service to build on the national network of victim assistance agencies and court-based services. The minister of justice affirmed that this National Victim Service would ensure that vulnerable victims get "their own dedicated case worker, responsible for pulling together various public services—such as housing, health, employment or social services—and for referring them quickly to specialist support."[15] This service will support victims' third inalienable right by providing universal coverage with permanent employees who will be able to make a career focused on victim support. The second initiative was to replace the rotating victim champion with a permanent victim commissioner to oversee the National Victim Service and make recommendations for improvements (in accordance with the eighth inalienable right).

The next chapters look at the eight inalienable rights in detail to propose where further improvements can be implemented and to present best practices that can be followed by governments around the world in order to rebalance justice in their own jurisdictions.

DEMANDS FOR LEGISLATORS

There is much in common between the proposals agreed on at the United Nations, the recommendations and actions in the United States on VOCA and VAWA, and the European framework decision.

Legislators must update their legislations and programs to ensure that they are consistent with the proclamations that represent a consensus internationally.

Legislators in North America and most countries of the European Union can learn a lot from Japan about taking recommendations off the written page and putting them into practice in order to make a real difference in every victim's life.

Legislators should adapt the model of the British Code of Practice for Victims of Crime, for Britain's National Victim Service goes further than any other to ensure universal services with external and independent review. It provides an inspiring solution for how to meet victims' needs for counseling and other basic services.

Legislators in Europe may look to the United States for ways to measure and research the needs of victims as well as focus on the prevention of violence against women, to France for giving victims a voice in the process, and to Japan for pulling most of it together into one effective package. Legislators must ensure that prevention of victimization is a part of these issues.

Legislators should endorse a proposal to develop a convention on victims' rights and services. In the meantime, they can use the legislation in the appendix as a check list to ensure that they are implementing the core inalienable rights on which there is international agreement.

③

FIRST IN AID

Victims at the Zenith of Law Enforcement

On our television monitors and silver screens, cops are busy heroes, fighting vicious bank robbers and heartless international traffickers of drugs and humans. Yet, for the victim of a crime who calls 911, the real-life police are always available twenty-four hours a day, seven days a week. And not only are they *there*, but they're there to help—or so victims believe. The police call paramedics, ambulances, and fire departments. They can separate the parties in a dispute and, at long last, provide safety for victims of domestic violence. They may be able to recover property or, at the very least, confirm its loss to the insurance company. Police officers may protect victims from the aggressor and arrest the suspect.

With more than one million sworn officers and another quarter of a million civilian personnel in the United States, expenditures on law enforcement have grown rapidly over the past two decades. It is estimated that today these exceed $100 billion annually in the United States. The U.S. National Research Council (NRC) estimates that about 60 percent of these funds—a whopping $60 billion—are spent on responding to 911 calls.[1]

For all the $100 billion spent each year, and for all the constitutional amendments and laws passed by state governments that purport to assist victims, there is little evidence as to whether law enforcement is itself obeying the laws in relation to how they treat victims. In the 1990s, the rhetoric of "community policing" was all the rage. Unfortunately, its main concept (that law enforcement must collaborate with the community) did not extend to concrete steps to provide victims of crime with information, support, or explanations on what happens next.

However, a common item in state laws is to require the police to give timely information to victims of crime. Since 1985, the crime victim rights act for Michigan has included the following:

> Within 24 hours after the initial contact between the victim of a reported crime and the law enforcement agency having the responsibility for investigating that crime, that agency shall give to the victim the following information in writing: (a) The availability of emergency and medical services, if applicable; (b) The availability of victim's compensation benefits and the address of the crime victims compensation board.

Some police departments require officers to respond to these points on the occurrence form, but many do not. I have not found any scientific evaluations that show whether victims were actually given this information. This lack of accountability to victims continues despite the sophistication of victimological surveys and numerous proclamations and proposals made by police forces' own leading professional bodies such as the International Association of Chiefs of Police (IACP)—the largest police executive association in the world—and the National Sheriffs' Association (NSA), both of which have more than 20,000 members. Progressive thinking from professional bodies such as the IACP and NSA has not led to facts that the police are providing this service.

Undoubtedly, victims of crime themselves are paying the price for law enforcement practices that are still focused only on criminal justice. Victims are not given information in a universal and timely manner about services, restitution, and compensation, and so too many cannot take advantage of them.

While law enforcement in the United States is not being reprimanded for such shortcomings, it is paying the price in lost reports, low victim satisfaction rates, and low arrest rates. Recognizing that this is the reality—no matter how well intentioned individual officers may be—this chapter calls for rethinking the overall mission of policing in order to strike an effective and just balance between enforcement and serving the needs of victims of crime.

POLICE RESPONSE

Let's return for a moment to the composite case taken from the 1982 President's Task Force that I shared with you in the first chapter about a fifty-year-old woman who had just had a man break into her home in the middle of the night, rape her, and then rob her. Now let's look at the composite case description of the police phase of this crime:

> Terrified, you rush to the first lighted house on the block. While you wait for the police, you pray that your attacker was bluffing when he said he'd return if you called them. Finally, what you expect to be help arrives. The police ask questions, take notes, dust for finger-prints, make photographs. When you tell them you were raped, they take you to the hospital. . . .
>
> You have lived through the crime and made it through the initial investigation. They've caught the man who harmed you, and he's been charged with armed burglary, robbery, and rape. Now he'll be tried. Now you expect justice. You receive a subpoena for a preliminary hearing. No one tells you what it will involve, how long it will take, or how you should prepare. You assume that this is the only time you will have to appear. But you are only beginning your initiation into a system that will grind away at you for months, disrupt your life, affect your emotional stability, and certainly cost you money; it may cost you your job, and, for the duration, will prevent you from putting the crime behind you and reconstructing your life.

The composite case above illustrates how the victim may be treated by the system. Just how much of this scenario could be experienced in 2010 is not clear; governments have not invested in the research to check up on how victims are treated by the police and courts today, so we may never know. Unfortunately, victims who do report to the police today can still expect just as much disruption, expense, and trauma as they can increased support and justice.

Victims' frustration and pain are too often left to fester. They will be lucky to get any sympathy at all from the police or the justice system as a whole, even if an individual officer or lawyer empathizes with their pain and frustration. What's worse, the unfortunately few victims who will be used as witnesses will go to court when it suits the judge and lawyers—not at a time that is convenient for the victim. Their concerns will not be heard, they will lose income and have to pay most of their own travel and other expenses, and they will be forced to live with their fears for their own safety. We'll look at these in more depth later on in this chapter.

WHY MANY VICTIMS DON'T CALL FOR HELP OR ENFORCEMENT

The relationship between law enforcement and victims of crime appears to be simple. If you have been a victim of crime, then you will call the police. You will get protection from the accused because the police will catch and their system will convict and (if necessary) incarcerate the perpetrator. Right? Maybe not. While a moral obligation to report crimes may have been a reality at one point in time, today the issue is not so black and white.

Low Rates of Crime Reporting

The first problem is that many victims of crime do not even call the police for a variety of reasons. Fifty-one percent of persons who are victims of a property crime and 66 percent of persons who are victims of a violent crime do not call the police in the United States.[2] These nonreporting rates have remained steady for many years in the United States and in England and Wales, but have gotten worse in Canada.[3] For a property offense for which one has insurance, the trend in nonreporting drops to 6 percent nonreporting for auto theft and 27 percent nonreporting for house burglaries—confirming that one common reason for reporting is to claim insurance.

In figure 3.1, I present comparisons between the proportions of victimizations not reported to the police by victims of auto theft, burglary, robbery, and assault, using the International Crime Victim Survey (ICVS). Overall, the results show that a disturbing proportion of victims do not report their victimizations. It shows higher rates of nonreporting for robbery and assault, where the victim is not insured.

The ICVS asked victims who did report their crimes about their satisfaction with the service they received from the police. Unfortunately, *less than half* of victims who reported their victimization to the police were satisfied with the response they received. Victims repeatedly expressed disappointment in the lack of interest that police took in their personal

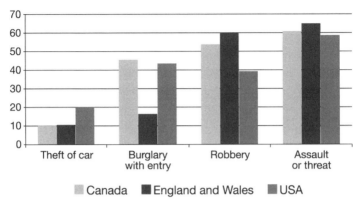

Figure 3.1. Proportion of victimizations not reported to police for auto theft, burglary, robbery, and assault

situation, and were also disillusioned by the police's lack of action on their cases. Forty percent also complained about the lack of information they got from law enforcement.[4]

Clearly, many of the core needs discussed in chapter 1 are regularly going unmet. One of the most disturbing statistics is the high nonreporting rates of rape and sexual assault. In the survey of violence against women by Kilpatrick mentioned in chapter 1, a staggering 84 percent of those raped did *not* call the police. For rape on college campuses, the proportion was even higher. What's more, in over 60 percent of domestic violence cases, the victim did not go to the police. It is clear that many fewer female victims of violence report to the police than male victims. These statistics should set off alarm bells about how police respond to victims of crime.[5] Fortunately, this chapter will discuss some best practices to provide options and remedies.

Low Rates of Crime Resolution

Reporting is just one of the challenges that the all-enforcement model of policing faces. Clearance rates—the proportion of crimes known to police for which there is a known perpetrator—have been dropping over the decades. For property crimes, less than 20 percent are cleared. For violent crimes, the proportion is closer to 50 percent,[6] but this reflects the reality that the victim has often seen the perpetrator firsthand, and in some cases (such as violence between intimate partners), the victim *knows* the perpetrator and can identity him to the police.

The cumulative impact of victims' decisions not to report their crimes to police, as well as the police's inability to effectively resolve crimes, results in only a small proportion of victims having their cases go to criminal courts. Further, many cases do not result in a conviction. Even in cases where the victim has seen or knows the offender, it is still difficult to get a conviction. Cumulatively, only 3 percent of victimizations result in an offender being convicted.[7] In figure 3.2, I have shown the extent to which sexual assault victimizations will reach the police, will result in an offender being identified, and then an offender convicted. This figure combines data from the National Crime Victimization Survey and the important survey undertaken by Kilpatrick with data from the FBI on the extent to which police departments solve cases.

The National Crime Survey asks victims who reported to the police *why* they reported to the police. As shown in figure 3.3, the dominant reason given by victims is that they want to ensure their own personal safety and prevent the offenses from occurring to them or to others again. This response reinforces our understanding of victims' core need to recover their confidence in their safety and security. It also reflects their concern that the victimization they suffered painfully should not be suffered by others.[8]

When police arrest an offender, they are able to stop him from committing crime while he is in custody. But if the court releases the offender on bail, the victim may be disappointed by law enforcement and the justice

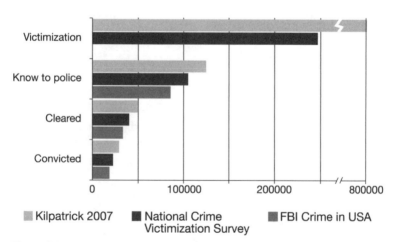

Figure 3.2.   Proportion of rape victimizations not reported to police and the impact of unsolved cases on conviction rates

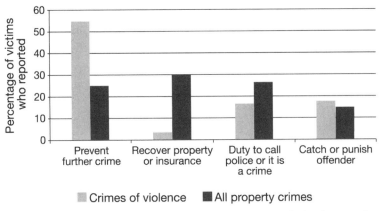

Figure 3.3. Reasons for victims to report their victimization to the police

system and will likely feel that their own (and others') security is again at risk. While studies have had difficulty proving that police actions actually do have a sustained impact on preventing future crimes, victims would undoubtedly feel more assured if a commitment to this objective was at least made clear by officers and law enforcement in general.

The second reason that victims give for reporting to the police is that they want to recover their stolen property, get damages repaired, and collect insurance. We have already seen the core need of victims to get reparation, and they hope that the police can assist them directly with this. However, it seems to me that the police have not been good at getting stolen property returned, judging at least by the amount of goods sold in police auctions. However, there is a lack of reliable research to confirm or disconfirm this. But what the police *are* undeniably good at is providing insurance companies with assurance that victims' property was indeed stolen, and so the police do facilitate victims' need to collect insurance payments and, by extension, reparation.

We will see in chapter 5 how this collection of reparation relates to victims' getting restitution from the offender. It is important to note that this particular National Crime Survey question about reasons for reporting to police does not allow for victims to respond to different options in terms of how they want to be reimbursed.

Some victims call the police because they feel it is their duty to do so and because it is a crime *not* to report to police. While in the past victims may have been expected to go to the police out of civic duty, today that response is no longer the reality. Victims are busy with other things and are increasingly realizing that a sense of duty alone is not motivation enough.

As we can see in figure 3.3, punishment of the offender is the least frequent motivation for reporting to police. Less than 20 percent of victims give this reason, which should raise questions about governments investing all of taxpayers' money in law enforcement, criminal justice, and corrections—most of which have the sole purpose of doling out appropriate punishment to offenders. However, some of these expenditures also provide safety from the accused, which is definitely part of victims' prevention response.

While it is important to make arrests wherever possible, for law enforcement to fully succeed in enforcing laws it must look at better ways of getting convictions. This may require investing in the improved treatment of victims so that they cooperate with evidence and as witnesses. It is also possible that if more crimes were reported to the police, then more information would be made available to them from which they could analyze patterns and so make more arrests.

Victim advocacy groups often focus on reforms in terms of prosecutors and judges. However, we must also look at those law enforcement officers who are first on the scene of a victimization. What can they do to directly meet victims' needs on the ground level? That is what we will consider in the remainder of this chapter.

THERE TO HELP: VICTIMS' EXPECTATIONS OF LAW ENFORCEMENT

When victims call the police following their victimization, it is often the first time that they have had contact with the criminal justice system. They are often in need of medical assistance, protection, and crisis services. If they have had property stolen, they want it returned. Not surprisingly, the victim's emotional trauma is often the most brutal effect of the crime.

What Information Do Victims Need from Police Immediately Following a Victimization?

The police are well situated to extend crisis support to victims. Because police officers are often the first officials to talk to the crime victim, they are able to reassure the victim of his or her safety and refer the victim to the appropriate crisis services in the community. However, for police officers to effectively do this, there must be guidelines and standards they can follow to help them balance the needs of the victim with the need of getting the details to catch the perpetrator. All frontline officers must know how to strike this balance.

Police officer training must include much, much more than simply sensitizing officers to the needs of victims. It must focus on what all police officers should do to reassure victims, how they can provide victims with basic information, and how they should refer them to services such as mental health care and social support. Officers must also be trained in how to provide assistance and referrals in terms of practical issues like repairs.

The police, available around the clock, have sophisticated communications equipment linked to central dispatchers. Clearly, police officers are in a position to extend help to victims when they need it the most, and with the proper training and resources, there is no reason why they should not facilitate the first steps in helping victims recover.

What Information Do Victims Need from the Police in the Medium Term?

After the initial victimization event, victims of crime will want information as to the progress of the police investigation. At the time an offender is identified by the police, victims may be concerned that the offender is going to retaliate because they called the police. They often express considerable disbelief if they find out that an offender who has just been caught has also just been released. Notably, victims want to know what criminal procedures they can expect to unfold. Victims can be unfamiliar with the courts and therefore want information as to where to go and what will happen during the court proceedings. Sometimes, victims want to present their views about these processes (and have them heard).

Victims also have a core need to receive information about how to prevent crime in the future. For instance, they might want to know how to make their homes more secure from burglars. Consequently, an important service that must be made available to victims is to be presented with reliable and valid information on victimization-prevention measures, which can be backed up with research and evidence—not just gut feelings.

Laws to Ensure That Victims' Needs for Information Are Met

It is surprising (and somewhat disheartening) to me that the points mentioned above about what information police officers can—and should—provide to victims in the short- and medium-term still need to be argued in 2010. In fact, many of these issues have been addressed by laws in the past (albeit to limited effect). The longest-standing and most common laws to help crime victims are those requiring police to provide victims with information. Some constitutional amendments require action by law enforcement, and many state laws specify in detail how police should react. But we have no idea where or when these laws are enforced (or if they are at all).[9]

Heads of law enforcement agencies are in full agreement that such measures which correspond to victims' core needs must be unconditionally met. When the IACP adopted its "bill of rights" as early as 1983, it urged police leadership to "establish procedures and train personnel" to implement the "incontrovertible rights of all crime victims," which call on police to treat victims as "privileged clients" by ensuring that victims are to be:

[a] Free from intimidation;

[b] Told of financial assistance and social services available and how to apply for them;

[c] Provided a secure area during interviews and court proceedings, and to be notified if presence in court is needed;

[d] Provided a quick return of stolen or other personal property when no longer needed as evidence;

[e] [Given] a speedy disposition of the case, and to be periodically informed of case status and final disposition; and, wherever personnel and resource capabilities allow, to be notified in felony cases whenever the perpetrator is released from custody; [and]

[f] Interviewed by a female official in the case of rape and other sexual offences, wherever personnel and resource capabilities allow.[10]

Unfortunately, even though this IACP bill of rights comes from those professionals who know the law enforcement industry the best, it is one of many examples of wishful thinking when it comes to support and justice for victims of crime. Did police leaderships train personnel? The odd few did. Did police agencies establish procedures? Too rarely.

And most unfortunately, these guidelines, which have the ability to concretely respond to victims' core need for information, were ignored during some key law enforcement reformations in recent years in the United States. For example, were these guidelines part of Compstat's goals? No. Were they adopted by high-profile police reformers such as former New York City mayor Rudy Giuliani or William Bratton when he was the chief of police of New York or Los Angeles? No. Did Chicago incorporate them as part of the well-known Chicago Alternative Policing Strategy that sought on-the-ground implementation of community problem-solving policing tactics? No. Did then president Bill Clinton make them part of the Community Orienting Policing Service Office? Again, the answer is no. Sadly, even the authoritative U.S. National Research Council study on the fairness and effectiveness of policing could only manage one measly index entry on victims, and that is on the characteristics of victims—not their treatment.[11] This is hardly fairness to victims of crime!

Real Solutions That First-on-the-Scene Officers Can Employ

The National Sheriffs' Association (NSA) calls for a focus on its own three needs of crime victims, which are close to three of the core needs in this book. They identify the need to feel safe, the need to express emotion, and the need to know what comes next.[12] It has proposed specific actions that law enforcement officers can take to better respond to victims. Similarly, the British code of practice for victims of crime sets out standards for police response to victims.

The most obvious step is to require that every officer responding to a 911 call make the victim aware of whatever services are available to them with a short and simple leaflet. This concept has been working effectively in England and Wales. Alternatively, the simple step of requiring the responding officer to provide the victim with a card would greatly assist victims in identifying the key telephone numbers of such services as the local distress center, locksmiths, the criminal injuries compensation authority, the regional crime prevention unit, and a service that could refer the victim to other community services. Ideally, this card would have empty fields in which the officer would identify both the file number of the case as well as the name of the responding police officer.

In terms of further solutions, much greater use could be made of modern wireless and communication technologies to ensure that the individual patrol officer can efficiently inform the victim of available services. Responding officers, while still with the victim, should be able to request details from their dispatchers about victim services such as the availability and location of emergency welfare services, rape crisis centers, transition homes for battered women, victim support units, and criminal injuries compensation authorities.

We know from the International Crime Victim Survey that only 4 percent of victims who reported to the police had their core needs addressed by formal victim service programs (even though, as we will see in chapter 4, these programs succeed in meeting multiple needs of crime victims). This is likely because many victims were simply not made aware of the availability of these services. Similarly, the major reason why eligible victims do not access compensation from the state following a violent victimization is that they were not made aware of these programs, as we will see in chapter 5.[13] Thus, there is a real and immediate need for law enforcement to disseminate this information in an easily accessible way.

In addition to providing the victim with information about services, police officers can provide immediate emotional support. The NSA's guide calls for listening to the victim and encouraging them to talk freely about what happened. As obvious as this may sound to any person with a reasonable amount of sensitivity, officers do not consistently extend this much-needed support to victims and, by failing to do so, are overlooking a simple yet important solution to meeting victims' core need for emotional support.

Another simple and effective solution for meeting victims' core need for information is to keep them informed about their cases. A recent study of co-victims—in this case, the family members of persons murdered in cases for which an offender was never arrested—showed that most were never informed when the file was transferred to a different detective or when the police decided little more could be done. One recommendation of this report was to inform the co-victims of such changes. Again, while it may seem an obvious solution to ensuring that co-victims' needs for information are met, this courtesy is not universally extended for reasons that I cannot begin to accept.

We know that these solutions work. Indeed, the effectiveness of these simple and inexpensive procedures has been demonstrated by some police departments. As early as the 1970s, the City of Edmonton's Police Services in Alberta, Canada, initiated a procedure requiring responding officers to provide victims with a card that identifies the phone number for the victim assistance unit and a list of services it provides. By 1980, this approach was assisting 3,000 victims a month in a city of 600,000 that had approximately 1,200 police personnel. One indicator of the program's effectiveness is that it doubled the number of claims to the Alberta Victims Compensation Board in the first year of its operation. Clearly, the card was successful in putting more victims in contact with the services they required.

A major reason for the victim services card program's success was the personal commitment of Edmonton's chief of police at the time to create a program for victims. Two other reasons were that the patrol officers were *required* (not requested) to give victims a card, and that the victim assistance unit gained full access to all police incident reports.

Edmonton's police services unit can provide a successful model for initiatives to meet other victims' core needs. Special efforts were made to train officers in victims' issues and to provide them with guidelines so that they could respond to victims in a more sensitive manner. Guidelines were also in place to link victims to a central unit that had more than a hundred volunteer victim advocates who may be called on twenty-four hours a day to assist victims suffering severe traumas such as sexual assaults, armed robberies, break-ins, and the violent deaths of family members.

Edmonton has implemented simple and effective methods for meeting two of the core needs of victims—the need to receive information and the need to have a sympathetic ear. Japan's National Police Agency has gotten even more involved in victim issues, not only by establishing various programs to support victims of crime, but also by taking on the primary responsibility for providing compensation to victims of crime. So we know that law enforcement across North America and around the world *can* implement real solutions. The only question that remains is, will they?

CRIME VICTIMS AS THE ZENITH OF LAW ENFORCEMENT

In 1999, the International Association of Chiefs of Police identified some of the global challenges for responding to victims of crime in the twenty-first century. Three of these were to enact and enforce consistent, fundamental rights for victims; to provide victims with access to comprehensive and quality services; and to integrate victims' issues into all levels of the nation's law enforcement and legal education systems.

In 2006, the Commission on Accreditation for Law Enforcement Agencies updated Standard 55 on victims and witnesses. Unlike the code of practice in England and Wales or the legislation in Michigan, it does little to specify *how* police officers will inform victims of crime of the services that are available. It is written more in terms of the victim serving law enforcement than law enforcement serving victims as clients. It does, however, mention cooperation with community agencies.

Now, the IACP wants to make crime victims the zenith of its work. In 2009, the IACP published four practical reports in its series, *Enhancing Law Enforcement Response to Victims*.[14] These emanated from a grant from the U.S. Office for Victims of Crime. The OVC's purpose in funding these reports was "not to create a separate victim unit but put crime victims' interests and needs at the 'zenith' of the response to crime."

Much of the content of the four IACP reports is built around seven critical needs of crime victims, which are similar to the core needs that I identified in chapter 1. In figure 3.4, I have presented an overview of law enforcement actions that would enhance the response to the victim's core needs, which I now discuss using particularly the IACP and NSA materials.

Law enforcement actions that enhance the response to core needs

	Core Needs for Victims of Crime	Right to legislation and implementation to provide
Support		
1	Recognition and emotional support	Trained informal and professional crisis support; Gendered response
2	Information on criminal justice, their case, services and personal developments	Timely information on: law enforcement, criminal justice and corrections; case
3	Assistance to access practical, medical and social services	Emergency calls
Justice		
4	Help to pay bills caused by victimization	Emergency funds; Ticket for restitution from offender
5	Personal safety and protection from accused	Prevention of revictimization and protection from accused
6	Choice to voice in justice	Provide evidence for criminal and civil cases
Good Government		
7	Best public safety	Modern strategies that reduce crime and prevent victimization
8	Implementation	Leadership, partnering, training and standards, performance assessment

Figure 3.4. Law enforcement actions that enhance the response to core needs

Victims Need to Feel Safe (Core Need Number 5)

The first major need identified by the NSA is for victims to feel safe and be protected from the accused. This seems closer to the common image of the professional cop who is trained to respond to violence, separate brawlers, make arrests, and use weapons such as guns and Tasers. The victim may also be looking for a referral to a safe place, such as a transition house in instances where a woman has been battered. Overall, victims need to be assured of their protection from an offender who may return to intimidate them, and they may also require advice on ways to protect themselves and their property in cases where locks or doors have been broken. In a broad sense, this need for security includes victims' need to receive reassurance from police that they will make it through the crisis and won't be alone.

Victims Need to Express Their Emotions (Core Need Number 1)

The second major need of victims identified by the NSA is that they must be able to tell their story. They need to get a sympathetic ear when a police officer responds to their call for assistance. While the idea of a tough cop being a sensitive listener may seem like an oxymoron, the victim's need in this instance is not for in-depth counseling but rather for a few extra minutes of active listening. This approach makes up an important component of the recommendations for reform from both the IACP and the NSA.

Victims Need to Know What Comes Next (Core Need Number 2)

A third major need of victims is to gain understanding about what is going to happen in the enforcement and criminal justice processes and what is happening with the accused. They also want to know how they can get medical care and what services are available. While it is normal for a police officer to call for medical help, it is not as normal (but just as necessary) for an officer to provide information about what will happen next and to refer victims to agencies that can help with repairs and provide services such as counseling.

To Serve and Protect Victims of Crime

The IACP's original 1983 bill of rights left enforcing the law as the principal mission of policing. Today, the IACP is making important proposals to shift the police's focus on victim assistance from a side matter to a mainstream issue. Under its executive director Dan Rosenblatt, former president and elected board member of the National Organization for Victim Assistance, the IACP's long-overdue proposals bring victim issues out of the shadows and place them on center stage.

If the IACP proposals were to be enacted, professional policing would not just be about law enforcement anymore, but would be about reducing the number of crime victims and assisting victims to get support and balanced justice. If this shift could be achieved, it would be a wonderful breakthrough toward assuring that victims of crime receive reliable and practical responses to their core needs while balancing policing's commitment to enforcing laws and arresting dangerous offenders.

The slogan of many North American police services is *to serve and protect*. However, my view is that the reality of police operations is more focused on response than service, and more on investigation than protection. After all, police resources in the United States are roughly committed 60 percent to responding to 911 calls and 20 percent to investigating the offense in order to arrest a perpetrator where possible.[15] The other 20 percent of police resources are allocated among many competing priorities, too few of which have to do with service and protection.

In contrast to this actual tendency of law enforcement *to respond and investigate*, the IACP proposals would truly make serving and protecting victims of crime a reality—thereby transforming the victim of crime into the privileged client of policing. The service would occur when officers respond to the crisis, provide information, and treat victims with respect in the investigation. The protection would be present when law enforcement protects victims of crime where necessary and contributes to public safety. What victim advocates and the IACP are proposing is a new and achievable police mission.

The good news is that these calls are coming from the International Association of Chiefs of Police. Don't forget, this association represents more than twenty thousand police executives from eighty-nine countries—all of whom are in leadership positions in policing across the United States and around the world. What's more, the IACP knows that their proposed strategies will work. In 2004, it developed a preliminary strategy and tested it in three police departments of different sizes. This on-the-ground pilot testing led to the guidelines for implementation, and also resulted in a resource kit for other police departments to use as a model. So, we know that we can achieve a newly focused police mission through reasonable means. But will policing ever truly change to better balance the needs of victims? We will have to see. It is certainly in policing's interest, if not in its tradition.

One of the most impressive parts of the IACP proposals is to follow up and check on whether these goals are being met in accordance with victims' eighth core need, which should be the inalienable right for implementation. They propose doing so by measuring whether victims of crime are *actually* getting the service they should be. The assessment must be done by surveys independently administered directly to victims. This step on its own would catapult crime victims into the forefront of policing as clients of law enforcement. Victims and citizens must demand this shift in focus. After all, until these proposals are actually implemented in police departments, they remain only words, not action.

Helping Victims Helps Law Enforcement: A Collaborative Approach

The IACP makes the argument that helping victims of crime is, in actuality, helping law enforcement. It proposes opportunities for law enforcement to increase its efficiency and effectiveness by fostering greater collaboration with victim service providers. While this may get victims increased access to services and compensation, it also frees the officers to investigate crimes. Other examples of how helping victims in turn helps law enforcement are that police officers who can understand crisis and trauma reactions will enhance the cooperation of victims, as well as improve the overall image of the police in the community.[16]

Evaluation

The IACP is clear that success in enhancing law enforcement's response to victims of crime requires measurable performance indicators. Their suggestions to achieve an effective form of evaluation include measuring victimization and repeat victimization rates, recording numbers of victims accessing services, and analyzing the number of requests filed for compensation from the state. While the IACP has a clear vision for ways forward, there is still work to be done in developing and implementing its evaluation methods. For example, even though the IACP highlights a seven-point inventory of victim needs in its report, the means for measuring success in terms of these seven points is not identified.

However, an effective evaluative tool could easily be within our grasp. For instance, safety was the first IACP need. So, any survey should look at the extent to which victims had this need met through analyzing the numbers of placements in transition houses, instances of receiving assistance to get locks repaired, arrests of perpetrators, and bail decisions that recognized the needs of the victims.

GENDERED RESPONSES FROM LAW ENFORCEMENT

Given the extreme reticence of most women to report sexual assault and rape to the police, combined with the hesitation of many female victims to report domestic violence, there is a need to radically change the procedures and image of policing. While police knowledge of such assaults may not always lead to fewer assaults and prevention, it is well established that many men are involved in more than one sexual assault.

There are likely many factors that contribute to the high nonreporting rates among female victims of sexual and domestic assault. For example, women do not always have the confidence that their reports will be taken seriously by police. If they know the perpetrator, then they are often concerned about his reaction. Furthermore, their social circle may not be supportive if it becomes public that they have reported being sexually assaulted—let alone by a common acquaintance.

In 1983 the IACP called for a female officer to be available to female victims of rape. If implemented, this would have been a good start, but I want more. We can learn a lot from developing countries where all-female police stations are providing a safer and more sympathetic reception for female victims of gender-related crimes. In 1983, Brazil's State Council on the Status of Women advocated for action because so many Brazilian women had been the victims of violence and so few went to the police. So, with the support of the Brazilian Bar Association and various nongovernmental women's organizations, the state council came up with a number of solutions, one of which was intended to empower women and to increase the proportion of offenders who came to the attention of the police.

The State Council on the Status of Women proposed that police stations staffed only by female officers be created in the poorer areas of Brazil. In 1985, the world's first all-female police station, mandated to receive complaints and investigate crimes against women and children, was established in São Paulo. Brazil had a system of appointing police chiefs from outside the police ranks, and so female lawyers, judges, and others were appointed as chiefs to these all-female stations. Importantly, these all-female units provided victimized women with social and psychological support services, emergency shelter where necessary, and an all-female patrol car.

As a means for meeting female victims' needs, all-female police stations are extremely successful. Reporting of violence against women at the all-female police station in São Paulo increased from 2,000 complaints in 1985 to over 7,000 in 1989. In Brazil, there are now three hundred such police stations, and several other countries (including Argentina, Costa Rica, India, the Philippines, and Pakistan) have adopted similar measures to great success.

Another important way to decrease rates of female nonreporting is to provide sustainable funds to sexual assault crisis centers so that professional staff can work with victims of rape and sexual assault. Trained staff members can then help victimized women report to police when (and if) they choose and with the professional support they need. One study in Chicago found that rape survivors who reported to police exhibited higher levels of psychological and physical distress than did victims who went to rape crisis centers instead. Sadly, about half of victims in this study described the legal system as being harmful to them.[17] This cannot continue.

In the 1970s, some police departments in North America developed partnerships between police officers and social workers. A police officer and a social worker would respond jointly to cases such as domestic violence and sexual assault. In some cases, the social worker was hired by the police department directly, and in others, she was employed by a separate group.

The Metropolitan Nashville Police Department provides an encouraging example of this strategy in action. In 1975, it started a victim intervention program in which a social worker or mental health worker was hired to provide free crisis counseling to victims of violent crime.[18] Building on

the success of this program, the department created a separate domestic
violence division to respond to the needs of victims of domestic violence
in 1994. This division has an effective collaboration with the local prosecutor's office. This program is believed to be the largest of its type in the
nation, with thirty-two specially trained professionals who handle thousands of cases each year. The Metropolitan Nashville Police Department
believes that this program contributed to a reduction in domestic violence
by 40 percent over two years.

Surprisingly, the movement toward community policing and problem-
oriented policing has not picked up on these partnering strategies. However,
other strategies are gaining ground in the interim. The authors of a four-
volume series on violence against women point to the seismic changes that
have occurred across the United States in responding to domestic violence.
One such strategy is the creation of specialized domestic violence courts in
some states. What's more, in some exemplary cases, police action focuses on
safety plans for victims. Many of these safety plans include a period of time
in a transition house or refuge, and funding from VOCA and VAWA in the
United States has led to many more transition houses in operation. Furthermore, as we will see in chapters 4 and 7, institutional cooperation between
such key players as law enforcement, prosecutors, transition houses, and
treatment programs for batterers provides avenues to achieve real solutions
in both assistance to victims and prevention of victimization.[19]

Other Ways to Make Victims of Crime Clients
of Law Enforcement

The police in Japan are responsible for distributing emergency funds
to victims of crime and running the criminal injuries compensation board.
Since 1981, they have had extensive experience with these responsibilities.
Such an approach would overcome the principal obstacle in getting compensation in North America, which is that eligible crime victims rarely find
out about compensation programs.

I understand that in the Netherlands, police are able to give tickets to
order offenders to pay restitution to the victim. The logic of this is obvious.
It works like a parking ticket, so if the police have good reason to suppose
that a particular person stole the property from the victim, they make out
a ticket. The offender can either pay or contest the ticket in court. As in

the case of parking and speeding tickets, there are limits on the value of the restitution order than can be made out.

Another important challenge faced by police departments is to engage in modern strategies to prevent victimization by reducing crime, as will be discussed in chapter 7. Much of this has to do with using their resources to analyze crime patterns in collaboration with social services, schools, and other programs that are in a position to tackle the causes. Police can also invest in training for citizens in schools and universities to teach ways for people to intervene as Good Samaritans. Given the rapid advances in technology such as cell phones with cameras, citizens can learn how to use this technology to protect lives and property.

If police leadership seriously wants *to serve and protect,* then it must shift policing from a reactive agency with little accountability to victims to one that serves victims and the general public. After all, they are the folks who pay police budgets and suffer the consequences when their core needs go unmet by law enforcement.

DEMANDS FOR LEGISLATORS

Victims of crime are important clients and funders (taxpayers) for law enforcement services. Modern police agencies have highly skilled personnel with great potential. They must provide victims with safety, support, information, and more as overviewed in figure 3.4. The majority of victims—particularly women impacted by violence—are not reporting crime to the police. The IACP is rightly aiming to put victims at the zenith of policing. Not only will policing benefit, but (more importantly) the core needs of victims will also be met.

Legislators must reinforce the significant progress that has been made by law enforcement to provide protection to victims of domestic violence.

Legislators must hold law enforcement accountable for providing information in a timely manner to victims. A protocol must establish what information is to be provided to which victims and how, and must identify when a victim is to be referred to a community agency.

Legislators must require law enforcement to develop and follow protocols to better meet the needs of women and children who are victims of sexual assault or other gender-related crimes. These victims must be respected and supported in their interactions with law enforcement. Best practices include the all-female police stations in Brazil.

Legislators must develop a timetable to implement the IACP strategy to enhance the law enforcement response to victims of crime. This will include the core elements of police leadership to make the changes, partnering between police and other agencies, training of personnel to pre-established standards, and monitoring performance. Best practices include the IACP test sites such as Charlotte-Mecklenburg.

Legislators must ensure independent surveys of victims who report to the police (as well as those who do not) to measure the extent to which their core needs were met.

Legislators must foster the greater use of modern technology to facilitate the safe intervention and provision of evidence by Good Samaritans.

Legislators must encourage research and development, and exchanges with other countries on innovative ways to meet the core needs of victims of crime. Best practices include England and Wales (specifically, the code of practice referred to in chapter 2), Japan (police's role in compensation from state), and the Netherlands (restitution from offenders through citations).

Legislators must prepare standards that put victims at the zenith of law enforcement and require police departments to meet those standards.

(4)

CARING FOR VICTIMS

Support, Mental Health, and Assistance

In chapter 1, we saw the extent of the losses as well as physical and mental health injuries that are caused by crime, and I grouped the core needs under eight headings. In this chapter, I will look at how victim services respond to the core needs of recognition, emotional support, and assistance with accessing practical, medical, and social services. These services also meet the needs for information about criminal justice and, in the case of domestic violence shelters, offer personal safety and protection from the accused. Once again we will see the limits of current data and the importance of the core need of ensuring implementation.

This chapter is divided into three parts. In the first, I will discuss those who care for victims of crime who are not specialized victim service providers—our friends, neighbors, and medical and mental health professionals. In the second, I will review the types of victim service providers that are available to all victims of crime. These generic services include victim assistance agencies in the community. In the third, I will look at services that are specialized to respond to the needs of victims of domestic violence, sexual assault and rape, child abuse, and elder abuse.

Obviously, victims of violent crime need to get care for their physical wounds from the health care system. But what are the financial and other costs of this care? What about care for the post-traumatic stress disorder that they acquired as a result of the ordeal? How can victim assistance organizations *actually* assist and protect victims? How can specialized crisis centers (such as those established for sexual assault victims, battered women, and abused children) be strengthened, reorganized and sustainably funded to better meet the needs of victims?

GENERAL CARE FOR VICTIMS

Family, Friends, and Neighbors

Victims have a need for emotional and psychological support in order to recover from their traumas. Often the first person to whom victims turn after a crime is a person with whom they're living, but they may also turn to friends and colleagues at work. They are looking for someone who can provide emotional support and help them sort out what to do next. Were they injured enough to go to a hospital? Should they call the police? What should they do about the broken window?

We do little to train friends, neighbors, and the general public to be able to give this emotional first aid. For some, it comes naturally, while for others, their own emotional reactions (or lack thereof) may make things worse for the victim. We must help people to gain the active listening skills necessary to help victims by increasing the frequency and quality of open discussions about victimization, and we must also disseminate basic knowledge about the presence of victim services so that any individual can help a victim.

We also need to help victims be aware of their own reaction to the event so that they can seek help if needed. Witnesses of violence and trauma or those who have listened to a victim can often experience the same (or even worse) reactions as the principal victims. One of the curious realities about witnesses of violence is that victims may recover more quickly than witnesses who failed to intervene.

Medical Care for Physical Injuries

Let's continue following the composite case compiled by the U.S. President's Task Force on Victims of Crime. Remember, you are a fifty-year-old woman who has been raped in her own home:

> Bleeding from cuts, your front teeth knocked out, bruised and in pain, you are told that your wounds are superficial, that rape itself is not considered

an injury. Awaiting treatment, you sit alone for hours, suffering the stares of curious passersby. You feel dirty, bruised, disheveled, and abandoned. When your turn comes for examination, the intern seems irritated because he has been called out to treat you. While with you, he says that he hates to get involved in rape cases because he doesn't like going to court. He asks if you "knew the man you had sex with."

The nurse says she wouldn't be out alone at this time of night. It seems pointless to explain that the attacker broke into your house and had a knife. An officer says you must go through this process, then the hospital sends you a bill for the examination that the investigators insisted upon. They give you a box filled with test tubes and swabs and envelopes and tell you to hold onto it. They'll run some tests if they ever catch your rapist.

Finally, you get home somehow, in a cab you paid for and wearing a hospital gown because they took your clothes as evidence. Everything that the attacker touched seems soiled. You're afraid to be in your house alone. The one place where you were always safe, at home, is sanctuary no longer. You are afraid to remain, yet terrified to leave your home unprotected.[1]

In the last hundred years, advances in general medicine and in emergency and intensive care mean that victims who are injured as a result of violent crime have much better chances of surviving gun and knife wounds and recovering from cuts, bruises, and broken bones. The AIDS epidemic has improved treatments for infections such as HIV and Hepatitis C. Generally, such medical care is universally available. This is all good news.

In North America and Europe, emergency response systems exist that include the widespread availability of a national emergency number such as 911 that links police, paramedics, and fire services directly to the victim or witness. In some cities in France and Spain, a special mobile emergency medical service exists that is led by doctors trained in emergency response. They have much more equipment and training than paramedics in North America. They travel in special ambulances to help the victims where the tragedy is happening.

In the United States, there are potentially major difficulties that victims of crime need to overcome when seeking physical health care following their victimizations—namely, who will pay for the services. Many victims of violence who are poor or out of work will not have state or private insurance to pay for this care. While most medical centers will not turn a person away, receiving care can lead to ballooning costs. These medical expenses leave victims with a tremendous financial burden incurred through no fault of their own. As we shall see in chapter 5, in the United States, 52 percent of victim compensation paid by state programs goes to medical bills, but even this is not sufficient in alleviating victims of the financial burden that may plague them long after their attack.[2] Some of this will change with the adoption in 2011 of the Affordable Health Care Act.

In Canada and England and Wales, the vast majority of emergency and health care expenses are covered under their national and universal health schemes. However, victims may find themselves paying out of pocket for ambulance services and prescription drugs. In these countries, the criminal injuries compensation programs that I will discuss in chapter 5 usually reimburse these expenses—if the victim is aware of the programs and applies for them, that is.

As we will discuss later in this chapter, the recent development of Sexual Assault Nurse Examiners (SANE) in North America has systematized the care provided to victims of sexual assault and rape—at least in instances when a trained nurse is available. More good news is that VOCA took a long-overdue step forward to ensure that victims of rape and sexual assault are not required to pay for their own rape kits such as those used in SANE procedures. In the United States in 2008, the states reimbursed $30 million in response to 50,000 claims to compensate victims for the costs of forensic sexual assault programs.

Logically, if government pays for universal police, judicial, and corrections services, it should also pay for the medical services necessary to help victims recover from physical injuries. Yes, the government might recover these costs from the offender or from a fund benefiting from fines against offenders, but the bottom line is clear: victims should not have to worry about whether or not they will get or be able to pay for medical care for physical injuries.

Victim Control versus Mandatory Medical Reporting

When accessing medical health care, mandatory reporting policies compromise victims' confidentiality and self-determinism. For victims of crime who have already been disempowered by their perpetrators, it is important for them to be able to choose how far they want to go with medical, social, and enforcement agencies. So, the laws that make reporting mandatory for doctors can inadvertently make victims hesitate to seek assistance for themselves.

In all jurisdictions in North America, the medical professions are legally required to report certain cases of intentional violence. For example, medical staff must report instances of violence against children to the child protection agency in the jurisdiction where they suspect the child is being abused. There are similar provisions for the elderly and often for vulnerable adults who are not able to speak out for themselves. There are also special regulations for reporting domestic violence, although these are less clear.

The intention of these laws is to enable protection agencies and law enforcement to intervene to protect victims who are not able to protect themselves.[3] But they leave the victim who *is* able to make choices for herself in a dilemma as to whether to seek medical help or avoid it altogether, as it will automatically lead to dealing with the criminal justice system. These mandatory reporting regulations may also dissuade parents from seeking care for their child if they were responsible for their child's injury, such as in a case of shaken baby syndrome or other forms of child abuse.

The American Medical Association (AMA) rightly puts this reporting into context by suggesting that medical professionals be trained to recognize the indicators of abuse, know their legal obligations, and know how to use the agencies and services available to help victims such as sexual assault crisis centers, transition houses for battered women, child protection agencies, and victim service agencies.

If doctors do not intervene, they have to weigh the likelihood of a suit for *not acting* being brought against them. In one recent case, a doctor was found civilly liable for $11 million because he did not take action to protect two young sisters from being sexually abused by a sibling molester in Lake Placid, New York.[4]

The ability of the victim to choose how far they want to go with law enforcement is very important. One good advance has been the introduction of a "Jane Doe" rape kit in some sexual assault clinics and hospitals. This approach enables rape or sexual assault victims who are not prepared to report the assault to law enforcement (for whatever reason) to still receive medical care. Victims and clinics are not forced to report the crime to the police, and victims keep the forensic evidence in case they choose to report to the police at a later point in time.

Similarly, some colleges and universities allow for students to confidentially report sexual assaults. This privacy policy enables victims to share what happened to them without forcing them to report to law enforcement. The college can still track the factors that led to the crime, such as where the assault took place and under what conditions. So, while an incident may not lead to criminal justice action, it may still be able to assist the college in taking preventive measures to avoid other sexual assaults in the future. As I have shown in *Less Law, More Order*, prevention is often much more effective than enforcement in reducing the number of victims of crime.

CARE FOR MENTAL HEALTH INJURIES

Post-Traumatic Stress Disorder

The unfortunate truth is that it is common for victims to suffer some type of mental health disorder following their victimization. Of these disorders, post-traumatic stress disorder (PTSD) is the most universally recognized today. However, many victims will not be able to afford the services to treat their PTSD, and many of these untreated victims will not be able to recover on their own.

As described in chapter 1, PTSD is a well-established psychiatric disorder. PTSD describes common symptoms that follow a traumatic event that is typically lived by the victim as having been life threatening. For crime victims, this traumatic event may be a robbery, a sexual assault, or a motor vehicle crash. The sufferer may be the direct victim of the crime or an indirect victim such as a witness, a family member, or a friend.

It is considered normal to feel shock, numbness, and disorientation after a traumatic event. Some people process these emotions and make sense of their experience without many recurring symptoms. On the other hand, a victim is described as having PTSD when symptoms persist. The symptoms include having difficulty sleeping, mentally reliving the experience, and needing to avoid normal situations that remind the victim of the original trauma. Experiencing flashbacks of the event, having recurring and intense physical reactions such as rapid breathing or nausea, or being easily startled are just some of the disturbing symptoms of PTSD that are well known.[5]

What can be done to help victims recover from PTSD? Experts are still looking into the matter. The prestigious U.S. Institute of Medicine of the National Academy of Sciences assembled a panel of experts to review the studies on PTSD and came to the conclusion that the evidence is inadequate to determine the effectiveness of most treatments.[6] They looked at various drugs, psychotherapy (including cognitive restructuring, coping skills training, and eye movement desensitization), and family therapy. The panel did not reject any of the treatment programs, but they did positively focus on the therapies known to work. For example, a gradual exposure of patients suffering from PTSD to situations that create their symptoms allows them to eventually tolerate the situation. Thus, the good news is that experts do have at least some knowledge of how to help PTSD sufferers live lives that more closely resemble their lives before the crime.

The expert panel called for more refined research into PTSD, and so over the next ten years more definitive conclusions may come to light. The panel was particularly concerned about the experiences and treatment of war veterans. In light of this, I would like to call for more research that focuses on victims of crimes, and in particular, research that looks at the differences between PTSD in males and females, and the differences in sexual assault victims as opposed to victims of nonsexual violence when it comes to PTSD.

Unfortunately, the widespread recognition of PTSD does not necessarily go hand in hand with sufficient services to treat it, nor with the financial resources to pay for the treatment. In some jurisdictions, there will be qualified psychiatric and psychological services for victims to access. In others, this will not be the case. Either way, the challenge must be to ensure that the services are not paid for by the victim of the crime.

Just as we need better data on the extent of PTSD among crime victims, we also need estimates of the gap between victims' core needs and victim services, and ultimately what the costs would be to fill in that gap. In chapter 1, we saw economists' estimates of the costs of providing these mental health services—approximately $5 to $10 billion annually in the United States—but these estimates did not provide how much of this sum was paid for by victims or other sources.[7]

The next section will take a closer look at the state of victim assistance services.

SUPPORT AND ASSISTANCE FOR VICTIMS

Victims need emotional support, assistance with material repairs, advocacy to reach services, and information about what will happen next. While there are more rape crisis centers and victim assistance units than ever

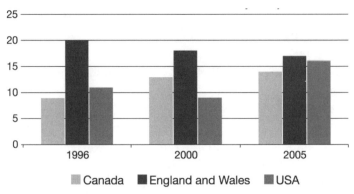

Figure 4.1. Percentage of victims reporting needs that did access services

before, there are still not enough; victims are not all able to access them, and they are frequently not well or sustainably funded.

Every five years, the International Crime Victim Survey interviews a small sample of the general population in many of the developed countries. It identifies those who have been a victim of crime and then asks them a series of questions about the impact of the crime on their lives and what actions they took in response to the crime. One question focuses on those victims with particular needs, and the results show that only a small proportion of victims actually access these services. In figure 4.1, we see the gradual rise from 1996 to 2005 in the proportion of victims in Canada and the United States who accessed services. In England and Wales, there has been a slight drop. However, overall, more than 80 percent of victims who are in need of victim services are not getting those services.

Not only are victims' needs going unmet, but so too are the needs of victim service providers. When community victim assistance agencies are dependent on annual grants, it can be difficult to retain skilled staff. When the budgets are below what is needed, understaffing and overwork leads to burnout. All too often, workers are specially trained at these units but, when they come to terms with the fact that they will not be well-compensated for their expertise or will perpetually lack job security, they leave for significantly better-paying jobs in other sectors. Sadly, the salaries for those providing victim services are not even close to the professional salaries of those providing services related to or for criminals, such as police officers, lawyers, judges, or prison guards.

Victim Assistance in New York City: A Look at Safe Horizon

What's encouraging here is that at least some victim assistance agencies (such as Safe Horizon in New York City, the largest victim assistance agency in the world) are able to overcome these challenges and go a long way toward meeting the physical, mental, and emotional needs of many victims in their catchment areas. Safe Horizon's programs include a mental health counseling center that helps crime victims cope with their reactions to their traumas. Specialists are on hand to help victims who are feeling overwhelmed mentally, physically, and/or emotionally, and also to assist with health issues such as significant increases or decreases in appetite, sleeplessness, grief, shock, flashbacks or nightmares, or increased alcohol consumption.

The overall aim of Safe Horizon is to help victims with their emotional and psychological recovery by promoting healthy behaviors such as eating right, exercising regularly, and following daily routines. Safe Horizon has the ability to refer victims who are feeling overwhelmed to experienced mental health counselors, and it also suggests strategies for struggling victims such as trying to rest, relax, forgive themselves, and communicate their feelings to people they trust.

Unfortunately, unlike victim services in many European countries (and even in some provinces in Canada), Safe Horizon is not a government service. So, it needs to be reimbursed by programs such as Medicaid, Medicare, the Crime Victims Board, Child Health Plus, and private health insurance companies. The good news is that the staff at Safe Horizon will gladly assist victims in completing all the forms that they need to submit. It also has a sliding-scale fee based on income for individuals without insurance or other coverage.

Victim Assistance Generally in the United States

Victim assistance services have a long history in the United States. In the 1970s, the federal government established a massive program known as Law Enforcement Assistance Administration to invest billions of dollars into long-overdue criminal justice reforms at the state and local level. Noticing problems getting witnesses to testify in court, they allocated a small amount of seed money to start half a dozen different support programs for victims and witnesses across the United States. These programs included initiatives to help witnesses testify in court, projects to ensure that victims of domestic violence would get a police officer and a social worker to respond to the home to make it safe and seek solutions, centers to assist victims of sexual assault, and services to help child victims cope with the system.

Thirty-five years later, these services have proliferated to over ten thousand programs.[8] Many communities have a victim assistance program, and some police departments have a victim services unit. The main vehicle to proliferate victim assistance services across the United States today has been the Victims of Crime Act (VOCA), passed in 1984. This landmark legislation created the Office for Victims of Crime (OVC). Starting with only $68 million in their first year in 1985, VOCA allocated ten times that amount in 2009 to multiply the availability of victim assistance services such as generic victim support programs, rape crisis centers, shelters for battered women, and services for children, as well as state compensation programs.

VOCA has inspired and initiated many wonderful innovations that complement its role in multiplying compensation and services. It could not have succeeded without the brilliance, leadership, and persistence of Marlene Young and those she inspired through the National Organization for Victim Assistance (NOVA). In the 1980s, NOVA produced a legislative guide that put each of the fifty states' victim legislations into one document to enable comparison of progress. It also brought together descriptions of pioneering programs to highlight benchmarks and shortfalls.[9] Notably, it started training programs to turn crisis intervention into a recognizable skill that could be acquired. NOVA organized annual conferences to perfect assistance workers' skills, to lobby for change, and to enable victim assistance workers to achieve their own emotional and psychological recovery from the many traumas they regularly witness in their professional lives.

Today, NOVA still exists to provide networking, advocacy, training, and crisis intervention across North America. It is the principal source of energy and expertise behind the progress that has been made in the United States toward meeting the core needs of victims of crime. It is the focal organization for those who respond to victims in communities, in courts, and in special sectors such as violence against women. NOVA became a leader in technical training through preparing curriculums and organizing professionals with unique skills to provide training. It has also played a critical role internationally in responding to widespread victimizations, fostering national crime victim programs, and training police, victim support workers, grassroots victims' organizations, and others who respond to victims of crime.

In 2004, a report was produced on the extent to which the services funded by VOCA met the needs of victims. It brought together results from two national studies that had contacted service administrators, visited twenty-four communities in twelve states, organized focus groups with victims, and undertaken telephone surveys with over 1,800 victims. (It should be noted that these surveys were limited to those who had reported their victimizations to law enforcement and so do not give information on the significant number of victims who did not go to law enforcement.) One of the studies looked at the proportion of victims who sought assistance from victim service providers.[10] Overall, the evaluation showed that only 4 percent of victims had gone to service providers—a percentage even lower than that reported by the International Crime Victimization Survey. And don't forget, this was the response of the victims who *did* report the crimes to the police in the first place. The reasons given for these low numbers were that victims were not made aware of them—a theme that repeats itself time after time—and when they were made aware of them, they did not know how they could be of specific help.

The promising news is that, in the cases where victims did contact victim service agencies, they found the services to be fairly comprehensive and highly satisfactory. One major survey emphasizes the importance of agencies being able to provide for all of victims' core needs.[11] It cites the provision of a comprehensive range of services that covers active listening, material repairs, information and referral, safety issues, and criminal justice information as being of primary importance.[12] They point to the need to do more to make victims aware of services at the earliest point in time.

Overall, while there are many promising services across the United States today, there is no guarantee that every community across the country will have access to these services—or that there will be the permanent staff and funds available to sufficiently run them. Undoubtedly, there is still much more work to be done.

Victim Support Schemes: The British Model

Sadly, even with all the good work that agencies such as Safe Horizon and the myriad of victim service providers in the United States do, American victims of crime are not treated as well as their counterparts in Europe, where the universality of support services for victims is more accepted. For example, in England and Wales, Victim Support is a nongovernmental organization that provides victims with emotional support, practical help, and information about what will happen next. The essence of its work is to listen and provide recognition to the emotional experiences of victims of crime so that the victims can better cope with their victimization and so recover practically, mentally, and emotionally.

Today, England and Wales have a universal system of victim assistance services called "support schemes." These started in earnest with the first schemes in 1979. Thirty years later, they provide a seamless network of victim services across the country. Originally the schemes employed professionals who trained volunteers to assist with victims' emotional recovery and to provide them with information about what would happen next. A milestone in the evolution of support schemes was the first evaluation of a victim support program undertaken in the 1980s by the University of Oxford.[13] The evaluation became the subject of a major conference of volunteers and professionals involved in victim support, and undoubtedly helped such organizations get additional funding, more professional workers, and increased status.

Victim Support is made up of a network of 375 local offices, where trained staff and volunteers provide services. It also offers a nationwide telephone support service to provide emotional support and healing to victims of crime. Victim Support's services are free to the user. The primary source of funding is an annual grant of $70 million (45 million pounds) from the British Justice Department. This costs the average British taxpayer $1.25 each year—arguably an affordable expense to ensure the overall mental and emotional support for victims of crime. In April 2010, Britain's minister of justice announced the consolidation of a national coast-to-coast victim support service that would employ full-time professionals—something that should be the envy of all victim advocates in North America.

Victim Assistance in Canada

In the 1980s, Canadian provinces passed legislation to promote victim services. Most followed a model of using fines against offenders to pay for them. Quebec was the only province to institute a government-run agency to help victims of crime—now one of only a few of its kind in North America. Despite the growing number of services for victims of crime in Canada, these initiatives remain largely a patchwork.

In 2008, Statistics Canada tried to do a complete census of victim service providers in Canada. They reached about 90 percent of the 884 service agencies. Of these, 40 percent were found to be based in police agencies, 23 percent in the community, and 8 percent based in courts. Another 17 percent were sexual assault crisis centers. Overall, Canadian agencies provide a range of specialized services for children, aboriginal populations, women, the elderly, and those with mental or physical disabilities. The survey showed that they all meet the core needs of providing emotional support and general information. There were more than 3,000 paid employees who, along with volunteers, served more than 400,000 victims annually.

Although these numbers may seem impressive at first glance, they are hiding a lot of information. For example, less than ten percent of adult victims sought services. While not all victims need or want services, surely more than this small fraction would benefit from emotional and psychological healing services. It would seem then that Canada, too (like the United States) has some large strides to make toward ensuring support for all victims of crime.

The Future of Victim Assistance: The Japanese Model

Japan provides an important model of how to ensure universal and basic services for victims of crime and how to meet all victims' physical, psychological, and mental health care needs. But the good news continues. In 2004, the central government implemented a comprehensive Victim of Crime Act that required both central and local governments to implement victim support services (including psychological and emotional health services) and to assist victims seeking to make claims for damages. It also required that victim assistance be integrated with the general health and welfare sectors. In 2005, the act was followed by the Victim Basic Plan, which turned the central government's legislative words into concrete action by introducing a strategy to ensure the implementation of the principles—surely a model for countries around the world (and especially in North America).

GENDER-RELATED SUPPORT

Victim experiences differ significantly because of the natures of the crimes. The Office on Violence Against Women (OVW) focuses on domestic violence, sexual assault, stalking, and human trafficking. These crimes differentially affect women more severely and generally have worse consequences for female as opposed to male victims. Further, the attitudes of predominantly male agencies such as law enforcement mean that women may not be treated sympathetically. Beyond this, gender is a factor that has a significant effect on how services should respond to the victimization.

The United States' Violence Against Women Act (VAWA), passed in 1994, has the dual purpose of reducing violence against women and serving the needs of victims of violence against women better. The act established the Office on Violence Against Women (OVW) to orchestrate and manage its programs. It has also added programs that deal with the particular needs of female victims with disabilities and female victims residing on Indian territory. An important component of the act is the requirement for the OVW to demonstrate to Congress how the funds are reaching their targets and assess their effectiveness in reducing violence and serving victims' needs.[14]

Domestic Violence

While domestic violence can involve violence against both women and men, over 80 percent of domestic crimes are against women, who also tend to be injured more often. Today there are more than 2,000 community-based projects in the United States that provide emergency shelter to 300,000 women and children annually.

The victims who can secure shelter at these safe havens stay for a period of a few days to several months. Victims of domestic violence are seeking protection and a range of counseling, safety planning, and legal assistance services. Those who do receive these services are overwhelmingly satisfied.[15]

VOCA provides more than half its victim assistance funding (so, $150 million annually) to domestic violence cases. This sounds like a large sum, but in reality it is a drop in the bucket compared to what is needed.

A special one-day census on victims of domestic violence looks at how many women and children are in shelters and how many were turned away on a given day. On average, there are approximately 10,000 women and 10,000 children residing at shelters across the country every day. Unfortunately, 9,000 victims are refused services daily because the programs are overburdened and simply do not have the resources.[16] This is a serious gap that cannot continue.

Canada has much greater capacity to support victims of domestic violence proportionate to its population. In 2008, approximately 101,000 women and children were admitted to 569 safe houses. The number of admissions has remained relatively stable over the past ten years. Over 4,000 women and 3,000 children reside in shelters on an average day.[17] If the United States had the same capacity, it would have close to a million women and children going through each year—that's 65,000 on an average day, or over three times its current capacity. Even so, Canada still needs to double its shelter capacity to fully serve the needs of victims.

In the United States, the largest recipient of funds through VAWA is the STOP program (Services Training Officers Prosecutors), which provides a proportion of its funding to community victim services agencies with mandates to help victims of domestic violence heal. Much of the money is used to pay 3,500 specialized staff and train 300,000 others who are involved in the victim support field (of which, approximately 100,000 are members of law enforcement). However, this is only a tiny step forward considering the 2.5 million persons working in law enforcement and the judicial and correctional systems in the United States. Still, even this handful of support workers is making good progress. The annual report on the effectiveness of the STOP program shows an overall increase in victim service agency activity in direct response to victims' healing needs.[18] These funds also work toward changing societal values, thus preventing violence before it occurs.

Sexual Assault

One of the strongest examples of positive action to meet the needs of victims of crime is the work done by countless dedicated individuals in sexual assault crisis centers. In the 1960s, women's groups began to provide support to victims of rape through sexual assault crisis centers across North America. In the 1970s, the center in Seattle was recognized for having the best practices among them. By the 1980s, more and more centers had opened, but all too often they lacked sustained funding. Without a doubt, pioneers in the sexual assault crisis field were struggling uphill, but their self-determinism and focus on the physical, emotional, and psychological needs of rape victims has paved the way for a variety of other victim support services around the world.

By the time of the passage of VAWA in 1994, there were over 1,315 rape crisis centers in the United States. While that may seem impressive at first, again consider that there are a million victims of rape every year in the United States, and more than one-third of all American adult women have been raped in their lifetimes.[19] As a result, the United States has nowhere near the capacity to support all of these victims, many of whom struggle to find the resources to get their emotional and practical needs met. When these centers *can* serve the needs of victims, however, they focus on raising awareness as well as supporting victims. In cases of sexual assault, support means accompanying the victim to the hospital and, if the victim decides to report to law enforcement, dedicating lots of time to meeting with police and going to court.

One small piece of good news is that sexual assault victims are a step closer to having their financial needs met in terms of paying the bills incurred by their victimization. One of the recent programs promoted by both the VAWA's and the VOCA's compensation programs would see victims' sexual assault examinations paid for by the government, primarily through the Sexual Assault Nurse Examiners (SANE) program. SANE programs now exist in every state of the union, with about five hundred programs in the United States and others in Canada. All SANE programs treat adults and adolescents, and about half of them treat children as well. SANE programs also typically handle sexual assault victims of both sexes.

Importantly, SANE programs provide healing services in a nonjudgmental atmosphere. In a review of the empirical literature examining the effectiveness of the SANE program in the United States, one researcher has found positive evidence that sexual assault nurse examiners are effective at assisting victims with their psychological recovery because they minimize trauma, preserve dignity, allow victims to make self-determining decisions, and assist in providing medical care. In fact, 75 percent of sexual assault victims described their contact with the SANE nurses as "healing" in and of itself. SANEs also improve the potential for a successful prosecution because they collect evidence in a useable manner, as well as foster interagency collaboration to improve responses to rape.[20]

SUPPORT AND ADVOCACY FOR CHILD VICTIMS

We know that there are 800,000 children identified by child protection agencies as being abused or neglected every year in the United States. In addition, there are unknown numbers of children twelve and under who are victims of crimes committed against them by non-family members. The law enforcement and criminal justice process is confusing and frightening to adults and can be even more so for children—especially when they don't necessarily have family members like parents that they can turn to anymore. The combination of the emotional shock of being a victim and a frightening judicial process justifies many special measures, not least of which is the provision of a central care unit that can handle the many agencies involved in the child protection process. For example, unless care is taken, a child victim might be interviewed many times in many different places about the same set of facts, and so a child victim advocacy unit is necessary to minimize the stress and impact on the child.

There are more than 350 child victim advocacy clinics across the United States today that work to ease the child victim's experience. In these clinics, police, child protection workers, prosecutors, and victim advocates are able to interview child victims in one consistent "child-friendly" environment. Sometimes a video recording will be made so that repetition can be avoided, and other times professionals can watch an interview through one-way glass so that the child is not disturbed.

These child-focused clinics concentrate on the short- and long-term emotional and psychological health and well-being of young victims. They facilitate treatments by various child welfare agencies and other specialized health care workers, and some even have facilities for medical examinations.[21] Child victim advocacy clinics are lauded for this one-stop approach to working with children who have been victims of violence because they are able to ensure that already-traumatized children are exposed to as few new and unfamiliar circumstances as possible during the judicial process.

Being a witness to a crime can have serious and long-lasting effects on a child. Safe Horizon in New York talks about the case of Andy, who as an eighteen-month-old child watched his father kill his six-year-old brother and then commit suicide. It is easy to see how this experience could—and indeed did—affect Andy as he grew up. The agency was able to help Andy and his grandmother cope with his own frequent violent outbursts.

Knowing the emotional distress that can be caused to child victims by the judicial process, the Child Witness Project in London, Ontario, Canada, helps children and adolescents who must testify in criminal court (usually in cases of physical or sexual abuse). The protocol includes caring for young victims' emotional health by ensuring that their stress levels are reduced, introducing them to coping strategies, and providing emotional support and advocacy. Since its inception, the project has provided services to almost 1,000 children and adolescents.

All initiatives to prepare child victims to participate in the criminal process *must* ensure that young and vulnerable witnesses are not traumatized by the legal process—preventing, not just minimizing, the trauma. After all, children will already be going through a tremendous amount of emotional stress, and there should be absolutely no acceptance of any processes that revictimize these young witnesses.

SUPPORT AND ADVOCACY FOR ELDERLY VICTIMS

Much less attention has been focused on elderly victims of crime than has been on other types or groups of victims. Even though the elderly are at considerably less risk of becoming victims of property and violent crime than individuals in the younger age groups, when victimizations do happen to them, the effects are often even more damaging. As victims, they are more likely to be injured and their injuries are more likely to have severe consequences.

Typically, the victim service response to elderly victims occurs within generic victim service agencies. However, many recommendations exist about how to tailor health services specifically to the needs of the elderly, including increasing the size of print in brochures and paying attention to compounded health issues. Still, little research has been done on the extent to which their particular needs are met within existing victim services programs, and whatever strategies have been put into practice in specialized instances have not been taken up by mainstream victim assistance programs.

As the proportion of the population over sixty-five grows, so do the confirmed reports of elder abuse. Much of the elder abuse that occurs is inflicted in the elderly person's place of residence by a family member or a caregiver. In the most recent survey in the United States, adult protective services confirmed 191,000 cases of elder abuse, but estimates by experts suggest a figure between one and two million is more accurate. More recent data are not available, and one major obstacle in the way of gaining more information is that the definitions of "elder abuse" still vary widely.[22]

The research has not kept up with the increasing trends toward elder abuse. The U.S. National Research Council was asked to develop a research agenda for issues on violence against the elderly. It could point to only fifteen studies undertaken by the National Institute on Aging. Hopefully, research in this area will advance and come up to par with the research on domestic violence and child abuse issues.

Solutions are gradually surfacing. Hotlines are increasingly available for the elderly to report their abusive situations. Unlike an abused child, elderly victims are able to call adult protective services or the police for assistance, but like a battered wife, they are often very conflicted about getting a family member or caregiver charged with a crime. If they have a network of friends or companions who visit them, their risk of being abused is likely decreased, and at the very least they will have a network of trusted individuals to provide them with a means to get help.

DEMANDS FOR LEGISLATORS

Victims face core needs to get emotional support and mental health assistance, information and referrals to services, and advocacy and assistance in accessing material, medical, and social services. Many services do exist for those who know about them, have access to them in their geographic areas, and can afford them.

Legislators must get schools and universities to teach citizens about how to provide emotional support to victims of crime. Adult education through the public media will also help this response.

Legislators must ensure that the medical care for physical and mental health trauma (such as emergency response services and treatment for PTSD) is available at no cost to the victim. This must include related costs of prescription drugs, ambulance services, and other related fees.

Legislators must ensure that comprehensive services for victims of crime are available to support all victims through their crises. These services must provide victims with material assistance, information about what happens next, and advocacy to make other services available in the future. Best practices include Safe Horizon in New York City, as well as the national victim support schemes in England and Wales and now Japan.

Legislators must invest in regular surveys to measure the gaps between the core needs of victims and the services provided to them. Specialized surveys are needed for domestic violence, sexual assault, and child and elderly abuse. Best practice includes the twenty-four-hour census of domestic violence shelters and services.

Legislators must shift more funding from general revenue into the full range of victim support services to provide sustainability and career possibilities in the specialized field of victim support services.

Legislators must allow for more discretion by medical and mental health practitioners on decisions to report victimizations to law enforcement so that victims of crime will not be dissuaded from getting the help they need. Best practices include those that allow victims of sexual assault to assure evidence from a sexual assault evidence kit without the obligation to report to the police.

(5)

MAKING GOOD THE LOSS

Reparation from Offender, State, and Civil Suits

Victims expect our systems of justice to order the perpetrator to repair the damage that he or she has caused. As we saw in chapter 3, seeking restitution from the offender is one of the main reasons why victims call the police to report crimes in the first place. Indeed, one of the core needs of victims of crime identified in chapter 1 is to be able to pay the bills that accumulate from the crime. These bills cover a wide spectrum, from replacing the lock that was broken to mental health counseling, loss of wages, reparation for pain and suffering, and more. They include the deductibles that insurance companies do not pay on insured damage and loss to property.

Another core need is for victims to search for justice. By definition, a crime is an intentional act by a perpetrator. So our culture assumes that there is an obligation on the perpetrator to make good the losses he or she caused. Certainly in primitive societies, restitution from the offender was a significant—if not the only—consideration. Unfortunately, our systems of law enforcement, criminal justice, and corrections today focus immense resources on punishment, deterrence, and incapacitation, and consequently do little to get restitution from the offender. This is epitomized on the website of the California Department of Corrections—a massive correctional machine with an embedded and highly successful system for collecting restitution. On the one hand, its annual report admits their limited ability to correct offenders by pointing to the fact that 60 to 70 percent of their prisoners are rearrested within three years of release, but forgets to mention its own success in collecting more than $20 million in restitution for victims. This focus must be rebalanced.

Unfortunately, the chances of victims recovering reparation from anyone other than an insurance company are not good in the United States, and are not much better in most parts of Canada. The majority of victims of crime are unlikely to recover anything even remotely close to what they suffered in medical costs, mental health costs, or loss of wages from their offenders—let alone their lost quality of life (pain and suffering) or peace of mind. If there is one issue that epitomizes the failure of legislators to guarantee one inalienable right for crime victims, it is the inability to get judges to order restitution from the offender—an essential step in getting restitution to be paid. I will show how leaflets prepared for the Office for Victims of Crime describe precisely what is being done successfully in some places for some victims, so we know it could be done everywhere for all victims.

Perhaps the most astonishing fact is that every year, the OVC creates a resource guide that is replete with statements such as, "Too few victims receive compensation and court-ordered restitution," and "Some courts . . . fail to order restitution."[1] These statements imply that victim advocates should be cajoling judges to obey the local laws and constitutions rather than expecting judges to apply the law. How is it a demonstration of fairness and dignity when victim advocates have to go out of their way to fight to have the inalienable rights of victims, as set out in state laws and constitutions, respected by the courts?

WHAT IS LOST: THE VICTIM'S CORE NEED TO BE REIMBURSED

It is known from the National Crime Victimization Survey that victims of property crime suffered $18 billion in property loss or damage in 2007 alone.[2] Some of this loss was goods that were stolen, such as television sets, laptop computers, and cars. The remainder was damage to property such as broken locks, shattered windows, or damage to recovered stolen cars. The average loss in a household burglary is $2,000, in a car theft $7,800, and in a simple theft $500.[3]

The economic impact of the crime on the victim will vary significantly with each particular victim's wealth and income. The average loss for persons earning under $15,000 a year is close to $600, which is significant for them. On the other hand, the average loss for persons earning over $75,000 a year is $1,700, which may be proportionately much less significant, particularly as they are more likely to have paid the premium for a private insurance policy that will reimburse the losses over a certain deductible. But note that these losses are not beyond the means of many offenders.

In chapter 1, we saw that the actual financial losses incurred from crime are much more than the value of the property that is lost or damaged. The costs of medical care for victims are estimated at $18 billion annually in the United States—an amount coincidentally similar to property loss and damage. Information taken from the NCVS suggests that 36 percent of this total is not paid by private insurance or public health programs. Some victims are left worse off than others. For example, almost half of the persons injured in the $15,000 to $25,000 family income range did not have insurance coverage, and thus covering their medical costs would be a weighty financial burden for them to bear. Overall, there is a $7 billion annual shortfall to be covered out of the pockets of victims of crime.

In addition to the costs of medical care and lost property, there is a combined total of $70 billion annually from lost wages, mental health services, and other related expenses. On average, this works out to be $1,000 per victim for lost property value and medical expenses, and $3,500 per victim for lost wages and mental health services. But keep in mind that thinking about losses in terms of averages is misleading; many victims have losses of little significance to them, while others suffer enormous losses that they may never be able to recoup or recover from in their lifetimes.

The Truth about Restitution and Compensation

In the United States, like in Canada and in England and Wales, victims of crime may benefit from some of the same programs as nonvictims, such as workers' compensation or medical insurance. Beyond these, there are five other avenues that victims of crime can pursue to recover their losses, which I will discuss in this chapter. These are:

1. an order of restitution (called a "compensation order" in England and Wales) made by a criminal court as part of the sentence;
2. a payment made by a state compensation board;
3. a civil suit brought against the perpetrator of the crime;

4. a civil suit brought against a third party who might have prevented the crime (or their insurance company); and

5. restorative justice—when the victim and offender may meet and work through the victimization and explore ways for the offender to make restitution.

There are several questions that come up regularly about the concept of criminals making restitution to victims. Is it a myth that criminals cannot pay the sums ordered? Do rich offenders pay more? Is compensation from the state adding insult to injury because it is too slow, too accusatory, or too little? Could insurance companies do more? Can third parties be sued successfully because they did not take steps to prevent the crime? How can restorative justice be applied in a situation to act as a true solution for victims instead of just an easy way out for offenders?

JUST RESTITUTION FROM CRIMINALS

In the last thirty years in the United States, every state has passed legislation to get criminal courts to order restitution from the offender. In addition, most state constitutions include a right for the victim to get restitution from the offender. Yet no basic statistics exist on how often restitution is ordered, let alone paid.

Innovations have occurred at the federal level to encourage criminal courts to order offenders to pay victims back for some of the losses incurred from the crime. The most recent is the 2004 Justice for All Act. But even here, we have yet to see how it works in practice, despite evaluations by the Government Accountability Office.[4]

Unfortunately, it is the same story for the records of ordinary state and local courts. I searched the Bureau of Justice Statistics website for data on restitution ordered and paid, to no avail. The information was simply not available. Indeed, very little is known by experts about the use of restitution. The latest official reference on the subject is from 1996.[5] How are governments supposed to consider serious improvements if there is not even any data to serve as a base starting point?

Criticism about the lack of enforcement of restitution payments is coming from other camps as well. In 1998, a report assessing progress on the implementation of the recommendations made by the President's Task Force on Victims of Crime had this to say:

"Despite the passage of federal and state legislation, restitution remains one of the most under-enforced victim rights within the criminal and juvenile justice systems. Evidence of this is apparent both in decisions to order restitution and in efforts to monitor, collect, and disperse restitution payment to victims."[6] Sadly, it seems little has changed since then. But with no new information collected since 1996, how could it?

As we will see in a moment, the National Center for Victims of Crime shows that for the average victim, the tangible losses are approximately $3,000—not an impossible sum. So, it is likely that it is much easier for criminals to come up with the funds to pay restitution than many legislators and judges think.[7] The reason why they are not held accountable for doing so, then, remains a mystery. The next section will present ways forward for making sure it happens.

GETTING RESTITUTION FROM OFFENDERS PAID TO VICTIMS: SEVEN EASY STEPS

A wide variety of measures exist at the state level to get restitution into the hands of victims. This inconsistency in ways of collecting restitution across the United States leads to immense frustration for victims. There is a deplorable lack of statistics and reliable research on which of these strategies works best to recover damages.

The OVC sponsored the National Center for Victims of Crime (NCVC) to explain the legal issues surrounding restitution in plain language for everyday citizens. These bulletins politely show how the avoidable legal confusion at the state level has led to many victims losing out on restitution. They go on to describe how to make restitution work and get it ordered using examples from states that have been successful. Many of their examples are taken from California, which has a system that is impressive, though not as exemplary as Vermont's, where the fines on offenders are used to establish a trust fund that in turn pays victims of crime court-ordered restitution without the need for the victim to do much more. Here, I have turned the NCVC's negative findings into seven essential elements for success.[8]

1. Victims Must Request Restitution

Victims must prepare a written request so that the court knows that the victim is expecting restitution to be ordered. Victims must be informed of this obligation soon after the victimization so that they can prepare the request.

2. Victims Must Demonstrate Losses

Victims must bring together the necessary receipts and justifications to substantiate their claims. They may need to seek help to prepare this request. Minnesota has a handy form that victims need to fill out to justify the restitution they are seeking. Unfortunately, this assumes that offenders will not be asked to pay for pain and suffering when I would like to see this considered wherever possible.

3. Identify Assets, Income, and Liabilities of the Offender at the Beginning

The court must be informed about the assets and income of offenders *before* the court considers restitution. In California, for example, the victim is entitled to see a defendant's disclosures on assets, income, and liabilities. This obvious precaution facilitates the court, probation officer, or victim advocate in knowing the ability of the offender to pay and so to determine whether the offender is unable to pay or is simply avoiding the responsibility.

4. Make Restitution Payments Automatic

Some justice professionals act as if all offenders are indigent and thus cannot afford to pay the restitution ordered. They may drop restitution when they are plea bargaining. To limit this breach of victims' rights, the California Court of Appeals ruled that restitution must be part of every sentence.[9] If the offender is unable to pay, that becomes a matter at the collection stage. Indeed, some offenders who are indigent today may turn their lives around and have the means to pay later.

5. Monitor Payments

In Wisconsin, the state's Department of Justice is responsible for setting up an account for each restitution order; the offender pays into the account and the department pays the victim. Similar systems are used in California and Florida. In this way, the state is aware of what has been ordered and what has been paid.

The Court-Ordered Payment System (COPS) is an automated collection system located on the mainframe computer of Florida's Department of Corrections. It is linked directly to the offenders' criminal histories and supervision/inmate records. The program requires offenders to make payments to the state, which are then converted to government checks and disbursed to victims. COPS links all of the state's 155 probation offices, 51 major justice institutions, 32 community correctional centers, and 43 road prisons, work camps, and forestry camps. The department uses a 4 percent surcharge collected on all court-ordered obligations to defray the costs of processing payments from offenders.

6. Enforce Compliance

In Wisconsin, if the victim is not paid then there is a restitution advocate who will investigate and sort out a solution. California garnishes part of the wages of offenders from work in prison or outside of prison to pay restitution. This system relieves a lot of the burden for compliance from the victim. Before the end of the sentence, the probation officer may be asked to report to the court on the progress in making the payments. The court may extend probation or parole in order to continue to supervise payments by the offender.

The lack of interagency agreements stipulating who is responsible for monitoring, enforcing, collecting, and disbursing restitution means that, in many states, payments fall through the cracks, leaving the victims with no real means of following up. Restitution orders can also be converted into civil judgments, but this puts the onus on the victim to get to know the civil court procedures and to sue the offender who will often be hard to find—really, it's fool's gold.

7. Make Restitution Payments the Priority

Restitution orders are not the first priority of court-ordered payments; in some states, offenders are expected to pay court fees, fines, costs of salaries for justice officials, costs of their incarceration, and other financial obligations before they make restitution payments to victims. The victim is left carrying the onus of collecting restitution—a burden that often becomes too cumbersome to bear. What is most depressing about these measures is that means for improving them are well known and inexpensive, but are still not widely used by legislators.

COMPENSATION FROM THE GOVERNMENT

In some cases, the offender will not be able to pay full or even partial restitution—at least not for a very long time. So, governments have set up compensation programs to make payments when such restitution is not fully paid. Typically, however, these programs have been limited to victims who have suffered a physical injury. As mentioned in the introduction, these programs came from the lobbying of Marjory Fry, a magistrate in England. She wanted victims of crime to get compensation at a level that was similar to workers who were injured on the job.

Inspired by her pamphlets, New Zealand started the first state compensation program for victims of violent crime in 1963. England followed suit a year later. California created its program in 1965, which led other states to do the same, followed by some Canadian provinces and Australian states. These programs were modest so that governments could avoid paying out more money than they could afford. Most are still modest today in North America, and have only just recently started providing information on websites to attract applicants.

The expansion of these programs in the United States was very slow. It was only when the VOCA legislation was adopted that the federal government began to provide funding so that states would start compensation programs. Though the amounts of money paid and the criteria for payment remain very restrictive, VOCA has enabled every state in the United States to have a compensation program.

While compensation is available in every state, the proportion of reparation paid through state-run compensation programs is small. The maximum amount payable in many states is only $35,000 and must be the last resort after insurance and other claims. This must be stretched between five main types of expenses: medical and hospital care (and dental work if necessary), mental health counseling, lost earnings due to crime-related injuries, support for dependents of a deceased victim, and funeral and burial expenses. Payments are not normally allowed to compensate for pain and suffering. About half of all compensation payments in the United States goes toward reimbursing uninsured medical costs.[10] About 8 percent goes toward reimbursing mental health costs. Some of the funds are used to pay for forensic exams for sexual assault victims—about $29 million out of $461 million in 2008.[11]

WHAT DOES THE GOVERNMENT SPEND ON VICTIMS' COMPENSATION TODAY?

The total amount paid out by state compensation programs on an annual basis in the United States has now reached $461 million, paid to 178,000 victims. That is an average of $2,590 paid per victim. In addition, programs paid more than $30 million for forensic sexual assault exams.

When comparing this average payment to those made to victims in other leading countries around the world, the payments in the United States are paltry as shown in figure 5.1. For example, the British Criminal Injuries Compensation Authority paid out $376 million dollars to 57,000 victims in England and Wales, which works out to approximately $6,600 per victim (or more than double what is paid in the United States). In Canada, the average payment in the province of Ontario is $10,000 and in the province of Quebec it is an impressive $14,000 (over five times what is paid in the United States). And keep in mind that these per-victim costs do not have to go toward much of victims' medical expenses in Canada or in England and Wales because they are already paid by their public health care systems.

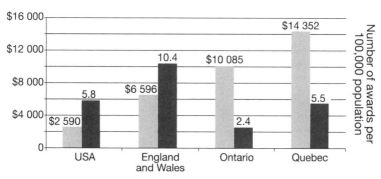

Figure 5.1. Comparison of average compensation payments from government contrasted to the number of awards per population

We must also keep in mind that another major difference between the United States and other leading countries relates to the lower proportion of eligible victims who apply for compensation in the United States. If American victims applied at a similar rate as they do in England and Wales, there would be over 300,000 victims claiming compensation every year in the United States—that's close to double the current number. Though we unfortunately do not have an accurate measure of victims who are eligible for state compensation in the United States, the NCVS identified 596,000 individuals who reported receiving medical care as a result of injuries sustained during violent crimes. Compare this to the mere 178,000 who received government compensation.

The reasons why victims do or do not apply have to do with being aware of the programs and getting help with the application. In chapter 3, I showed how the Edmonton Police Department had doubled the number of applications to their provincial compensation program by informing victims of their eligibility. Pennsylvania was worried about the underutilization of its compensation program, and its review confirmed that the major cause of its program's underutilization was that eligible victims were not aware of the program's existence. They found that victim service providers saw the process as too complicated, and so did not encourage victims to apply.[12] Unfortunately, Pennsylvania's study did not look at the role and availability of online information, which is a significant source for information-gathering in the twenty-first century.

We might look to England and Wales for a solution to simplify the process of applying for government compensation, as they have initiated a website with an electronic filing procedure to make the entire process easier on victims.

As mentioned, the United States provides only $2,590 on average per victim. If the United States reached as many victims per capita as England and Wales do, then there would be over 300,000 cases coming forward for compensation, and if all of these received an award comparable to the average British award, then the cost would be $2 billion annually. This is not a significant amount of money when compared to the $225 billion spent on reacting to crime. Some might argue that special fines on offenders could be used to defray some of these costs. I argue that it must come from general revenue, as in other countries, in order to deliver balanced justice.

Compensating for the True Cost of Crime

If we are ever going to figure out the *actual* compensation needs of victims in the United States, then the NCVS must include specific questions for those injured, and must also undertake in-depth studies to assess the true financial needs of victims. After all, despite the importance of compensation, no study has been done since 1977 to arrive at realistic assessments of victims' financial needs.

We know that legislators can recognize the importance of compensation to the lives of victims and their families if they so choose. For example, 11,000 victims of the World Trade Center attack in New York City were recently offered $712 million—this is an average of $65,000, which is a figure that comes much closer to actually representing fair compensation than what they would have received from the New York State Compensation system for their horrendous losses.

There does not seem to be any logic for why the payments to victims of one type of international violence should receive much less than victims hurt by terrorists.

We can look to England and Wales for an example here. Their compensation scheme has maximum compensation awards of close to $450,000 per victim. So, when terrorists killed a number of passengers on the subway in London in 2005, the compensation scheme was able to provide them with more adequate and fair compensation without having to pass special legislation.

I can sense the legislators getting their backs up at this point. They are going to warn that large payments to victims of violence are expensive and, as such, are beyond VOCA's budget. But I would advise them not to forget that the expenditures on compensation in England are *only 2 percent* of the government's expenditures on law and order and come from the same general revenues as policing and prison expenditures. Two percent of the U.S. expenditures on law and order would be approximately $5 billion— more than the $4 billion we have just estimated to catch up with England and Wales. This is not a proportionally large sum to recognize the losses to victims of violent crime. Even if the programs were well used (that is, sufficiently publicized and victim service providers helped victims to fill out the forms if necessary), the amount spent would still remain a small percentage of total expenditures on law enforcement, justice, and corrections.

So, to legislators, I would respond that the issue is not money, but rather balancing priorities on current spending. Victims of violent crime and their families pay taxes and vote, and they need to receive just compensation for what they went through.

Unfortunately, the news is not much better north of the border. In Canada, vast inequalities persist from one province to the next. Estimates suggest that in Canada, less than $250 million is paid out to victims of violence out of the $15 billion spent each year on law enforcement, courts, and corrections. Total payments to victims are also significantly less than the additional $400 million that the federal government recently promised to invest in additional police services alone.

The province of Ontario had a compensation program broadly similar to many programs in the United States. Only one in forty eligible applicants applied. Around 2005, victims of violent crime began to complain to the government's ombudsman about their treatment and delays in getting compensation. The ombudsman investigated and in 2007 released a scathing report entitled *Adding Insult to Injury*, which embarrassed the government just before an election.[13]

The ombudsman's office made numerous recommendations for simplifying and improving the efficiency of the Criminal Injuries Compensation Board. The attorney general responded by increasing the budget of the compensation board by about 10 percent. Furthermore, the board is required to submit biannual reports to the ombudsman's office on its progress in implementing the recommendations, as well as undertake regular surveys to see whether victims of crime are aware of and accessing the services that had been promised to them as inalienable rights.

As shown in chapter 1, the medical care costs for victims of violent crime are $18 billion annually, of which one-third (or $7 billion) may not be paid by medical insurance. In addition, victims have to bear the costs of lost wages and (often) mental health care, which combined is close to $70 billion. So, if the research was done carefully, the real need for criminal injuries compensation in the United States would be closer to this figure. It is much harder to convince governments to pay this amount for compensation programs even though it is about what is spent on incarceration and less than spent on law enforcement. I will argue in chapter 7 that the size of these losses is a compelling argument for investing in modern and proven strategies to prevent victimization and so reduce the amount of compensation expenditures necessary to repay for pain and suffering while still compensating victims fairly.

CIVIL SUITS AGAINST THE PERPETRATOR

Another source of funds to pay for victim services and compensation is civil suits, where restitution can be ordered as well as punitive damages.

On June 17, 1994, the NFL football star O.J. Simpson was charged with the murder of his wife, Nicole Brown Simpson, and a friend, Ronald Goldman. Ninety-five million television viewers watched as the police chased Simpson in his white Ford Bronco along L.A. highways. One year later, Simpson was acquitted of the charges by a jury in a criminal court. The jury effectively decided that the charges had not been proven *beyond a reasonable doubt*. Reality television has nothing on the real-life drama that unfolded during this case.

The two families of the murder victims then sued Simpson for wrongful death in a civil court. In 1997, a different jury decided that the evidence proved that Simpson had caused the wrongful deaths. The court then ordered Simpson to pay $8.5 million in civil damages for the loss of life and $25 million in punitive damages.

But the story does not finish there. Curiously, in California, Simpson could live on a $25,000 per month pension—that is, the courts could not take any of that $25,000 a month pension to pay the court-ordered damages to the victims' families. As a result, little or none of the payment has ever made it to the families of the two victims.[14] So, if there is a moral to the Simpson story, it is that civil suits can bring court-ordered restitution for victims, although they do not necessarily ensure that any of that money will make it into the victims' hands.

Understanding Civil Suits

The arguments for using civil suits to bring about restitution in the United States have now been put into an easy-to-read guide on civil justice for victims of crime, produced by the National Crime Victim Bar Association.[15] This association points to important differences between criminal and civil cases. For instance, victims themselves (not the state) are the litigants in civil cases, and as such they can influence court dates, have a say in what evidence is going to come forward, and be guaranteed a part of any settlement. In a settlement in a civil case, it is possible to get payments for damages that go beyond tangible losses, and can also include damages for pain and suffering. Furthermore, in some cases there will be punitive damages, such as those that were ordered in the O.J. Simpson case. These are an order for the culprit to pay what amounts to a fine because of their responsibility for what happened.

Some victims of crimes pursue civil suits because they cannot get a conviction in criminal courts. As we saw in chapter 3, police did not make an arrest (or were not in a position to make an arrest) in 83 percent of property crimes and 60 percent of violent crimes.[16] Furthermore, in some sorts of crimes such as sexual assault, it is difficult to get an accused convicted because it is problematic to present proof beyond a reasonable doubt in a situation that often occurs behind closed doors and with no other witnesses. This is one important advantage of the civil suit—that the burden of proof is based on a *balance of probabilities* (as opposed to *beyond a reasonable doubt*). This was the key in the outcome of the O.J. Simpson civil suit.

However, it is still rare for victims to use civil courts to sue offenders, in part because many victims do not have the money to pay their own lawyers, but also because after they have waited for a resolution of the criminal case, they often do not have the momentum to start their own legal action. They have to collect their own evidence, navigate the civil court process, and risk expensive legal fees—all to collect reparation that offenders may or may not deliver in the end.

In chapter 6, I will argue that victims should have much more control than they presently do in criminal cases. We can turn to different examples around the world to see how this might work. For many decades, victims of crime in France have not had to choose between a criminal and a civil process, as both are combined into one proceeding. In practice, the details of the criminal investigation by the police and the examining magistrate are available to the victim, who is a party to this process. The sentences in as many as half of cases in front of criminal courts are settled when the offender provides proof that the victim has received payment of restitution. As far as the victim goes, oftentimes justice is considered served as soon as they have received restitution (we can recall that the motivation given by many U.S. victims of property crime was to receive restitution). So, why could the systems in Anglo-American traditions such as those in Canada, England and Wales, and the United States not follow France's lead?

CIVIL SUITS AGAINST THIRD PARTIES

In 1974, the popular singer Connie Francis was singing at a music festival on Long Island. On the fourth night of the festival, she became the unfortunate victim of an offender who was able to enter her hotel room. He proceeded to rape her at knifepoint over the next couple of hours. Although she reported it to the police, they were unable to obtain the identity of the offender and nobody was ever charged for the crime.

By chance, Francis's lawyer learned that there had been several break-ins at this particular hotel. So, Francis brought a tort action against the hotel for not taking sufficient safety precautions. Connie Francis won the suit and was reputedly awarded $3 million. Still, she never sang again.

Basically, the purpose of third-party suits is to recover the damages and costs of pain and suffering from a company or agency that has the means to pay. These suits focus on negligence by the party, as in the case of the hotel chain in the Connie Francis case. Frank Carrington was the pioneer of third-party suits. He was the founder of the Crime Victims' Legal Advocacy Institute, Inc., which later became the Victims' Assistance Legal Organization (VALOR). He wrote his book on crime victims in 1975 and was later a member of the President's Task Force in 1982. His life was devoted to finding ways to get rights and restitution for victims of crime.

Today, there is a crime victim bar foundation in the United States that provides technical assistance to lawyers wanting to sue third parties. This is an important tool for victims seeking payment for pain and suffering and other costs which government has not chosen to compensate. It also encourages governments, universities, and private companies to ensure that they are taking reasonable steps to prevent victimization.

RESTORATIVE JUSTICE FOR VICTIMS

Internationally, there is a growing movement for "restorative justice." The concept is appealing. Its proponents talk about the need to help victims and offenders work through their feelings and reach a resolution. It is expected that this will help to restore the victims' emotional condition to what it was before the crime. It talks about the crime being not only a violation of the victim but also of the community as a whole, and so it also goes a ways in advancing the restoration of the community.

There are several different models for restorative justice. The basic elements include some type of meeting between the victim and offender, with a professional coordinator or mediator organizing the meeting. Some types of restoration are called "victim-offender reconciliation" because the main objective is to reach reconciliation between the victim and the offender. Other types are called "circle sentencing" because community members sit in a circle and listen to the victim, the offender, and the community members talk about what happened before deciding on a sentence for the offender.

While the rhetoric of restorative justice is appealing to victims, the practice has one major flaw. The offender has many sources of support available to him, including legal advice from his defense lawyer paid, if necessary, by the state. Yet the victim will not have access to a lawyer paid for by the state, and often the victim will not have a professional advocate providing any support. So, if the victim and offender cannot work out an arrangement that is suitable for the offender, then the offender can always go back to the criminal court in hopes of a resolution that better suits his needs. However, the victim cannot do the same because the victim has no standing in that forum.

Nevertheless, the evidence supporting the satisfactory effects of restorative justice for victims is strong. There is also impressive evidence to suggest that restorative justice sessions can reduce the likelihood of offenders committing future victimizations—something difficult for massive corrections systems such as those in California to achieve. It seems that the offender who understands the harm that he or she has caused victims becomes motivated to work out how to avoid criminal tendencies in the future.

Research shows that victims feel much less angry after going through this process than if they went through the standard criminal court process.[17] This is important, as it reduces the need to waste more money on prison construction and operation in the name of victims' rights.

We can look to Australia, Canada, and Europe for successful examples of restorative justice in action. In the Netherlands, HALT, a program that began as a small one-off project, has spread to become a national institution. Originally launched in Rotterdam in 1981, juveniles involved in vandalism were required by the police or the prosecuting authorities to repair the damage and seek assistance. This approach has now been multiplied across sixty-five sites. Today, there is a national agency that provides coaching and technical assistance to local HALT projects. The reductions in repeat victimizations are 70 percent.

In 1986, when other countries were just taking up the fight to focus on victims' rights, France was already emphasizing both assistance and mediation. Its national mediation organization, L'Institut National d'Aide aux Victimes et de Médiation (INAVEM), was established as a national voluntary organization to coordinate and support victim assistance and mediation throughout France. Today, INAVEM leads and coordinates a network of 150 local mediation organizations that help seek out restitution between victims and their offenders.

In 1998, France went a step further and set a new benchmark for other countries. It created 20,000 positions for community social mediators. Essentially, young persons who were unemployed were hired to work with various government sectors at different levels to help resolve conflicts between individuals and between individuals and various state agencies. The nature of their roles, expertise, and future as mediators has been the subject of various reports.

DEMANDS FOR LEGISLATORS

The core need for victims of crime to be reimbursed for tangible losses is indisputable. Once again, legislative rhetoric is in abundance without having workable and affordable systems in place.

Legislators must implement programs that follow the seven key steps identified for ordering and collecting restitution from offenders and paying this to victims. Best practices include systems in California and Vermont, as well as in France.

Legislators must upgrade the amounts of compensation paid by the state to meet the basic tangible costs borne by victims of violent crime and some of the pain and suffering. States should also consider simple electronic filing procedures to make the entire process easier on victims, as has been implemented in England and Wales. Best practices include England and Wales, as well as some Canadian provinces.

Legislators must ensure that victims of crime are informed early on about the procedures for restitution and compensation, through means discussed in chapters 3 and 4.

Legislators must provide legal aid to assist victims of crime to bring civil and third-party suits to recover the costs of pain and suffering.

Legislators must develop mediation and restorative justice programs that respect the core needs and inalienable rights of victims, with evaluations to survey the satisfaction of victims and changes in rates of repeat offending.

Legislators must call for research and statistics to show the extent to which victims are informed of restitution, compensation, civil suits, and restorative justice avenues, as well as the extent to which they apply for and get court orders and receive payments.

(6)

STAKING CLAIMS

Victims Represented and Heard

In chapter 2, I showed the national and international consensus about the inalienable rights of victims to have both protection from the accused and access to justice (a "voice" in the process). A recurring theme in chapters 3, 4, and 5 has been that many of the inalienable rights for victims of crime are overlooked and ignored. This chapter looks at the arguments for providing victims with the rights to have participation and representation in criminal courts. This participation and representation would go much further than a mere victim impact statement could. These measures would match and surpass the provisions adopted in 2008 in the California victim rights amendment known as Marsy's Law, as they would allow victims to litigate the outcomes and so directly protect their interests.

In 1982, the U.S. President's Task Force said that "[g]overnment must be restrained from trampling on the rights of individual citizens. Victims of crime have been transformed into a group oppressively burdened by a system designed to protect them." It then proposed a modest remedy with an addition to the sixth amendment of the U.S. Constitution. The addition stated "Likewise, the victim, in every criminal prosecution, shall have the right to be present and heard at all critical stages of judicial proceedings." The "likewise" referred to due process safeguards for an accused in the same sixth amendment.[1]

It has been surprisingly difficult for criminal lawyers to embrace the notion of the victim being present and heard in the United States, England and Wales, and Canada. While the core needs and interests of crime victims were not so clear in 1982 when my colleagues and I began our *magna carta* campaign, they have become abundantly clear through my research and advocacy, as I have shown in the earlier chapters. Furthermore, constitutional amendments and state laws (particularly Marsy's Law) have clarified them even further.

Victims have an inalienable right to be safe and be sure that their safety is amply considered when judges make decisions about the release of a potentially violent accused, such as at bail hearings, sentencing, and parole decisions. Bail hearings occur soon after the arrest of the accused to decide whether (and under what conditions) the accused may be released, pending the trial.

As we've seen, victims want to be respected in the criminal justice process because the crime was perpetrated against *them*, not against the state. Respect for victims means considering their needs when deciding court dates, returning property, agreeing to a plea of a lesser charge, and more. In sum, victims desperately want court decisions to recognize what was done to them.

THE INTERESTS OF VICTIMS THAT GO UNMET

In 1982, the constitutional amendment proposed by the President's Task Force talked about the various opportunities for victims to have their voice heard during the justice process. There are (or at least, there should be) a surprising number of these, which I will illustrate using quotes from the President's Task Force's composite case that we have been following throughout the book.

1. Police Investigation

The first opportunity for victim input is presented when the victim reports the offense. The police may investigate the crime and look for a person to arrest. In the Anglo-American systems, the police are exclusively in charge of an investigation over which victims have no influence and about which they may know absolutely nothing. Influence during an investigation becomes important in relation to any civil suit. If an accused person is arrested and charged, the victim will not necessarily be informed. This is a great injustice for victims, who tend to have a lingering fear that the perpetrator may come back to attack or intimidate them. So victims need influence during the investigation and knowledge about an arrest.

2. Bail Hearing

The next opportunity for victim input should exist at the judge's decision on whether or not the accused person should be released on bail. One of the most common complaints of victims of crime is that they are surprised to find that the accused has been released on bail without their knowledge, as in the case of Marsy's mother and many, many others that we will see below. For now let's go back to the composite case:

> At least you can be assured that the man who attacked you is in custody, or so you think. No one tells you when he is released on his promise to come to court. No one ever asks you if you've been threatened. The judge is never told that the defendant said he'd kill you if you told or that he'd get even if he went to jail. Horrified, you ask how he got out after what he did. You're told the judge can't consider whether he'll be dangerous, only whether he'll come back to court. He's been accused and convicted before, but he's always come to court; so he must be released.[2]

In some cases, the offender's release on bail can lead to the victim feeling intimidated. It is promising that, since this composite case was compiled in 1982, some improvements to bail consideration have taken place in some jurisdictions (although not nearly enough).[3] The judge is supposed to consider not only whether the accused person is likely to turn up for trial, but also if he will be dangerous if released and if his release will bring justice into disrepute. Typically, however, the judge will make this decision without any direct consideration of the victim's concerns for safety or justice. Certainly, the victim does not have a right to talk directly to the court. Even in cases of intimate partner violence, a battered woman does not have standing to present her concerns. She may only find out by chance that the man has been released.

3. Case Scheduling

The next critical stage happens when (and if) the case goes to court. The victim may not even know that the case is scheduled, and so may not have the opportunity to choose to attend. But if they *do* know and choose to attend, the whole situation likely brings more feelings of frustration than of justice and closure for the victim. While some improvements are happening, let's not forget what the composite case felt like:

> Now the case is scheduled for trial. Again there are delays. When you call and ask to speak with the prosecutor, you are told the case has been reassigned. You tell your story in detail to five different prosecutors before the case is tried. Months go by and no one tells you what's happening. Periodically you are subpoenaed to appear. You leave your work, wait, and are finally told to go home. . . .
> Continuances are granted because the courts are filled, one of the lawyers is on another case, the judge has a meeting to attend or an early tennis match. You can't understand why they couldn't have discovered these problems before you came to court. When you ask if the next date could be set a week later so you can attend a family gathering out of state, you are told that the defendant has the right to a speedy trial. You stay home from the reunion and the case is continued.[4]

4. Plea Negotiation

During these continuances (when court appearances are postponed or canceled), the lawyer for the accused and the prosecutor are negotiating a plea. Basically, it is a strategy game, where the prosecutor looks at the chances of getting a conviction for a certain charge given the need to prove it beyond a reasonable doubt. The prosecutor is also looking to have the case completed to ease his workload. The defense lawyer is doing the reverse, hoping to get a lesser sentence for the accused and realizing that delays may get a softer judge or higher payment for legal defense services. It is not surprising, then, that many victims begin to feel like they are caught in the middle of a game over which they have no control—they are.

5. Sentencing

In terms of sentencing, if there is a conviction, the role of the victim at most will be relegated to providing a statement about the impact that the crime had on them. This might be a written statement or, in some cases, a brief oral statement. Across Europe and North America, legislators are proud of this concession to victims—even though researchers say that an impact statement makes little difference to the length of the sentence of an offender. Many victims are not even informed of their option to submit an impact statement, and even if they do submit one, this token action falls far short of their inalienable right to be present and heard with legal representation, as the system provides for in France. After all, having been disempowered by the offender, victims want nothing more than to be empowered and to have a voice in the justice system. And why should this be denied to them?

6. Prior Convictions

Other aspects of what happens every day in the justice system also seem like a strategy match. If there is a conviction, then previous convictions of the convicted person can be shared, resulting in a longer sentence overall. For many victims, it is hard to understand why a history of rapes would not be allowed as evidence into the court room—particularly when, until only recently, the sexual histories of rape victims could be used by defense lawyers to suggest that the victim had somehow facilitated the horror of being raped. Many factors seem stacked against the victim, with the perpetrators' rights trumping their own in the justice system. I'll return to this injustice in chapter 8 when we look at the urgent need to balance the different interests of victims and accused rather than always allowing the accused's interests to pull rank. The composite case continues to shed some light on what is at stake:

> You are stunned when you later learn that the defendant also raped five others; one victim was an eight-year-old girl. During her testimony she was asked to describe her attacker's anatomy. Spectators laughed when she said she did not understand the words being used. When she was asked to draw a picture of her attacker's genitalia, the girl fled from the courtroom and ran sobbing to her mother, who had been subpoenaed by the defense and had to wait outside. The youngster was forced to sit alone and recount, as you did, each minute of the attack. You know how difficult it was for you to speak of these things; you cannot imagine how it was for a child.[5]

RIGHTS OR BAND-AIDS?

The good news is that the face of criminal justice has changed at least somewhat in the United States in the last twenty-five years, thanks to the amazing success of the National Victims Crime Amendment Passage (NV-CAP), which got state legislatures and voters to approve constitutional amendments in thirty-three states. You can see the specifics of these amendments by going on the website of the applicable state attorney general, or to the NVCAP website, where information about each state's amendment is easily accessible.[6] Information about developments and improvements in the enforceability of the amendments, as well as new amendments such as Marsy's Law, are also available on the NVCAP website.[7]

NVCAP succeeded in getting Presidents Bill Clinton and George W. Bush to endorse the principle of the victim rights amendment. The operative paragraph of the amendment included principles typical of many state constitutions:

> Victims of violent crimes shall have the rights to timely notice of any release, escape, and public proceeding involving the crime; not to be excluded from such proceedings; to be heard at release, plea, sentencing, commutation, and pardon proceedings; and not to be subjected to undue delay, or to decisions that disregard their safety or their just claims to restitution; nor shall these rights be restricted, except when, and to the degree that, compelling necessity dictates.[8]

Unfortunately, this clause—as sensible as it is—was never added to the Constitution, as it was not adopted by the U.S. Senate—a very sad day for victims of crime in the United States.[9] It was also a letdown for victims in other countries who might have looked to the United States for leadership. If the amendment had been added to the Constitution, then victims (citizens, voters, and taxpayers) would have gained the right to go up to the Supreme Court to ensure that their inalienable rights as victims are enforced. Their ability to do so is long overdue, and there is no reason to keep this from them.

One needless concern that ended up blocking the bid was the fear that this amendment would set back *defendants'* rights, which had been centuries in their development. But this fear was wholly unfounded, as the NVCAP added the qualifier that the protection of these rights for victims would not "abridge the rights of those accused or convicted of victimizing them." It became clear that single-minded senators concerned only about rights for the accused would not agree to even modest additions to the Constitution that specifically recognized the importance of inalienable rights for the victims as well. This is not balance.

In the end, NVCAP pursued a smaller step forward, which became known as the Justice for All Act and was signed into federal law on October 30, 2004. One section of this act (named in memory of crime victims Scott Campbell, Stephanie Roper, Wendy Preston, Louarna Gillis, and Nila Lynn) specifies eight rights for victims. The rights are similar to those in the victim rights amendment that failed to be adopted by the U.S. Congress, but with some minor clarifications and two additional rights—the reasonable right to confer with the attorney for the government in the case, and the right for the victim to be treated with fairness and respect in terms of dignity and privacy.

Importantly, the approval of the Justice for All Act was accompanied by the authorization of funds to ensure that these rights were implemented. The Government Accountability Office (GAO) was to assess whether the objectives were achieved, and also recommend practical improvements. Unfortunately, the assessments are vague because the GAO had difficulty contacting victims to seek their input.[10]

MARSY'S LAW

On November 4, 2008, the most recent and detailed constitutional amendment (known as Marsy's Law) became law in California after it was approved by 53.9 percent of voters.[11] It begins with a preamble that describes the tragic case of Marsy to show why such an amendment is needed. It then goes on to elaborate seventeen principles to remedy a justice system that fails to fully recognize—and adequately enforce—the inalienable rights of victims of crime. It includes an enforcement mechanism in the court where a case is being heard.

Consistent with my eight core needs that I identified in chapter 1, there are some notable themes running through these amendments. One is the core need to get criminal justice to pay attention to public safety—and particularly to the protection of victims from their accused. A second dominant theme is that victims of crime have a core need to have a voice in that criminal justice system. The amendment explains:

> It is named after Marsy, a 21-year-old college senior at U.C. Santa Barbara who was preparing to pursue a career in special education for handicapped children and had her whole life ahead of her. She was murdered on November 30, 1983.

Following her murderer's arrest, Marsy's mother was shocked to meet him at a local supermarket, learning that he had been released on bail without any notice to Marsy's family and without any opportunity for her family to state their opposition to his release.

Several years after his conviction and sentence to "life in prison," the parole hearings for his release began. In the first parole hearing, Marsy's mother suffered a heart attack fighting against his release. Since then Marsy's family has endured the trauma of frequent parole hearings and constant anxiety that Marsy's killer would be released.[12]

This preamble to Marsy's Law identifies many of the common problems that have been faced by victims of crime for many decades—and are still faced by victims today. These include "the failure of our criminal justice system to notify them of their rights, failure to give them notice of important hearings in the prosecutions of their criminal wrongdoers, failure to provide them with an opportunity to speak and participate, failure to impose actual and just punishment upon their wrongdoers, and failure to extend to them some measure of finality to the trauma inflicted upon them by their wrongdoers."[13]

In figures 6.1, 6.2 and 6.3, I have compared the eight rights in the federal Justice for All Act with the rights in Marsy's Law, which covers provisions that are found in other constitutional amendments (albeit in more detail). My aim is to enable you to see what is included in both as strong steps toward balancing justice.

Justice for All Act 2004	Marsy's Law, California, 2008
(1) The right to be reasonably protected from the accused.	2. Protection from the Defendant To be reasonably protected from the defendant and persons acting on behalf of the defendant.
	3. Victim Safety Considerations in Setting Bail and Release Conditions To have the safety of the victim and the victim's family considered in fixing the amount of bail and release conditions for the defendant.
	16. Safety of Victim and Public are Factors in Parole Release To have the safety of the victim, the victim's family, and the general public considered before any parole or other post-judgment release decision is made.
(2) The right to reasonable, accurate, and timely notice of any public court proceeding, or any parole proceeding, involving the crime or of any release or escape of the accused.	15. Notice of Parole Procedures and Release on Parole To be informed of all parole procedures, to participate in the parole process, to provide information to the parole authority to be considered before the parole of the offender, and to be notified, upon request, of the parole or other release of the offender.
	12. Information About Conviction, Sentence, Incarceration, Release, and Escape To be informed, upon request, of the conviction, sentence, place and time of incarceration, or other disposition of the defendant, the scheduled release date of the defendant, and the release of or the escape by the defendant from custody.
(3) The right not to be excluded from any such public court proceeding, unless the court, after receiving clear and convincing evidence, determines that testimony by the victim would be materially altered if the victim heard other testimony at that proceeding.	7. Notice of and Presence at Public Proceedings To reasonable notice of all public proceedings, including delinquency proceedings, upon request, at which the defendant and the prosecutor are entitled to be present and of all parole or other post-conviction release proceedings, and to be present at all such proceedings.
	11. Receipt of Pre-Sentence Report To receive, upon request, the pre-sentence report when available to the defendant, except for those portions made confidential by law.

Figure 6.1. Comparison of the rights in the Federal Justice for All Act with those in Marsy's Law in California (part 1)

Justice for All Act 2004	Marsy's Law, California, 2008
(4) The right to be reasonably heard at any public proceeding in the district court involving release, plea, sentencing, or any parole proceeding.	8. Appearance at Court Proceedings and Expression of Views To be heard, upon request, at any proceeding, including any delinquency proceeding, involving a post-arrest release decision, plea, sentencing, post-conviction release decision, or any proceeding in which a right of the victim is at issue.
	10. Provision of Information to the Probation Department To provide information to a probation department official conducting a pre-sentence investigation concerning the impact of the offense on the victim and the victim's family and any sentencing recommendations before the sentencing of the defendant.
(5) The reasonable right to confer with the attorney for the Government in the case.	6. **Conference with the Prosecution and Notice of Pretrial Disposition** To reasonable notice of and to reasonably confer with the prosecuting agency, upon request, regarding, the arrest of the defendant if known by the prosecutor, the charges filed, the determination whether to extradite the defendant, and, upon request, to be notified of and informed before any pretrial disposition of the case.
(6) The right to full and timely restitution as provided in law.	13. **Restitution A.** It is the unequivocal intention of the People of the State of California that all persons who suffer losses as a result of criminal activity shall have the right to seek and secure restitution from the persons convicted of the crimes causing the losses they suffer. B. Restitution shall be ordered from the convicted wrongdoer in every case, regardless of the sentence or disposition imposed, in which a crime victim suffers a loss. C. All monetary payments, monies, and property collected from any person who has been ordered to make restitution shall be first applied to pay the amounts ordered as restitution to the victim.

Figure 6.2.   Comparison of the rights in the Federal Justice for All Act with those in Marsy's Law in California (part 2)

Justice for All Act 2004	Marsy's Law, California, 2008
(7) The right to proceedings free from unreasonable delay.	9. **Speedy Trial and Prompt Conclusion of the Case** To a speedy trial and a prompt and final conclusion of the case and any related post-judgment proceedings.
(8) The right to be treated with fairness and with respect for the victim's dignity and privacy.	1. **Fairness and Respect** To be treated with fairness and respect for his or her privacy and dignity, and to be free from intimidation, harassment, and abuse, throughout the criminal or juvenile justice process.
	4. **The Prevention of the Disclosure of Confidential Information** To prevent the disclosure of confidential information or records to the defendant, the defendant's attorney, or any other person acting on behalf of the defendant, which could be used to locate or harass the victim or the victim's family or which disclose confidential communications made in the course of medical or counseling treatment, or which are otherwise privileged or confidential by law.
	5. **Refusal to be Interviewed by the Defense** To refuse an interview, deposition, or discovery request by the defendant, the defendant's attorney, or any other person acting on behalf of the defendant, and to set reasonable conditions on the conduct of any such interview to which the victim consents.
	14. **The Prompt Return of Property** To the prompt return of property when no longer needed as evidence.
	17. **Information About These 16 Rights** To be informed of the rights enumerated in paragraphs (1) through (16).

Figure 6.3.   Comparison of the rights in the Federal Justice for All Act with those in Marsy's Law in California (part 3)

All eight rights of the Justice for All Act can be found in Marsy's Law. For instance, Marsy's Law rights 2, 3, and 16 elaborate on ways to better protect victims from the accused. Rights 12 and 15 cover notice being given to the victim. Rights 7 and 11 call for the victim to be present and to have input. Rights 8 and 10 allow for the victims to express their views. Right 6 calls for collaboration with the prosecutor. Right 13 gives priority to restitution from the offender. Right 9 focuses on a speedy trial. Right 1 calls for fairness and respect.

Marsy's Law adds three other aspects that are not found in Justice for All. Marsy's Law rights 4 and 5 protect the victim's information. Right 14 calls for prompt return of property, and right 17 requires victims to be informed of all the other rights.

There is still room for improvement, however. It appears that the crucial guideline for law enforcement to inform victims is not clearly stated here, so many victims may not be informed in a timely manner. Marsy's Law does not talk to the core needs relating to information, support, and services that were discussed in chapters 1, 3, and 4. It points to restitution, but not to compensation from the state as discussed in chapter 5.

NEW INITIATIVES TO ENFORCE RIGHTS

The detail in Marsy's Law is impressive, as are the provisions to enforce it. As many of the provisions were already in place, we can expect that these provisions will be implemented. Unfortunately, as necessary and as just as these rights are, the few teeth added may or may not be enough to ensure comprehensive enforcement. The law does not provide for an office to actually enforce the rights, and compliance costs money, so we will have to see how much funding is authorized for enforcement.

Many states are following the example of Arizona by having an enforcement officer. Others are looking into mandamus proceedings, which would allow for victims to appeal to a higher court to have their rights respected and implemented, as have fortunately been adopted in Oregon and are being considered for Illinois.[14]

Apart from enforcement, I would also like a regular survey undertaken to see to what extent victims are aware of their rights and take advantage of them. Given the sophistication of our knowledge about reaching victims with surveys, it's clear that we do know how to measure whether these laws are in fact working or not. So, although we are making some modest progress in terms of increasing respect for victims' inalienable rights, we must use evaluation tools to our fullest advantage to ensure that our laws are actually meeting their goals.

GIVING VICTIMS A VOICE: MODELS FROM FRANCE AND AROUND THE WORLD

From my perspective, one of the most disappointing aspects of this amazing social movement—the movement to have victims' inalienable rights respected around the world—has been its inability to get victims real standing in criminal courts in North America and other Anglo-American systems. Courts continue to accept mere victim impact statements as a substitute for victims' true voices throughout the process. Even the Justice for All Act and Marsy's Law only provide victims with the right to confer with the prosecutor—not the right to have actual standing in a manner equal to the accused, as exists in France and was recently proposed by Victim Support Europe when commenting on implementation of European standards for victims of crime.

What's most frustrating is that we know that it *can be done*, and we know that it *works*. France, for example, has given victims a role in criminal proceedings for more than forty years. It is a system little known and barely understood outside of France. What it entails is that victims have an enforceable right to standing in a French criminal court. While their standing comes from being the civil party in a criminal justice process (for as we have seen, France can combine the criminal and civil proceedings), victims have the opportunity to defend their interests while they pursue truth, reparation, public safety, just sentencing, and related issues. Furthermore, victims are able to raise concerns about their personal safety and force a more thorough investigation of the offenses against them.

Another piece of good news in France is that victims can be parties to the investigations by asking questions of those in charge and, if necessary, going to a judge if their assertions are not taken seriously. This enables victims to have access to evidence brought together by law enforcement for the civil aspects of the case. Furthermore, when decisions are made about what charges should be brought, the French victim can be heard.

Although the laws in France are not that different from those in other countries in Europe, the provision of legal aid to victims of crime is one of the main factors that changes legal rhetoric into concrete action. As a result, French courts often have as many lawyers for victims as they do for defendants.

I, and many other victims' advocates, strongly believe that this is as it should be. Imagine a court in the United States, Canada, or England and Wales with lawyers representing victims of crime to get respect for victims' inalienable rights in bail decisions, plea bargaining, continuances, and sentences. We can imagine how the nightmare for the victim in our composite case would never have happened.

But this is only part of the story in France. The existence of this active role for the victim has led to a large number of settlements where the victim and the defendant agree on the restitution that will be paid by the defendant. Officially, the court can sanction these agreements by binding over the criminal case indefinitely. This is a form of restorative justice that takes place directly in the courts instead of being relegated to the corridors of the courthouse.

Yet more good news is that France is no longer alone. Belgium, Germany, Japan, and Korea are just some of the countries that have adopted this system of justice, which retains a reasonable and focused balance on the rights and needs of victims. In the case of Korea, this victim-focused approach to justice has even been entered into its constitution. And why not? This all seems so obvious. And like many obvious notions of natural justice, the United Nations General Assembly has endorsed it.

Yet sadly, in the American, British, and Canadian systems, the idea of victims being represented and heard is still heresy. Law schools and other bastions that steadfastly defend the rights of accused and offenders tend to raise concerns over victim representation—even going so far as to say that allowing the views and concerns of victims to be presented and considered would delay justice. (It would seem that the accused's defense counsel's tactical delays are not of equal concern to the defendant-focused critics.) What's more, naysayers tend to warn that allowing the victim's voice in the courtroom would make criminal courts too emotional. Really? Surely, judges can cope with the emotions of victims if they arise—after all, as we have seen, crimes are committed against real persons with real emotions, *not* against inanimate states.

INTERNATIONAL CRIMINAL COURT PROVIDES VICTIMS WITH A VOICE AND MUCH MORE

Representatives of the Anglo-American legal culture use another argument to exclude victims from having standing in their criminal justice system. They point to the French criminal justice system being truth-seeking— how welcome for crime victims!—rather than adversarial (a system where the prosecution is pitted against the defense, as in the O.J. Simpson case). They claim that only the adversarial system can protect innocent persons from being wrongfully convicted, at least in any numbers. Somehow, these critics have hoodwinked policy makers into thinking that these differences in legal cultures stand in the way of Anglo-American systems giving victims standing, even though in my opinion these two concepts are not mutually exclusive and one doesn't impact the other whatsoever. And this is not only my own opinion; we can see systems that merge the best virtues of both approaches for the benefit of everybody involved. Indeed, Japan provides an example of a nation that has successfully combined an adversarial national justice system with a victim-centered approach.

Another important example is the permanent International Criminal Court (ICC) in The Hague, which has combined impressively the virtues of the Anglo-American adversarial system with a comprehensive approach toward protecting victims.

In the 1990s, the United Nations started discussions to develop a permanent international criminal court. On July 17, 1998, a group of governments adopted the Statute of Rome, which established the ICC as a permanent court to sanction persons who commit such heinous abuses of power as genocide, crimes against humanity, and war crimes. On October 9, 2002, at the same time that the court was officially opened, it adopted specific rules for procedure and evidence that outlined the role and treatment of victims within its courtrooms.[15]

In figure 6.4, I have highlighted the key provisions in the Statute of Rome, the Rules of Procedure and Evidence, and now the operationalization of the investigations, trials, and so on. I have grouped these under the headings of support, justice, and good government that I have used throughout the book for presenting the core needs and inalienable rights

Support

Victims protected and supported

Victims given response sensitive to gender, age and other issues

Justice

Victim participation and representation (grouped) paid by legal aid in adversarial trial and sentencing

Restitution paid to victims through trust fund fed by offenders and others

Good Government

Trust Fund contributes to awareness and prevention

Permanent infrastructure paid by governments with performance assessments

Figure 6.4. Participation, representation, support, protection, and restitution in the International Criminal Court

of crime victims. The figure shows how ICC embraces many of those rights, including rights to protection and support for generic and specific victims and good government performance measurement. There are also some gaps relating to police and service responses. However, my main purpose here is to focus on participation and representation. My argument is that if governments embrace rights for victims at the ICC, then they should embrace those same rights for victims of crime in their domestic jurisdictions, including participation and representation.

Like France has been able to do for many years, the ICC provides for victims to participate, to be represented, to ask questions, and to seek reparation. Its rules include wording similar to that in the original proposed amendment to the U.S. Constitution in 1982, but it goes much further in establishing services, protections, reparation mechanisms, and ways for victims to be represented. Importantly, it has provisions for victims to appeal to a judicial authority if their rights are not respected.

The debates that led to the establishment of the ICC pitted the governments dominated by the Anglo-American legal culture against the governments dominated by investigatory (truth-seeking) legal systems (namely, France). Lobbying for victims during these governmental debates were pioneers of the victim movement including Dr. Yael Danieli, and also leaders of the genocide victims' rights movement such as Carla Ferstman. The result of these intense debates is a hybrid court that combines the Anglo-American adversarial system to determine guilt with an active role and standing for victims of crime.

Victim Standing in the International Criminal Court

In the ICC, victims of the abuses of power have a role that goes beyond that of mere witnesses. They are guaranteed their rights to support, protection, reparation, and participation—truly, an example for national jurisdictions to strive for. One of the great innovations of the ICC is to provide an opportunity for the victims to present their views, address questions to the court, and observe. In sum, it is an inspiring example of what victim advocates such as myself should fight for in every jurisdiction.

In 2005, the ICC decided to set up an Office of the Public Counsel for Victims to ensure the effective participation of victims in the process. This office advises independent legal counsel and may also represent victims free of charge. Victims are provided with a list of legal counselors who will be able to meet the required standards. As many of these crimes involve thousands of victims, the legislation allows for the court to agree to group- ings of victims, and within this logistical limit, the victims have standing and are represented by lawyers.

Victim Services in the International Criminal Court

The ICC encompasses services and protections for victims that meet the standards of the very best services in the United States, England and Wales, and Canada. The court has created a special unit for victims and witnesses to provide support before, during, and after the trial. The services are delivered by well-paid specialists who are often salaried em- ployees of the court. The staff includes persons with expertise in trauma, including trauma from sexual violence. They also understand the special needs of certain vulnerable victims, including children and the elderly. When providing testimony, victims may also have support from family members, psychologists, or legal representatives, particularly if they are vulnerable because of age or the traumatic nature of the victimization.

These victim services specialists are also able to advise the prosecutors on appropriate security arrangements for victims. The court must take appro- priate measures to protect the safety, physical and psychological well-being, dignity, and privacy of victims and witnesses—particularly if they are vulner- able. The statute allows for identities not to be made public, testimony to be provided by electronic means, and the hearing to be confidential.

The statute also calls for the court to establish principles relating to "rep- arations to, or in respect of, victims, including restitution, compensation and rehabilitation," and to establish a trust fund which "works for victims by mobilizing people, funding opportunities for the benefit of victims, and implementing court-ordered reparations awards."[16]

The ICC is still in its early phases. Much of the initial work of the court since its inception has been to investigate alleged crimes. Only a few of these investigations have led to charges and arrests. So, it remains to be seen how the statute and the rules of procedure will be put into practice over the years ahead.

Overall, the ICC provides a successful example of a complex criminal justice system that is based on the Anglo-American concept of justice, but which has successfully incorporated the voice of victims into its proceedings. The fact that the United States is one of the few leading nations not to have

ratified the underlying statute does not take away from its model for victim
justice. One of the ICC's main visions is to empower victims and their families. It listens to victims and seeks to amplify their voices. It works with them
to find culturally relevant ways to recover and rehabilitate. It advocates for
reconciliation and to prevent reoccurrence of the horrors.

With this system to serve as an example, there should be no more excuses for why the criminal justice systems in the United States, Canada,
and England and Wales cannot adopt criminal justice systems that provide
victims with their inalienable right to have standing and a voice. The time
to act is now.

HOW WILL VICTIMS GET THEIR VOICE?

It is clear that victims of crime need standing in every court in every jurisdiction. We can see this when we listen to victims and when we look at
the promising examples provided by the ICC, France, and the growing
list of countries that are adopting means to empower victims within their
criminal justice systems. So we know what we need to do. The only question that remains is, how do we get there? How do we ensure that victims'
core needs are respected in our systems of justice? How can victims be
protected from the accused, get reparation, and have a real and valued
voice in the justice process? I believe they can, and here's how:

Step One: Ensuring Representation for the Victim

In the United States, Canada, and England and Wales, the first step is
to realize that a district attorney or a Crown prosecutor is *not* an attorney
for the victim. The interests of the district or the Crown are *not* the same
as the interests of the victim. Some confuse the lawyer representing the
state with a lawyer representing the victim, but this is far from the case.
As we've seen, the prosecutor in England and Wales, as well as in Canada, is called a "Crown prosecutor," making it clear that the lawyer actually represents the queen—not the victim of crime. While the interests
of the victim may occasionally coincide with those of the queen, in many
cases they do not. So, there must be a separate advocate for victims,
particularly in cases where the safety of victims is in doubt. This separate
advocate is also necessary to ensure that the victim receives restitution,

for if victims were represented at the time of restitution decisions, then the courts would order it.

Step Two: Gaining a Voice beyond an Impact Statement

The second thing we need to realize is that victim impact statements do *not* provide a sufficient voice for victims of crime. While they are seen by some victim advocates as a step in the right direction, they fall far short of providing victims with an actual voice in court proceedings. Disappointingly, impact statements do not allow victims of crime to request specific amounts of restitution or sanctions that will protect the victim or bring them closure. What we need to ensure is that there is a mechanism that enables the views and concerns of victims to be heard when their personal interests (such as safety, reparation, and justice) are affected. This mechanism would be a voice, not a veto or a final decision. The court would decide the final outcome after considering the interests of *all* parties—the accused, the state, *and* the victim.

If we succeed in opening the door for victims to gain representation in justice proceedings, it is also vital that the state provide legal aid so that victims can realize their newfound voices.

Step Three: Broadening the Court's Focus

This concept of considering all parties involved is not so different from the principles of family law, where the state has an interest in the family's well-being, as do the two spouses and their children. Following the initiative of the Violence Against Women's Act in the United States, experts are increasingly calling for domestic courts where criminal justice and family law are considered simultaneously because the decisions all arise out of a single set of facts.

Canada has amalgamated divorce (federal) and alimony (provincial) considerations into a single unified family court. A parallel experiment could also center the criminal and civil proceedings around one set of facts, so the prosecutor for the state would continue to litigate for the interests of the state and the broader community, while the attorney for the victim would pursue the interests of the victim in terms of safety, reparation, and respect. As we have seen in chapter 5, the advantage of using the civil system is that the victim is a party to the process and so has more control than in the criminal justice process, where only the prosecutor and the defendant have standing.[17] The solution, then, is not to keep this system of justice separate from criminal justice, but to join them.

DEMANDS FOR LEGISLATORS

Thirty-three states have adopted constitutional amendments and all governments have agreed at the General Assembly of the United Nations that victims must be present and heard whenever their interests are at stake. However, progress beyond victim impact statements at the time of sentencing has been slow.

Legislators must establish clear remedies for victims who do not receive services or treatment consistent with constitutions or laws. Best practices include the procedures in Oregon and those proposed for Illinois.

Legislators must provide funding for legal assistance so that victims can have their interests represented in court, request reparation in criminal courts, and pursue payment of restitution through civil courts and family law protections. One practice to look to is the Justice for All Act.

Legislators must pay for surveys to identify the extent to which victims get to realize the inalienable rights proclaimed through constitutional amendments. These surveys must also identify remedies for when these rights are ignored. Examples of best practices are the reviews done of VAWA and VOCA.

Legislators must experiment with joint criminal and civil court proceedings to empower victims to protect their concerns for their safety, convenience, need for services, reparation, desire for the truth, and right to justice. An important model best practice is the legislation, rules of procedure, and organization of the International Criminal Court.

(7)

STOPPING CRIME

Victimization Prevention as Return on Investment

The best way to help victims of crime is to prevent crime from happening.

In my earlier book, *Less Law, More Order*, I identified what prevents crime and reduces victimization according to reviews completed by such prestigious organizations as the World Health Organization, the United Nations Commission on Crime Prevention and Criminal Justice, and the U.S. National Research Council.[1] These reviews were particularly influenced by an accumulation of positive results from random control trials that compared prevention projects with the standard response of police and criminal justice.

The good news is there is strong evidence to prove that specific projects which tackle causes of crime before it happens can reduce victimizations from both violent and property crime. So victimization *is* preventable. Much of this evidence is based on careful experiments undertaken in the last thirty years in the United States. These experiments focused on reducing the number of young males involved in victimizing by enriching remedies to tackle negative life experiences such as abusive parenting, dropping out of school, and lack of positive role models.

Less Law, More Order shared this good news with taxpayers and voters so that they could hold legislators accountable for reforming policy. I argued that if we invested immediately, we'd get a significant return in reductions in victimization in the future, for there is no more important issue than preventing people from becoming victims. The bad news is that little of this knowledge is being used in the United States today. However, Canada and some other countries are beginning to invest big time in harnessing this knowledge. Governments around the world have agreed to do much more to prevent victimizations by applying the international knowledge base on what works to plan effective victimization prevention.

THE GOOD NEWS

The evidence for what predisposes young persons to become persistent offenders is strong and clear. Large-scale research projects have followed the personal development of males from birth through adolescence to adulthood. As the youths grew up, the researchers recorded data on life experiences such as inconsistent and abusive parenting, behavioral difficulties in primary school, abuse of alcohol and drugs, and skipping school as a teenager. When they considered males with these negative life experiences, they found that there was a much higher probability that these individuals would be involved in delinquency than those with fewer such experiences. The bright side here is that when advocates have deliberately set up programs to reduce those negative life experiences, independent evaluators have concluded that the young men were involved in many fewer crimes against victims.

The prestigious organizations mentioned above call for a combination of enforcement, community treatment for persons at risk of offending (such as tackling drug and alcohol abuse), and prevention. This three-pronged approach aims to get the best return in reductions of victimization. Projects that work to prevent victimization generally also aim to prevent violence against women, but they must be accompanied by specific programs to change male attitudes toward violence against women and to reduce the risky consumption of alcohol. The organizations endorse offering women more freedom to leave violent relationships through social and economic opportunities, liberalized divorce and family laws, and transition houses. As of yet, the evidence that these strategies work to prevent violence against women is not as strong as the evidence for preventing street violence, but this reflects a lack of evaluation more than weaknesses in the programs—a common shortfall when discussing rights for victims of crime.

Another piece of good news is that there has been a steady reduction in deaths at the hands of drunk drivers in the United States, from 30,000 in

1980 to 12,000 in 2008. Research on the successes in reducing fatalities on the road in Europe suggests that some of this reduction is due to a change in routine habits (that is, fewer persons driving when inebriated). The success in raising the legal drinking age is likely another contributing factor. Programs that tackle the common negative life experiences that predispose young persons to persistent victimizing would likely also contribute to reductions in the number of young people driving while impaired.

There is hope that the number of deaths can be even further reduced by programs prioritized by MADD. For example, random breathalyzer testing has brought about reductions in the number of impaired driving victimizations in Australia. It is also logical to focus on preventing drunk drivers from repeat offending through the installation of an ignition interlock (a device that requires drivers to pass a sort of breathalyzer test before their engines will start) in the cars of convicted offenders. Results of ignition interlock programs from New Mexico and Arizona are encouraging for persons convicted of being impaired at a blood alcohol level of 0.08.[2]

Research shows that addressing problems in the community does more to prevent victimization—and costs less—than sending even more people to jail or hiring more police and lawyers. *Less Law, More Order* illustrates the research with numerous practical examples of jurisdictions that have succeeded in reducing victimization *before* it happens. Hiring public health nurses, providing parent training through programs such as "Triple P," and investing in helping at-risk youth to complete school and get job training is better than hiring more police. Preventing family violence, reducing the need for handguns for self-protection, and dealing with drugs through public health saves more lives than incarceration. Getting neighbors to watch out for each other and implementing better urban design is more effective than packing our criminal courts. Smarter policing is better than more police. And combining smart enforcement with smart social prevention is better than more rhetoric.

We know that we can reduce the number of victims across the United States and around the world if we apply these strategies—strategies which we know work.

Other Returns on Investment from Preventing Victimization

What is missing is serious consideration by legislators of sustained investment in these programs, which we know to be both effective and cost-efficient at preventing victimization. The legislators seem addicted to doing more and more of the same thing. Yet, investment in smart (and thus effective) prevention reduces the numbers of victims and reduces the ballooning costs of dealing with crime. For every one dollar spent on proven programs that prevent a young person from turning to violence (such as parenting programs and programs to help at-risk youth complete school), it would take *seven* dollars to incarcerate that individual—not to mention the costs of caring for those he victimized. Even the legislators must see what an obvious solution victimization prevention is.

Less Law, More Order shows practical examples of cities whose legislators have worked with policy planning groups to diagnose the problems of victimizations in their cities. Working with this knowledge, they have then been able to successfully implement solutions where they are needed most. These city-wide initiatives tackle well-established negative life experiences of some of their residents (such as child abuse, behavioral difficulties in primary school, and dropping out of secondary school) by mobilizing services for housing, youth programs, schooling, and other social factors in targeted neighborhoods.

These effective and cost-efficient programs are stopping young men from growing up to be violent. The research suggests that, if current socioeconomic trends continue, these programs would achieve a reduction in victimization by *50 percent* within ten years. That's one in two victims saved the agony, the fear, the shock, the anger, the humiliation, and the degradation of being victimized. That's also one in two would-be criminals who are contributing to society instead of running from the law or maybe spending time behind bars. We know we can do this. Now let's make it happen.

MAKING IT HAPPEN

Even though these programs and strategies make obvious sense, a reduction in victimization cannot happen on its own. Simply knowing what is effective in reducing crime and knowing how to do it is not enough to get the sustained investment that is needed.

We know that present policies are tough on *victims*, not tough on crime. Too many children are still being abused, too many women assaulted, and too many people robbed and left scared in their own homes. What these present policies *are* tough on, however, are taxpayers, as the cost of law and order inexorably increases each year. The present systems are tough to use, and as we've seen throughout this book, they're tough on victims of crime.

Legislators must invest in changing the standard inefficient strategies that *don't* work into smart and effective strategies that *do*. Action to increase the number of programs and a strategy to prevent victimization and use taxes responsibly is long overdue. Action is needed to replace the antiquated policies that have led to us using mass incarceration as a blunt and expensive way to stop victimization. The United States in particular must get beyond its insatiable appetite for incarceration in order to get smart about proven ways to prevent violent crime and stop victimization.

In *Less Law, More Order*, I demonstrated how investing in smart strategies is feasible in even the most adverse of fiscal environments. It can be done by allocating the equivalent of only 2 percent of what is spent each year on *reacting* to crime after it happens. That's right—if we add a mere 2 percent more of our current police, criminal justice, and corrections budget each year for five years toward training personnel in prevention skills and implementing effective prevention programs, then we could cut the number of victimizations in half over the next decade. Whether the allocation of funds for policing, criminal justice, and mass incarceration is going up or down, it is still possible to find 2 percent to invest for the return on victimization reduction.

Less Law, More Order shows that there are affordable and sustainable solutions out there. It shows that each of those solutions can achieve large reductions in crime and victimization. Every chapter includes a success story that demonstrates a reduction in crime and victimization of between 20 and 50 percent. But these strategies are beneficial not only because they directly lead to reductions in crime; most of these measures would also improve the overall quality of life of children, youth, women, and whole communities. And what's more, they would achieve this at less cost than our expenditures, which are currently creating budget crises in California and many other states.

Barriers to Making It Happen

Legislators tell me that they believe the public wants punishment, not prevention. But those legislators could not be more wrong. Response to crime is not an "either/or" issue. The public may want punishment, or they may not. In actual fact, members of the public are split on punishment

issues. At election time, much focus is on particular sensational and exceptional cases that caught the attention of the media. Legislators say that the
criminals deserve to be behind bars. And maybe they do. But do not confuse that debate with the debate about how to prevent victimization from
happening in the first place. We have to accept once and for all that harsh
prison sentences are not a deterrent for other would-be criminals, though
an incarcerated felon does not commit crime while behind bars. Beyond
that, any link between reductions in victimization and penalties meted
out in criminal courts is purely coincidental. Yes, incarcerating significant
numbers of persons will reduce crime, but it will do so by busting budgets
and wasting lives—the lives of criminals and victims alike.

International victims' rights meetings often conclude that citizens need
to be made aware of the effectiveness of crime prevention policies. As
demonstrated in *Less Law, More Order*, it is the legislators who need to
be made aware of this, as the public already believes in the power of prevention, at least to some degree.[3] Most voters and victims of crime know
that victimization has multiple causes. Unlike the National Crime Victim
Survey, the British Crime Survey actually asks the question and shows
that the public see crime as being a multifaceted problem caused more by
bad parenting, drugs, and alcohol than law enforcement and the criminal
justice system.[4]

In sum, the public is much more in tune with the types of proven recommendations flowing from *Less Law, More Order* than the legislators.
Citizens understand and are supportive of the methods that work to reduce
victimization, including those that remedy negative life experiences for at-
risk youth, that change attitudes of men to stop violence against women,
and that tackle problems related to impaired driving, alcohol, and drugs.

We must continue to demand that our legislators act on the evidence-
based recommendations from a growing number of prestigious com-
missions showing that reductions in crime *can* be achieved. It is for our
educators in the media, universities, schools, and families to share what
can be done. It is for legislators to deliver one part of what the public
wants—less victimization and fewer victims of crime. Let's get smart and
leave our children with fewer scars from violence within the home, with
safer streets, and with a more sustainable way to deal with crime before
it happens. Let's use truth and good sense to invest in proven prevention.
Right now we might be thinking that the time to start was five years ago.
In five years' time, we will realize that the time to start was now. *Now* is

the time to invest in fewer victimizations and balanced justice. We cannot afford to put it off any longer.

IT IS HAPPENING ALREADY: SUCCESS STORIES

People often talk about "crime prevention," and we will here too. But we will call it by what it truly is—*victimization prevention*. As our legislators too often ignore, for every crime prevented, an equal or greater number of victimizations are also prevented.

In *Less Law, More Order*, I shared some amazing success stories from cities across the United States and around the world. I shared many pioneering projects that proved that using an evidence-based and collaborative approach succeeds in reducing the numbers of victims of violence by tackling the problems at their roots. I was able to talk about what key elements are necessary to make this happen—namely, a responsibility center that can mobilize schools, housing, social services, law enforcement, and families around the diagnosis of local problems. Using this knowledge, communities can plan and implement what is likely to work for their specific challenges. We will see here cutting-edge evidence to further support this approach. We will also look at cities and a province in Canada that are investing significant money to put what was proposed into action.

The new evidence is heavily concentrated around public health. In North America, the champion of public health approaches to crime reduction is the Centers for Disease Control and Prevention (CDCP). (Note that the organization has changed its title to add "prevention" to its name, and so I am adding the "P" to the acronym.) CDCP is best known for its expertise on epidemics such as cholera and flu, but it also has a long-term program focused on the prevention of violence and victimization. With 16,000 murders, 12,000 deaths at the hands of drunk drivers, and many other people injured by violence every single year, CDCP has had a National Center for Injury Prevention and Control for many years now. This center focuses on the prevention of youth violence, sexual assault, drunk driving, intimate partner violence, and child maltreatment.

CDCP has a program to pursue a public health approach to the prevention of violence. Basically, their program focuses on identifying the causes of violence, finding programs that are proven to prevent violence by tackling those causes, and promoting the implementation of programs that work. Since *Less Law, More Order* was published in 2005, there have been few new breakthroughs, but the ones that have arisen have added a significant focus on teen violence and gathered important new evidence on the prevention of child maltreatment.

Preventing Victimization from Street Crime

Successful programs to tackle street gangs and youth violence use the public health model at the city level. That is, they bring together key local agencies such as law enforcement, programs for parents, and youth services to diagnose the causes of the violence. They are then able to implement a strategy that works at the local level. The best-known success stories in reducing violence among young men have been led and coordinated by municipalities around the world.

The most impressive example is the City of Bogotá, Colombia. It followed the key elements of the public health approach: after diagnosing the patterns of victimization, it acted on recommendations to tackle those causes by imposing curfews, limiting access to alcohol, reducing the availability of firearms, and counseling victims to avoid revenge killings. In the end, street violence was reduced by 50 percent over a ten-year period. Clearly, crime prevention does not mean taking a passive approach to the law; it is an active, forward-thinking strategy that works.

Boston is another promising example. It reduced the number of homicides between young men by 50 percent within only two years of implementing its city-wide strategy. It used strategic approaches that combined existing police resources, programs to help young men complete school and get jobs, and the mobilization of mothers to pressure their sons to abandon violent associates. Beyond any doubt, Boston's success was built on much more than law enforcement.

Still, our entrenched law enforcement and justice systems resist these proven multifaceted strategies. In 2008, in advance of its initiative Project Safe Neighborhoods, the National Institute of Justice released a series of pamphlets on the prevention of gun violence. In these publications they commented on the success of violent crime reduction in Boston, although they only focused on the targeted law enforcement component of the strategy.[5] So, when the National Institute of Justice implemented its Project Safe Neighborhoods, only the law enforcement elements of this strategy were replicated; they did not invest in the prevention strategies that contributed so importantly to the success in Boston. They did not outreach to young men to encourage them to complete school, and they did not help them get job training and jobs. Nevertheless, there were still some reductions in rates of homicide in a handful of the cities—which is better than nothing, but the results were not as good as they should have been for an investment of $3 billion over ten years.[6]

It seems obvious why Project Safe Neighborhoods' results were less impressive than Boston's previous success: the implementation focused only on law enforcement—particularly the prosecution of gun crimes. The evaluators raised concerns about the sustainability of the program after it ended, noting that high rates of gun violence tended to recur in these cities—including Boston.[7] In my opinion, victimizations rebounded in Boston because of the lack of a sustained responsibility center to continue the all-important public health strategies that we know can successfully tackle the roots of the violence. A sustained focus on prosecution alone will make no inroads toward the prevention of victimization.

It is exciting to note that two recent examples have produced much more impressive results. One of these, code named "Operation Ceasefire," was based in Chicago and used two out of the three successful ingredients of the Boston strategy. Explicitly described as a public health approach, it was managed by the University of Illinois' School of Public Health. The program brought together a number of key partners and analyzed the data on Chicago so that the area's unique problems could be identified early on.

In contrast to Project Safe Neighborhoods, Operation Ceasefire did not involve manipulating law enforcement tactics. It was successful because it targeted that small group of persons most likely to be shot or to become a shooter. It recruited street-level workers who outreached to the target group to mentor them and help them to continue with their education, get jobs, and leave their gangs. It also mobilized the target groups' communities to focus on the unwanted presence of violence by engaging in rallies and prayer vigils and by educating everyone on the dangers of violence.

Operation Ceasefire was the subject of an independent evaluation by one of the best-known independent researchers in the United States, Dr. Wesley Skogan. His team focused on interviewing 300 of the high-risk individuals who were targeted by the program. He confirmed that 76 percent of those participants had needed a job before the program, and that 87 percent of those got help finding employment from their outreach worker. He also found that 37 percent had wanted to continue their education, and 85 percent of those got help doing so. What's more, 34 percent had long since wanted to disengage from their gangs, and every one of them received help in doing so.[8]

Operation Ceasefire was unique in that it provided support to at-risk victims and would-be offenders to prevent them from going down those roads. Skogan found that shootings declined by 17 to 34 percent in targeted neighborhoods, and that there was an overall reduction in victimizations. Given the five-year preparation period and the focus of the project, it is not surprising that it was successful by all measures. It's shocking, then, to learn that despite these impressive successes, the project was initially not able to get funding to continue. Sadly, this disappointing outcome is not unique. Many successful preventative programs often fail to receive permanent funding. We have already seen this in Boston. And unless our legislators can find the pulse of the nation, we will continue to see this in the future. Miraculously, what looked like another success story that would wither, funding was eventually found in Chicago. We will see how long this will continue.

The second recent example of successful prevention of victimization took place in Glasgow, Scotland. The city's government instituted a public health strategy to diagnose ways to reduce knife violence between young men. The strategy included programs to help parents provide consistent and caring education, efforts to persuade victims to change their lives to avoid revictimization, enforcement targeted at persistent offenders, and measures to prevent young men from carrying knives. The preliminary evidence is encouraging, and the program has become part of a government-wide strategy across Scotland. Although the program lacks an extensive evaluation, it receives its funding through the police department and so is able to continue.

Violent street crime between young men ages twelve to twenty-five tends to be concentrated in areas of disadvantage, social exclusion, and relative poverty. Extensive studies in many different countries have identified the life experiences that predispose some young men in these areas to become persistent violent offenders. Those with more negative life experiences are more likely to cause multiple victimizations.

Fortunately, several experimental projects have demonstrated that it is indeed possible for at-risk offenders to overcome their negative life experiences in order to live their lives without victimizing others. For instance, programs such as Quantum Opportunities reach out to young men who are likely to drop out of school. As a result of mentoring, more of these at-risk youths are kept in school, and acts of violence perpetrated by those men are reduced. A Canadian initiative, Stop Now and Plan (SNAP), helps children and parents regulate youth aggression. This program has been subjected to rigorous evaluations, many of which have demonstrated positive outcomes among children under the age of twelve. We can also look to England's Youth Inclusion Projects, a series of programs developed to reach the most difficult teenagers and significantly reduce their offending.

It is heartening to see successful preventative initiatives being developed around the world, because for every would-be criminal that we can stop from becoming an offender, at least one—and probably many—would-be victims are spared the trauma of being victimized. As obvious as that fact may be, we still need to help our legislators to realize that investing in stopping victimization gives a much better return on investment to victims (taxpayers) than does paying for victim services or footing the bill for mass incarceration, which by itself provides little sustained relief from crime.

Preventing Victimization against Women

Experts agree that violence against women is preventable.[9] The World Health Organization agrees on different types of risk factors that contribute to higher levels of domestic violence. "Individual" factors include heavy drinking, low income, and witnessing violence. "Relationship" factors include male dominance and poor family functioning. "Societal and community" factors include male patriarchy norms that support violence, as well as weak community sanctions against it.

There is some agreement among experts about what will work to tackle the risk factors, but there are few random control trials or reliable evaluations to hold up as "proof."

Trend data has shown a gradual decrease in the number of women murdered by intimate partners in the United States. To find out why, one influential study looked at trends in domestic violence across forty-eight cities over two decades since 1980.[10] The authors speculated that the declines were in part due to changes in family law and increased economic opportunities, as well as more spaces available in transition houses—all of which enabled more women to leave violent partners. The declines also correlate with the increased use of arrest for perpetrators and independent legal advocacy for women.

Unfortunately, the study also found that many common preventative approaches do not necessarily work to prevent violence against women. It concluded that court-ordered treatment of batterers does not reduce domestic violence any more than the standard responses.[11] On the other hand, the arrest of batterers may have some impact—but only on men who have something to lose.

The good news here is that there is some encouraging news for coordinated strategies such as those promoted with the Violence Against Women Act's STOP program funding. In one case, New Haven, Connecticut, police used aggressive enforcement of court protection orders to reduce intimate partner homicides from thirty-four in 1994 to nineteen in 2005. As a result, the program was adopted as a state model. In San Diego, California, intimate partner homicides dropped from thirteen in 1995 to five by 2005 with the opening of its Family Justice Center, which offers services for victims.[12] While these examples are undoubtedly promising, they are not yet the strong evidence that is really needed. But they are stronger than the evidence for any return on massive expenditures toward unfocussed standard reactive enforcement.

Unfortunately, the news about changes in the rates of sexual violence is not so positive. Experts do not believe that there have been decreases in the numbers of rapes and sexual assaults. They point especially to the high rates of victimizations among university and college populations.[13]

What's heartening here is that there is agreement among experts on what strategies are most likely to reduce the number of rape and sexual assault victims. For instance, if we can change male attitudes toward violence and women, then we can expect to reduce most common types of violence against women.

There are two strategies that stand out. The first is to change the attitudes of teenagers in high school regarding alcohol and drug abuse, violence, and sexual assault against women. This approach has been proven through random control trials, so we know it works.[14] The other strategy is the White Ribbon Campaign, where men work to prevent men's violence against women in an awareness campaign. In sum, men wear a white ribbon on their jacket to show that they are against violence by men against women. Although there are no evaluations for this program, there is a logic to this action, as we know that the male attitude toward violence against women is one of the contributing factors to its prevalence.[15]

Experts also propose a number of actions that individuals can take toward preventing violence against women. Some of these are university-targeted public awareness campaigns that aim to weaken the culture of support for violence against women and increase the support of female friends in risky situations.[16] Two examples we can look to are at the University of Kentucky in the United States and the University of Ottawa in Canada.[17]

Preventing the Victimization of Children

Violence against children within the family makes victims just as often as violence against a spouse does. Close to 3.3 million children are referred to child protection agencies in the United States for signs of negligence and abuse every year. Of these, 800,000 will be confirmed as victims of child maltreatment, which is only the tip of the iceberg. This means that a government agency has confirmed that the child had been a victim of physical, sexual, or emotional abuse, or was not provided with basic care such as food, housing, or medical care.

There is considerably strong knowledge about what works to reduce violence against children. Much of this has been brought together by the Centers for Disease Control and Prevention in the United States.[18] A key is to identify at-risk mothers (for instance, those who are young, or who have substance abuse problems) and direct prevention at them. For example, it has been well established that having public health nurses visit at-risk mothers reduces child maltreatment by 72 percent, and as a result there are 50 percent fewer violent crimes committed by their children during their teenage years.

However, it is also known that many parents who do not present the profile of an at-risk mother will maltreat their child, and so programs must focus on a broader target. The CDCP reports the completion of a major random control trial of a parent training program known as "Triple P." The program was implemented in nine out of eighteen counties with a population of fifty thousand to one hundred thousand. The results are very impressive: in an area with one hundred thousand children under eight years of age, Triple P could reduce child maltreatment by 688 cases, avoid 240 instances where the child would have had to be taken out of the home, and reduce the number of children taken to hospital emergency rooms by 60.[19] If programs like these work—and it seems clear that they do—then there is no reason why every parent in the country shouldn't have access to them.

Preventing Victimization from Property Crime

International crime data show that property crime rates have been decreasing over recent years in Europe, as they have been in North America. Experts point to preventing the occurrence of crime through such methods as the use of alarms in residences. In chapter 1, we saw that pain and suffering caused by property crime is important, but cumulatively not as widespread as it is for crimes of violence. However, joyriding often leads to injuries and fatal crashes, and so property crimes can have devastating spin-off effects.

Winnipeg is a city of 600,000 people in the center of Canada. In 2004, it had North America's highest rate of auto theft—over 1,900 thefts per 100,000 people. The annual cost to the provincial insurance company was $40 million. What's worse was that many residents were injured by reckless auto thieves.

Winnipeg's first step toward countering this plague was to establish a task force that brought together key players such as police, the insurance company, and a leading academic. Their in-depth diagnosis of the epidemic showed that most thefts were committed by young offenders, and virtually all the vehicles were stolen for joyriding.

The second step was to implement a three-pronged plan: intensive community supervision of high-risk youth; a program requiring compulsory vehicle immobilizers for the most at-risk vehicles; and youth programs to address the root causes of vehicle theft.

The third step was to evaluate results. Thefts declined by 29 percent in 2007, 42 percent in 2008, and an impressive 76 percent by 2010. Taxpayer savings are estimated to be an average of at least $40 million a year, and at least 10,000 crimes have been prevented annually. Clearly, preventative programs that take all facets of the root causes into account do have tangible results.

COMPREHENSIVE CRIME REDUCTION

For all intents and purposes, comprehensive crime reduction is actually comprehensive *victimization* reduction. It works by following a diagnosis of the problems facing the community, analyzing the evidence about what works, and developing strategies to get these programs implemented.

These strategies combine local schools, housing, social services, law enforcement, and many other facets.

We can look to Canada for examples of how to pursue comprehensive crime reduction strategies. In 2007, the province of Alberta (with a population of three million) established a task force to look at crime reduction, community safety, and public attitudes on these issues. After the results were in, the Alberta government announced its commitment to implementing a three-pronged strategy of enforcement, treatment, and prevention, committing an additional $500 million over three years as part of a long-term and comprehensive strategy.

The province recognized that enforcement, treatment, and prevention go hand in hand. As part of its all-in-one strategy, eighty new treatment beds in community mental health centers were created, $60 million was slated for prevention programs, and two hundred new police officers were hired. The province was also forward-thinking in establishing a community safety secretariat made up of senior-level bureaucrats from nine ministries, including housing, social services, youth, and health cooperating with law enforcement, justice, and municipal affairs. Comprehensive crime reduction strategies such as Alberta's are effective because they work on short-term actions to achieve long-term success. This is an important best practice to emulate.

In addition to this province-wide initiative, the mayor of Edmonton, Alberta, independently set up a task force in 2008 to recommend an action for the city to take charge of its own strategy of prevention to complement its police services. As part of its nine-point action plan, Edmonton has set up a permanent responsibility center to spearhead its investment in prevention. The objective of the ten-year plan is to create a culture of community safety in Edmonton within one generation.

Some of these Canadian success stories are the direct result of funding from the Canadian National Crime Prevention Center, which astutely provided a dedicated institute for the study of the prevention of crime at the University of Ottawa. This institute provides the means for communities to collaborate with national organizations and other cities to harness collective knowledge so that no communities are left trying to reinvent the wheel when it comes to victimization reduction. In 2009, the project produced a series of action briefs to educate municipal stakeholders about how to mobilize partners within their community to diagnose their unique problems and to implement strategies that will work. The briefs also provide solutions to street violence, violence against women, violence affecting aboriginal peoples, and property crime.[20]

PREVENTING REPEAT AND IMMINENT VICTIMIZATION

As we saw in chapter 1, two of victims' eight core needs are for personal safety, and so reduction of revictimization must become a priority. Legislators must make better investments in strategies that stop citizens from being victimized. We know that we have access to methods to prevent repeat victimization. For instance, it has been demonstrated that burglary reduction programs that systematically focus on repeat victimization can achieve as much as a 75 percent reduction in burglaries within a five-year period.

Another important example is the need to reach victims of violence before they retaliate. As we've seen, imbalanced justice systems can leave victims with feelings of anger that need to be properly treated before they can subside. In *Less Law, More Order*, I described the success of the City of Bogotá in its strategy to diagnose and reduce its alarming rates of violence. One item in the diagnosis was the number of men who were killing in retaliation against the murder of one of their family members or colleagues. So as a solution, social workers reached out to those victims to "immunize" them against retaliation. The program was a classic victim assistance program based on emotional support and psychological counseling to help the loved ones of the first victims cope with their anger and rage. This resulted in reductions of further victimizations.

In chapter 3, we saw that police leadership around the world wants victims of crime to be at the zenith of criminal justice policies. This means that police must also take to heart the need to protect victims wherever possible from imminent victimization. The following Jane Doe case illustrates what can happen if the police do not.

In 1986 in Toronto, Canada, a serial rapist was on the loose. Police knew that he had entered the apartments of four white women with dark hair who lived alone. They also knew of his modus operandi of entering over the balcony. Still, the police did not warn women in the area, even though the likelihood of further victimizations seemed imminent. So, when the rapist attacked a fifth victim, that victim successfully sued the police for not warning her; the Supreme Court had decided that police were responsible for informing potential victims of certain impending dangers posed by offenders.

This case shows that it is possible (with much pain and heartache) to get change and so enforce the inalienable right for protection against crime. To an ordinary citizen, it is obvious that the police should warn potential victims. To the police in a system that does not balance the interests of the victim, their role is too often focused on catching the offender instead of preventing the offense. For me, this is an important case to consider as it shows that preventing repeated and imminent crime, at least in some special instances, trumps catching repeat and imminent offenders.

PREVENTING CRIME, NOT RELEASING FELONS: SMART WAYS TO REDUCE INCARCERATION

In 2010, an increasing number of states (including California) started to release prisoners in order to balance state budgets without implementing any programs to prevent offending in the first place. It is no surprise that victims of crime are (rightly) criticizing Governor Schwarzenegger and other governors for releasing prisoners to cut state expenditures. It is also no surprise that the holus-bolus release of low-risk prisoners to save money reaps grim results. Innocent taxpayers and voters become the victims of repeat offenders, be it in California, in New York, or in other states that have resorted to this. On March 4, 2010, the *New York Times* headline was correct in saying that "Safety Is Issue as the Budget Cuts Free Prisoners."

When the evidence on prevention of victimization is so strong, it is clear that the strategy should be to invest in what works to prevent victimization and so reduce the number of persons committing crime and being sentenced to incarceration. Why is this not a concern for state legislators? And what's more, how can they be so shortsighted? It is clear to experts that these myopic policies will lead to higher—not lower—costs as these felons commit more crimes and are eventually caught, convicted, and incarcerated yet again. The real solution is to prevent these offenders from turning to victimizing in the first place.

DEMANDS FOR LEGISLATORS

The majority of victims of crime want prevention more than punishment. So does the majority of the public. The evidence on what reduces and prevents victimization is strong and hopeful. Figure 7.1 lists the main areas where victimization prevention is hopeful.

Investing in proven success

Reducing street violence

Reducing violence against women

Reducing child abuse

Reducing property crime

Comprehensive crime reduction

Preventing repeat and imminent victimization

Smart partnerships between law enforcement, youth outreach workers, and families

Smart ways to reduce incarceration

Figure 7.1.   Return on investment with proven and promising victimization prevention

Legislators wanting to save money must reach at-risk youth *before* they victimize innocent civilians.

Legislators must target the areas where street violence is most prevalent and must combine smarter use of the following: increased support services agencies to outreach to youth and young males, increased numbers of beds in treatment centers for those with addictions and mental health problems, and current law enforcement resources to tackle prolific offenders. Chicago Ceasefire is a best practice.

Legislators must reduce violence against women by providing women, particularly in disadvantaged circumstances, with economic opportunities, and options to leave violent relationships will reduce violence against them, as will safe houses and coordinated police and community anti-violence strategies.

Legislators must invest in changing male attitudes to be less coercive and more respectful toward women to reduce sexual violence against women. These approaches will succeed where rates of sexual violence are high, such as at universities and colleges, as well as in disadvantaged neighborhoods. Implementing programs such as university respect campaigns and white ribbon campaigns are important best practices.

Legislators must continue to tackle alcohol and drug abuse among younger adults to reduce violence on the streets, in our homes, and on our roads. Investing in more parent-training programs will continue to reduce maltreatment of children as well as decrease spin-off violence as this generation becomes adolescent and adult. Proven best practices include

Triple P programs and outreach to mothers in difficulty by trained public health nurses.

Legislators must shift crime policy from over-reliance on reaction to evidence-based preemptive strategies orchestrated by a small secretariat to assist agencies such as schools, housing, law enforcement, and the general public to collaborate on a diagnosis of the causes of crime and to implement an action plan to tackle the causes of victimization. This process must use the best evidence available. Best practices include Alberta's crime-reduction strategy involving nine provincial ministries, and the mayor's task force in Edmonton.

Legislators must require law enforcement to warn potential victims of the presence of repeat offenders, providing information to avoid repeat victimization, collaborating in intersectoral strategies to prevent crime, and collaborating with victim-assistance programs to avoid violent retaliation.

(8)

THE ACTION PLAN

Investment to Rebalance Justice for Crime Victims

This short book makes its readers expert in advocating rights for victims of crime by assembling the best current knowledge on the experience of victims of crime. It empowers taxpayers, voters and (potential) victims of crime to make the case to rebalance justice and support victims. It shows that many of us will be victims of property or violent crime, and, if you are a woman, a rape or domestic violence incident. And when these unfortunate incidents happen, it would be better if the reforms had already been made.

You can now use your democratic powers to ensure that victims have rights in practice and, importantly, have remedies for when governments fail to make good on their promises. While both adults and children are victims of crime, it is mostly adults who will read this book. Adults are the only ones who will be able to speak with their vote, pay taxes, and insist on policies that will do much better for both adult and child victims of crime.

This book applauds the laws in the United States and elsewhere that support victims by providing assistance, compensation, and protection from the accused, but criticizes inadequate implementation. Victims need action, not words. Police services must catch crooks but make victims their clients. Courts must balance rights for defendants and victims. Services for women, children, and elderly victims must be funded sustainably, not just on the backs of offenders. Restitution from offenders must be ordered and collected, not overlooked. Compensation from the state must change from a secret of the few to a fair payment to all who are eligible. The budget priority must be prevention of victimization, not mass incarceration.

Overall, the growth in programs and justice has been slow and deliberate. It is time to look at how to get more services, more reparation, and more balanced justice for victims of crime. Now is the time to go the last mile to get services for those in need. Now is the time to plan how to accelerate the provision of services so that they will be available and accessible to all who need them. Yes, this will require some new directions for law enforcement, criminal justice, and social services. These, in turn, will require clear standards for service which can be measured through performance reports and statistical surveys. Universities and colleges will have to foster up-and-coming public administration managers to have knowledge in this field, as well as train those embarking on a new range of professions as victim assistance providers, specialists on stopping violence against women, restorative justice coordinators, and reparation specialists. The legislative leaders, the ombudspersons, and the public must be supported by statistical surveys and independent institutes that can do the research and development to provide the evidence and renewed vision for further reform in favor of victims of crime. Yes, this rebalancing will require reallocation of funds—although not as much as the skeptics think—and more high-level responsibility centers to implement these changes and manage those funds. Yes, it will require more changes in constitutions and charters of rights to frame these actions, to provide effective remedies, and to ensure that the inalienable rights of victims are not blindly trumped by offenders' rights.

At the end of each chapter, I concluded with demands for legislators. I will first review the highlights. Then I will turn to how all of these can be made to happen in our current time of perpetually tight fiscal priorities. Solutions can—and must—be implemented today. There are no more excuses not to act.

AN AGENDA FOR ACTION THAT WORKS

In chapter 1, I showed that the majority of us will have the misfortune in our lifetimes to be a victim of a crime, from child abuse to residential burglary, from drunk driving to sexual predation or homicide. I argued that these crimes created eight core needs to which government must respond that were grouped in figure 1.4 under the headings of support, justice, and good government.

In chapter 2, I built on the integrative work of the group of fourteen eminent experts drawn from across the world to show the enduring consensus about what must be done in figure 2.1. With few variations, that consensus integrates the ambitions of the President's Task Force and VOCA and VAWA, the vision of the UN Resolution and Declaration, the pragmatism of the European Union standards, the brilliant hybrid innovation of the International Criminal Court, and the hard-nosed implementation in Japan and the United Kingdom. I also showed in figure 2.1 that the consensus among governments on what they needed to do would meet most of the eight core needs of victims originally identified in chapter 1, figure 1.4. That is, if governments were doing what they promised, they would indeed be providing adequate support, justice, and good government for victims of crime. But unfortunately it is only some governments, some of the time who might be able claim serious and full implementation.

In chapter 3, I focused on what policing must do to meet its responsibilities to respond effectively to victims' core needs and the consensus about what should be rights. Consistent with grounded proposals from the International Association of Chiefs of Police, law enforcement must put victims of crime at the zenith of policing, and by so doing, provide safety, information, support, and justice to victims.

In chapter 4, the main call was to get much greater and permanent funding for victim services in order to meet victims' core needs. These services cluster around generic support services, gender-specific support services (such as transition houses and sexual assault crisis centers), and those focusing on children and the elderly. The discussion included a greater need to respect the choice of victims to report to law enforcement and so engage (or not) with the criminal justice process.

In chapter 5, the main appeal was to get fair reparation paid to victims of crime by ensuring that restitution is ordered and collected, as several states are already doing, and by making compensation from the state as well known and adequate as it is in England and Wales. It called for legal aid for victims to use the civil process more often, and assistance to victims who want to follow a restorative justice solution.

In chapter 6, I called for innovations to ensure that victims of crime participate and represent their interests if needed at the charge, bail, plea, trial, sentence, and post-sentence stages of the criminal justice process.

New compliance procedures are a step in the right direction. Models that provide legally aided participation for victims exist in other countries— some with adversarial traditions like North America.

In chapter 7, I asked for greater investment in strategies that provide good returns in terms of prevention (and, so, reduction) in victimization. These will be effective in reducing street crime, violence against women, child abuse, and other crimes—far more efficient than mass incarceration for all offenders.

Where possible, I identified in each chapter some best practices that show how somewhere, some of the time, victims of crime have their core needs met. Some victims get recognition and emotional support, information on criminal justice and their case when they need it, and assistance from agencies that specialize in supporting victims of crime. Some victims get emergency funds, restitution from the offender, and compensation from the state. Some who need safety get it. Some in other countries get to defend their interests directly through their own advocate, not through a prosecutor for the state.

MAKING IT HAPPEN

Your first reaction may be that this list is too long or too costly. But I will show below how this can be done. In order to overcome the number of changes, we'll need an agency to lead the reforms, standards for service that will be the basis for training, a way of assessing what has been achieved, and further research and development to guide what has yet to be achieved. Then, we will need comprehensive legislation, fair funding, and (possibly) a constitutional amendment to avoid having the inalienable rights of victims of violent crime unnecessarily trumped by the rights of offenders.

RETOOLING: OFFICES FOR VICTIMS OF CRIME

There is a need for political leadership to bring about reforms, but also a permanent office to continue this leadership, such as an operational office for victims of crime to oversee the implementation. This office must have the capacity to multiply services in the community and to ensure that reforms are made by the police, courts, and corrections to make victims the zenith of their work.

The Office for Victims of Crime in the U.S. Department of Justice is an inspiring best practice of how such an office operates and so is a best practice for other jurisdictions, such as individual states or governments in other countries. It has used 95 percent of its funding (approximately $700 million) to increase the number of victim service agencies—possibly even doubling the number of victims of crime who receive these services—and ensuring that every state has a compensation program. It has used the other 5 percent of its funding (approximately $35 million) to leverage other actions that advance quality of services for victims in the United States such as conferences, training, and work by the IACP.

The Office on Violence Against Women plays a role similar to that of the OVC but focuses exclusively on the prevention of and response to violence against women. It can rightly claim to have dramatically altered the landscape for women who suffer sexual, domestic, and other forms of violence. It is funded out of general revenue and is now spending federal funds at a level getting close to that of the OVC. Its largest program of $150 million a year (STOP) focuses on stopping violence against women and holding offenders accountable.

WORKING WITH VICTIMS: STANDARDS, TRAINING, AND PROFESSIONAL DEVELOPMENT FOR SUPPORT, LAW ENFORCEMENT, AND JUSTICE WORKERS

As we saw in chapter 2, the British government has developed a basic code of practice so victims of crime know what they can expect to happen as part of the criminal justice process. Some states (such as Michigan) have had similar provisions for some time, but these are in need of updating. Standards must be developed at all levels and become the basis for training and professional development. Training without accountability to standards is not enough.

The OVC has already invested in some training programs, but much more is needed to ensure the universal delivery of adequate services. The National Victim Assistance Academy provides three components addressed to entry-level victim service providers (those with at least two years experience and leadership and management skills). Algonquin College in

Ottawa, Canada, has launched a graduate certificate in victimology with similar but more advanced objectives. In the United States, lawyers have access to a growing number of national and state victim law academies, such as the National Crime Victim Law Clinic at Lewis and Clark Law School in Oregon. National organizations such as the National Organization for Victim Assistance (NOVA), the National Center for Victims of Crime (NCVC), and the National Association of Victim Support Schemes (NAVSS) in England have provided information and resources to support young trainees in the victim-assistance fields. These need to be reinvigorated and focused on training to meet standards.

Ultimately, universities and colleges must be mobilized around advancing the training, education, and professional development of the new professions that are needed to meet the needs of victims of crime. Already, nursing schools have responded to the need to train nurses in SANE practices. We must commit to integrating crime victims' issues into all levels of the educational systems to ensure that police, lawyers, victim assistance workers, and crime prevention experts receive comprehensive training on victims' issues as part of their academic education and continuing training in the field.

MONITORING AND OMBUDSPERSONS

Governments must take appropriate action to monitor whether legislators' intentions and proclamations do indeed provide the inalienable rights discussed in this book. They must organize performance reports, periodic reviews, and evaluations of their legislation, regulations, and procedures, and also appoint individuals and offices to oversee the processes and implement action.

The OVC receives annual performance reports and organized one major progress report in 1998, which sought the opinions of those working in the field.[1] Through the National Institute of Justice, it recently funded two evaluations of the impact of its work, which talked to victims who had received services as well as those working in the field (as I discussed in chapter 4).

The performance reports show that nearly four million victims of crime—about half of whom were victims of domestic violence—had received services that year. It also noted that nearly 200,000 victims of violence received at least some compensation. We know that the victims of crime who got the services were better off, but we also know that these were a minority. Unfortunately, we do not know how many other victims needed those services but did not get them. As VOCA does not focus on the prevention of victimization, we can only assume that these services have not contributed to fewer victimizations.

In chapter 1, I emphasized that good reforms are often blocked by the bureaucratic imperative—that is, existing systems (such as law enforcement, criminal justice, and corrections) continue to get more resources. Unfortunately, those resources have been given without a requirement to deliver on their responsibilities to victims of crime—the citizens who pay their bills and should be privileged clients. This bureaucratic imperative tends to support the dominant legal culture that excludes victims of crime from having a voice.

So, it is vital that independent offices are established to review progress and make suggestions. Through these offices, crime victim ombudspersons or commissioners would play a dual role of ensuring that individual victims of crime get the services that are offered, and also identifying gaps that require more systemic reforms.

In 2004, the Justice for All Act contained a provision to create a Federal Victim Rights Ombudsman whose role is to help victims of crime get their rights realized. Though the effectiveness of this legislation was evaluated by the Government Accountability Office, it is not yet clear whether it is working successfully, which means we have to do better.[2] The state of Arizona is well known for its systems to enforce rights, but again, little is known about how to make this more comprehensive.

In 2010, the British government established the position of victims' commissioner to oversee the implementation of the code of practice in terms of the treatment of victims. This commissioner is also responsible for proposing additional solutions to enhance victims' rights. In 2007, the Canadian federal government established a Federal Ombudsman Office for Victims of Crime. This position is independent of the Federal Policy Centre for Victim Issues, which operates on behalf of the traditional justice bureaucracies in administering programs and revising legislation. The ombudsperson reports at the highest hierarchical level of the federal government, through the minister of justice.

The state of South Australia has long been at the cutting edge of actions to meet the core needs of victims of crime by implementing the provision of the *magna carta* for victims of crime. Recently, it adopted an act to establish a commissioner for victims' rights. Among the key functions of this office are to advise the attorney general on how best to use government resources to help victims, as well as to monitor and report on compliance according to the standards set out in the *magna carta*. There are lessons to be learned from this office, as its legislation is tested in practice by putting words into actions. However, they too agree on the importance of an independent victim advocate whose interests are disengaged from those of the current government bureaucracies.

Surveying for Success

Much of the success of the ombudsperson will depend on research, established standards, and data that can inform on systemic issues. Thus, it is essential that these individuals and offices have access to accurate, detailed, and up-to-date information. Regular national and local victimization surveys provide a general measure of the extent to which victimization occurs, whether it is increasing or decreasing, and what experiences victims have with the police, courts, and corrections systems. However, existing surveys must be adapted or complemented to measure the extent to which victims who report to the police or to other agencies (such as sexual assault crisis centers) do, in fact, receive the information, referrals, and practical support they so desperately need, in order to evaluate what works (and highlight what doesn't). We can look to Kilpatrick's work and the National Women's Survey in the United States and the Statistics Canada survey on violence against women for starting points.

More data on the economic impact of crime is needed to mobilize governments and advocates for action. Research is needed so that we can accurately estimate the costs of compensation programs that would more adequately reimburse victims for mental health care and pain and suffering. For those looking for best specialized surveying practices to follow, I would point to the study led by Ted Miller, which served as the basis for the cost of crime analysis in chapter 1.[3]

A strategy must be developed to highlight the annual results of these surveys in the media and on the Internet so that voters and legislators can be made aware of the trends. After all, governments and citizens cannot become engaged in supporting investments in victims' rights and services if they aren't made aware of the realities of victimization today.

RESEARCH AND DEVELOPMENT: INSTITUTES FOR VICTIM SERVICES AND RIGHTS

Much more action is needed in North America in order to realize respect for the inalienable rights of victims of crime. One mechanism that would help put jurisdictions in North America at the forefront of the protection of these rights would be the creation of a permanently funded institute. This institute must be independent of law schools, and while legal experts must contribute, it is social science research and expertise that is imperative to providing the evidence for how far we have come and what still needs to be done.

Such an institute would likely be based in (or at least have a hub at) a leading university that is dedicated to victim services and rights. It would be able to empower the networks of victim advocates and victim service practitioners. It would be a key partner in the work of communities, commissioners, and ombudspersons across the continent. It would assist in the analysis of surveys and the promotion of victim advocacy experiments (such as the unification of criminal and civil court proceedings, as discussed in chapter 6). It could also work with law faculties to educate future lawyers and judges on the inalienable rights of victims.

One best practice to which we can look is the International Victimology Institute Tilburg (INTERVICT), which was launched by Tilburg University in the Netherlands in 2005. It is an academic institute that is actively expanding the research base on victimization and victim assistance within Europe. This institute has conducted extensive evaluations of the implementation of victim legislation in European Union countries (such as the European framework decision, as discussed in chapter 2). It is a global leader in the emerging frontiers of victimization such as identity theft, human trafficking, and online victimization.

We can also look to Japan for an example. The Tokiwa International Victimology Institute (TIVI) was established in 2003 to conduct international interdisciplinary research and teaching in victimology. The president of Tokiwa University and the head of a victims' rights group combined forces to persuade Japan's prime minister to identify what extensive reforms were needed and to follow through with impressive and comprehensive concrete actions.

Such an institute in North America would support the range of national nongovernmental groups in Washington for the United States and those in

Montreal and Ottawa for Canada, as well as the networks of victim rights groups such as the Victims' Rights Working Group (VRWG), which is a partner of the International Criminal Court. VRWG has a network of over three hundred national and international civil society groups, academics, and other experts. It was started in 1997 as a coalition in support of the ICC. The group maintains an ICC victims' rights list-serv, where experts and advocates on victims' rights from around the world continue to exchange information related to the ICC and the status of victims of crime globally. The VRWG plays a continuous role in ensuring that the ICC does not stumble when protecting the inalienable rights of victims of crimes, as mandated in the ICC's statute.

NEXT STEPS: COMPREHENSIVE LAWS, PERMANENT FUNDING, AND INALIENABLE RIGHTS

There are three additional steps that must be taken in each state, province, or national jurisdiction before full provision of victim services and victims' rights can be ensured. One is to enact a *Law to Rebalance Justice by Implementing Effectively Rights for Victims of Crime* in each jurisdiction, which would update the myriad of laws that already exist—some of which date back to the 1980s. The second step is to ensure that there are adequate funds available to take the rhetoric and proclamations—as well as the progress so far—and put them into comprehensive actions. The third step is to make sure that the justified concern to respect rights of the accused does not trump the inalienable rights of victims of crime. Let's look at these in more detail.

MODEL LAW TO REBALANCE JUSTICE

In chapter 2, I discussed the work of the group of fourteen experts from across the world who met at INTERVICT in 2005 to discuss how the inalienable rights for victims of crime outlined in the *magna carta* could be implemented more effectively. They produced a cogent draft for an international convention that national governments would negotiate, ratify, and sign that integrated the various national and international agreements into one coherent document.

But I want action now. I want legislators moved to take rights for victims of crime seriously and implement legislation to achieve this. So I have adapted the work of the group of fourteen experts and the conclusions from this book into a draft for a model law in the appendix. It uses the sections of the draft convention that are relevant to North America and that could be adapted to any state, provincial, or territorial jurisdiction that wants to meet international standards. Figure 8.1 outlines the three facets that have run throughout this book into this model legislation so that it encompasses support, justice, and good government.

My model law starts with a relatively short preamble that draws attention to earlier laws and proclamations as well as commitments by all world governments to implement the *magna carta* for victims of crime. It points to the harm caused to victims from crime, the lack of effective strategies to reduce victimization, and the need to minimize harm when victims collaborate with law enforcement and criminal justice systems.

It stresses the importance of rebalancing justice and recognizing that crimes hurt people, not just the state. It defines who victims of crime are and, in particular, differentiates victims of crime who need special considerations and services because of issues such as gender or age. This law applies directly to victims of crime, their co-victims (such as family members), and others (such as Good Samaritans). It clarifies its scope as

Support
1. Right to Recognition
2. Right to Information
3. Right to Assistance

Justice
4. Right to Restitution and Repayment
5. Right to Protection from the Accused
6. Right to Participation and Representation

Good government
7. Right to Effective Policies to Reduce Victimization
8. Right to Full Implementation
   — Office for victims of crime
   — Standards and training
   — Evaluation and ombudspersons
   — Surveys for success
   — Research and development

Figure 8.1. Inalienable rights for victims of crime in draft model law

covering all the relevant adult and juvenile criminal codes. It includes commitments to preventing victimization through reducing crime.

The operational paragraphs of my proposed law define victims' rights and services. This includes how victims of crime would be provided with information, assistance, reparation, participation, and representation, as we have discussed in chapters 3 to 6. It points to the importance of preventing victimization in the most effective ways possible as in chapter 7.

The legislation has an important section ensuring good government and implementation that includes an office for victims of crime, ombudspersons, standards as the basis for all training, monitoring made possible through surveys, and an institute as discussed above.

In sum, it takes up the demands to legislators presented in each chapter of this book and puts them into wording that will help legislators develop their own laws and programs. It is important to note the comprehensive nature of the proposed law, and the integration of measures to ensure effective implementation (which, as we have seen, have been largely missing up to now). For instance, sections 5 and 6 of the proposed law are less detailed but are consistent with the federal Justice for All Act in the United States and Marsy's Law in California. The model law is not proposed to override those provisions already adopted. However, it is crafted with the most recent knowledge available, and thus goes much further toward meeting some inalienable rights of victims of crime that have not yet been included in even recent legislation.

FAIR FUNDING

A comprehensive and effective program of rights for victims of crime requires fair and permanent funding.

In figure 8.2, I have set out in the insert the impressive growth in funds available through VOCA and VAWA over the last twenty years. As we have seen, VOCA is funded through fines levied on offenders in the federal criminal justice system. At times it has not been clear whether or not these fines alone would be adequate to fund VOCA's programs, and while the fund has been fortunate to date in that it has regularly benefited from large penalties, its funding is not as secure as the funding to law enforcement or corrections, which is guaranteed through general revenues. As we can see

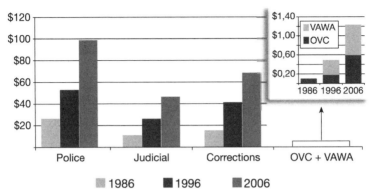

Figure 8.2. Comparison of expenditures on police, judicial, and correctional items with VOCA and VAWA

in figure 8.2, the VOCA and VAWA funds are dwarfed by the growth in expenditures on police, criminal justice, and corrections budgets.

Justice for victims of crime must be addressed and rebalanced in these budgets. Even given these grim numbers, it would still be possible to realize the actions I have called for with only modest increases or reallocations in spending.

In figure 8.3, I provide a schematic budget for the United States to show the order of funding that is needed to achieve much of what is proposed in this book—to rebalance justice for victims by ensuring their inalienable rights. I have listed the inalienable rights from chapter 2, figure 2.1 and indicated the relevant sections in the model law that correspond closely to the eight core needs. For each activity I have then provided a ballpark figure of what is needed to pay for the reforms. I have used the figure of $100 million in several of the boxes for activities that require more of a change in general orientation rather than hiring new personnel or paying for compensation.

From chapter 3, the actions needed to put victims of crime at the zenith of law enforcement require the implementation of the recommendations of the IACP report, but with an emphasis on ensuring that victims get timely information. This requires the development of standards and training, which are not expensive (but with approximately a million sworn officers in the United States, it would require some expenditures).

In chapter 4, I showed that more spaces were needed in transition houses for victims of domestic violence, but I was not able to identify a

Model Law (relevant section)	Law enforcement (chp. 3)	Assistance (chp. 4)	Restitution + Repayment (chp. 5)	Judicial + Courts (chp. 6)	Victimization prevention (chp. 7)	Assessment + Surveys (chp. 8)	Sub-total
Support							
1 Recognition of victims, co-victims, good samaritans	$100		$100			$100	$300
2 Information	$100		$100	$100	$100	$100	$600
Assistance - referral by police	$200	$100				$100	$300
3 Assistance - short term		$1 000				$100	$1 100
Assistance - medium term		$2 000				$100	$2 100
Special assistance because of age, gender, disability, race		$6 000				$100	$6 100
Justice							
4 Restitution from offender				$100		$100	$200
Restorative justice - respecting victim rights			$100			$100	$200
Compensation from state			$4 000			$100	$4 100
5 Protection of victims, witnesses and experts						$100	$100
6 Access to justice and fair treatment				$2 000		$100	$2 100
Good Government							
7 Commitment to reduce victimization)					$10 000	$100	$10 100
8 Implementation	$100	$100	$100	$100	$100	$100	$600
Subtotal	**$500**	**$9 200**	**$4 400**	**$2 300**	**$10 200**	**$1 300**	**$27 900**
Current budget (mid-point of estimates)	$100 000	$2 000	$1 000	$50 000	$70 000	$1 000	$224 000
Estimated percentage increase or re-allocation	1%	460%	440%	5%	15%	130%	12%

Figure 8.3. Preliminary sketch of possible additional investments needed (in millions of $) to implement the demands in each chapter, showing their relation to sections in the model law

precise number. So, I compared the higher number of beds per capita in Canada and suggested that this might be a useful target, pending surveys to give more accurate numbers. Similarly, there is a need for more sexual assault crisis centers, but here too estimates remain vague. So, the proposed increase of $1 billion for the short term, $2 billion for generic services, and $6 billion for gender-based services gives an idea of the order of magnitude of funds needed.

In chapter 5, I showed that the costs of implementing effective restitution collection measures are not large (although they are tremendously important to victims). They require some simple changes in procedure that already exist in some jurisdictions. However, I showed that compensation in the United States was lagging behind other comparable jurisdictions both in terms of average amounts paid and in numbers of eligible victims applying. I estimated an increase of about $4 billion to bring the United States up to the standards of England and Wales or leading Canadian provinces.

In chapter 6, the appeal for participation and representation does not require significant expenditures, though it does require some funds to pay lawyers to represent victims, cover the costs of experimenting with court provisions, and provide funds to empower more victims to use civil procedures.

Chapter 7 recalls and updates the significant knowledge about what works to reduce victimization, and so calls for a significantly bigger investment in what we know is effective. Clearly, it is better for everybody to reduce victimization in the first place than to pay for victims' other inalienable rights after they have been victimized. So I have proposed an annual investment of $10 billion.

Finally, I have included some funds to realize the measures identified in this chapter in the schematic budget.

We must put these totals in the context of current expenditures on law enforcement, criminal justice, and corrections, so I have tallied the total required spending for each chapter and calculated the percentage increase for rebalancing justice for victims of crime relative to current expenditures. I have used the current expenditures for corrections as the base for the percentage increase in victimization prevention.

Though the cost estimates are only ballpark figures, rebalancing justice in support of victims would require an allocation (or reallocation) of *merely 12 percent* of what is currently spent on law and order, and close to half of this is to reduce victimization. Starting with annual increments of

2 percent, within six years the budget for these actions would eventually reach the equivalent of 12 percent of what is currently being spent on law enforcement and judicial and correctional functions.

The time is long overdue for adequate funds to be invested by states across the United States to ensure that every victim has access to basic support and every law enforcement officer and prosecutor is qualified in how victims must be treated. It is time to ensure that the toothless bills of rights become principles of balanced justice that are enforced. It is clear that we need to act, and it is clear that acting is within our financial means.

VICTIMS' RIGHTS AMENDMENT

Many of the needs of victims of crime can be met without affecting any rights of the offender—that is, provided that governments are investing their general revenues in an equitable manner and that funds for victim support are not being taken away to pay for services for offenders.

The inalienable rights that I have identified in figure 8.1 do not require amendments to constitutions to be put into action, but it might be nice to put them into law so that victims will know they are guaranteed.

Many experts argue that there is no conflict between the interests of victims of crime and the interests of offenders. However, this is blatantly not true. Most offenders would prefer not to be incarcerated, whereas most victims of violent crimes would prefer that dangerous and violent offenders be incarcerated for as long as possible (or at least be provided with some type of effective correctional program that would make it safe for them to be in the community). This focus on victims' need for public safety has been a strong theme throughout federal legislation and the amendments of thirty-three state constitutions in the United States, particularly the Justice for All Act and Marsy's Law.

This overt conflict of rights is a fundamental issue, as it concerns the victim's safety. It applies to those cases where the offender has been violent. Currently, as we've seen, the victim is rarely able to communicate directly with the court in relation to bail decisions, sentence bargaining, and parole release. Many jurisdictions allow a victim to submit an impact statement at the time of sentencing or parole hearings, but this is not a presentation of arguments about the victim's safety if the alleged offender were to be released. If necessary reforms were to take place, however, and victims were given a voice in the justice process, then the victim would be able to put forth his or her concerns to the judge in terms of particular conditions or correctional programming.

The incorrect view that granting rights to victims of crime would unjustifiably take away from longstanding offender rights was likely the reason why the U.S. Senate blocked the proposed victim rights amendment in 2004. My view is that there needs to be a balance between these conflicting interests, and this balance must be decided by independent judicial authorities after the rights of the offender *and* the rights of the victim have been appropriately represented and heard.

But it is not just about having victims' safety concerns heard. Victims of crime also want to participate in criminal justice processes in order to get recognition for what happened to them and to see a sanction that is consistent with sentencing standards in that jurisdiction. Much of this is about process, but some is about outcomes. They want fair treatment and recognition.

Victims are also concerned with receiving restitution from the offender. They want to see offenders taking responsibility to pay reparation for the harm that they have done. The offender may not be in a position to pay at anything more than a token rate, but the victim needs to know what assets the offender has so that if he does not pay, appropriate action can be taken.

In light of these victims' interests, I am proposing the amendment to balance the rights for victims of crime and offenders, presented in figure 8.4. This is an amendment that would be made to jurisdictions that have a constitution or a charter of rights and freedoms. This amendment clarifies the right for victims of crime to have their voices heard. It recognizes their rights to protect their own personal safety, their interests

— to have the rights of victims of crime to safety, reparation and justice respected **and**

— balanced fairly, against rights of the accused or convicted offender, **and**

— heard through participation and representation equal to that of the accused

— **in all judicial and administrative proceedings**

Figure 8.4. The amendment to balance the rights for victims of crime and offenders

in reparation, and their need for justice. It proposes that judicial and administrative authorities balance the rights of the accused and of the victim, considering both fairly and not simply allowing the rights of the accused to trump those of victims.

RIGHTS IN REALITY: THE LAST MILE
FROM LEGISLATORS

Victims of crime have key needs that are recognized by large-scale surveys, constitutional amendments, and international consensus. This book has identified an agenda of actionable recommendations to succeed in providing support, reparation, protection, and justice for victims of crime. It has identified many best practices that are meeting those needs in some places, for some victims, some of the time. Now, it is time to go the last mile.

The commonsense recommendations presented in this volume will not happen on their own. They face the normal challenges—namely, that people resist reform, particularly if it is not well planned and the human resources have not been sufficiently trained and developed. My proposals will be diverted by some legislators who see victims' rights only as trampling on offender rights. My proposals will also face formidable resistance from those entrenched in the traditional way of responding to crime such as law enforcement, prosecutors for the state, and judges—many of whom still contend that their role does not include victims, that they do not have the time to deal with victims as well as offenders, and that they are fighting for victims by fighting against offenders. As we have seen, this is an outdated and imbalanced approach to justice.

This chapter has identified what must be demanded of legislators in order to implement reasonable and actionable recommendations so that every victim will have services to meet their basic needs, as well as rights that can be defended in courts of justice. Legislators must establish central offices for victims of crime in every jurisdiction to provide leadership, invest general revenues, and promote and provide services for victims. These offices must retool the functions of law enforcement, prosecutors, criminal justice—and yes, even corrections—so that support, information, reparation, and safety are central to their activities and budgets. They must establish standards for victim services so that the training and professional development of law enforcement personnel, lawyers, judges, victim services providers, and many others are sufficient to provide victims with what they need. They must establish ombudspersons to solve individual difficulties and to recommend systemic solutions. Legislators must invest in annual surveys to measure whether victims of crime are receiving the services and rights promised, and they must also call for more in-depth studies to understand how services and rights might be improved. They must promote institutes on victim services and rights to do the research and development on behalf of communities, governments, and victim services advocates.

Legislators will succeed in getting victims the services and considerations that are rightfully theirs by adopting comprehensive and model legislation such as that proposed in the appendix. They must pay the relatively modest bill for these actions. I proposed that these budgets be achieved by a modest 2 percent increase each year, which would eventually reach the equivalent of 12 percent of what is currently being spent on law enforcement and judicial and correctional functions. Most of these increases would occur at the state level in the United States. Constitutions must be amended to overcome those cases where the inalienable rights of victims of crime to safety, reparation, and justice might be trumped by rights for offenders that predated the realization that victims of crime matter.

Ultimately, what matters is that everyone who reads this book realizes that they have the power to get legislators to reform antiquated practices that made sense only when governments could overlook the loss, injury, and pain that so many victims of crime live with on a daily basis. The good news is that in some places, some of the time, some victims are being served and protected in ways that are both exemplary and a model for others to look to for what could—and must—be.

The challenge now is to get those services and rights accessible and used by all who need them. This book argues the case and spikes the counterarguments. There will always be excuses and reasons not to act, but the devastating consequences of crime merit our strongest efforts to guarantee basic rights for victims and to stop victimization through means that we know work. It is time to get our legislators to go the last mile to rebalance justice to implement effectively rights for all victims of crime all of the time.

Appendix

DRAFT MODEL LAW TO REBALANCE JUSTICE BY IMPLEMENTING EFFECTIVELY RIGHTS FOR VICTIMS OF CRIME

PREAMBLE

Recalling many proclamations in laws to provide rights for victims of crime and the commitment by all the world's governments in 1985 at the UN General Assembly (GA/RES/40/34) to take the necessary steps to give effect to the provisions contained in the Declaration of Basic Principles of Justice for Victims of Crime and Abuse of Power,

We the people adopt this law to rebalance justice by implementing effectively the inalienable rights for victims of crime, fostering modern strategies to reduce victimization, and minimizing hardship when victims assist in the prosecution of offenders.[1]

ARTICLE 1. RIGHT TO RECOGNITION

Crimes are not just against the state but impact millions of people, including many women and children, vulnerable groups, and indigenous populations, who are victims of crime, suffering, loss, injury, and mental harm each year. These persons may be victims more than once in that year; the rights of these victims still have not been adequately recognized, and they may, in addition, suffer hardship when assisting in the prosecution of offenders.

"Victims" means natural persons who, individually or collectively, have suffered harm, including physical or mental injury, emotional suffering, or economic loss in relation to violations of adult, juvenile, and other criminal codes.

A person is a victim regardless of whether or not a perpetrator is identified, apprehended, prosecuted, or convicted, and regardless of the familial relationship between the perpetrator and the victim.

Where appropriate, the term "victims" includes the immediate family or dependants of the direct victims and persons who have suffered in intervening to assist victims in distress or to prevent victimization.

The provisions shall be applicable to all, without discrimination of any kind, such as race, color, gender, age, language, religion, nationality, political or other opinion, cultural beliefs or practices, property, birth or family status, ethnic or social origin, or disability.

Where appropriate, persons who are vulnerable because of gender, age, race, disability, susceptibility to post-traumatic stress disorder, or other reasons will receive appropriate services.

ARTICLE 2. RIGHT TO INFORMATION

Victims will receive timely information from their first contact with law enforcement or other agencies.

The information will be provided in the most effective way, consistent with advances in technology. Such information shall facilitate an informed understanding for the victims and shall be at least as follows:

(a) the type of services or organizations to which they can turn for support;

(b) the type of support which they can obtain, including the availability of health and social services and other relevant assistance, as well as obligations on those services to report to law enforcement, and who will pay for the services;

(c) where and how they can report an offense and whether they can choose not to report;

(d) procedures following such a report and their role in connection with such procedures;

(e)   their role and the scope, timing, and progress of the proceedings
      and of the disposition of their cases, especially where serious crimes
      are involved and where they have requested such information;
(f)   how and under what conditions they can obtain protection;
(g)   to what extent and on what terms they have access to legal advice
      or legal aid;
(h)   requirements for them to be entitled to compensation from the
      state;
(i)   if they reside in another state, any special arrangements available to
      them in order to protect their interests;
(j)   where and how they can obtain more information.

Victims who have expressed a wish to this effect are to be kept informed of:

(k)   the outcome of their complaint;
(l)   relevant factors enabling them, in the event of prosecution, to know
      the conduct of the proceedings regarding the person prosecuted
      for offenses concerning them, except in exceptional cases where
      the proper handling of the case may be adversely affected;
(m) the court's sentence.

Necessary measures shall be taken to ensure that the victim is notified,
at least in cases where there might be danger to the victims, when the person prosecuted or sentenced for an offense is released, and when the victim requests it. Victims have the right to refuse to receive the information.

ARTICLE 3. RIGHT TO ASSISTANCE

Victims shall receive the necessary material, medical, psychological, and
social assistance through government, voluntary, community-based, and
indigenous means. Such assistance may be provided through specialized
agencies or comprehensive programs.

Networks of criminal justice, social services, health and mental health
services, victim assistance services, and other relevant groups or institutions may be established to facilitate referrals, coordination, and planning
among those providing assistance and to reach out to victims.

The following kinds of assistance are essential to victims:

(1) Immediate Assistance:
   (a) medical attention and accompaniment to medical exams, including first aid, emergency medical attention, and medical transport. Support services shall be provided to victims when forensic examinations are called for or in the aftermath of death. Such services shall be at no cost to the victim;
   (b) material support such as shelter, housing, transportation, or property repair;
   (c) crisis intervention, involving crisis counseling and problem solving;
   (d) information and notification about what happened to the extent that such information does not interfere with investigation, including notification of any immediate responsibilities to the criminal justice system. Assistance shall be offered in notifying family or friends of what happened;
   (e) protection from repeat victimization shall be provided through the development of safety and security plans. This may include information on police surveillance, relocation, emergency communication, and the like. It may also involve assistance with obtaining protection orders through the judicial system;
   (f) victims shall be protected from media intrusion;
   (g) general support and advocacy shall be offered when victims interact with social, justice, and medical institutions as well as appropriate referrals for urgent needs;
   (h) confidentiality and privacy shall be guaranteed to the extent allowable under current law and policy.
(2) Medium-Term Assistance:
   (a) the continuation of the services provided under (1) Immediate Assistance;
   (b) psychological health and spiritual interventions that may include post-trauma counseling, mental health therapy, pastoral counseling, or traditional healing intercessions;
   (c) assistance with financial needs or claims including filing and advocacy for compensation claims, restitution, insurance, or emergency funds;

(d) legal referrals for legal assistance in the criminal or civil justice systems. To the extent possible such legal assistance shall be at no cost to the victim.

(3) Long-Term Assistance:
   (a) the continuation of the services provided under (1) Immediate Assistance and (2) Medium-Term Assistance;
   (b) assurances and reestablishment of the victim's place in the community and in the workplace shall be encouraged;
   (c) language understood by victims shall be encouraged. If translators are needed, they shall be trained in the subject matter that they are addressing and victim support personnel shall be familiar with common terms that will be used;
   (d) assistance with regard to victims' roles in the criminal justice system, including the nature of information they will receive on the case status and their rights to participation or representation;
   (e) information and assistance on how victims can provide input at all critical stages of criminal justice proceedings, including: bail hearings, initial hearings, plea bargains, diversion programs, case disposition, offender status post disposition, and offender releases;
   (f) information, support, and assistance concerning options for participation in alternative justice forums.

ARTICLE 4. RIGHT TO REPARATION

Victims shall receive assistance to recover their financial losses through at least the following procedures:

Restorative justice respectful of victim rights shall endeavor to establish or enhance the systems of restorative justice, which shall seek as a priority to restore the victim. It shall emphasize the need for acceptance by the offender of his or her responsibility for the offense and the acknowledgement of the adverse consequences of the offense for the victim. It shall ensure that victims shall have the opportunity to choose restorative justice forums, which accord to victims' dignity, compassion, and the other rights and services in the Act. Support for the victim shall be equivalent to the legal and social support provided to the offender.

Restitution from offender shall make offenders or third parties responsible for paying fair restitution to victims, their families, or dependants. Such restitution shall include the return of property or payment for the harm or loss suffered, reimbursement of expenses incurred as a result of the victimization, the provision of services, and the restoration of rights.

(1) Victims shall request the criminal court to order restitution from the offender in writing with receipts and other documentation justifying the amount.
(2) The criminal court will obtain an assessment of the income, assets, and liabilities of the offender.
(3) The department of corrections will be responsible for collecting the restitution and paying it to the victim.
(4) In cases where the offender is under the legal obligation to pay restitution as well as other pecuniary sanctions, the former shall have precedence over the latter.
(5) In cases where the victim seeks restitution through civil remedies, the government shall expedite these proceedings and minimize expenses.

Compensation from the state will be paid when restitution is not fully available from the offender or other sources.

(1) It shall provide compensation to:
    (a) victims who have sustained significant bodily injury or impairment of physical or mental health as a result of intentional violent crime;
    (b) the victims' family, in particular dependants of persons who have died or become physically or mentally incapacitated as a result of such victimization.
(2) Compensation shall be provided for:
    (a) treatment and rehabilitation for care of physical injuries and mental health problems;
    (b) loss of income, funeral expenses, and loss of maintenance for dependants;
    (c) reasonable pain and suffering and other psychological injuries caused to victims.

(3) The establishment, strengthening, and expansion of national, regional, or local funds for compensation to victims. Funds will come
from general revenue, special taxes, fines, private contributions, and
other sources.
(4) These funds shall guarantee fair, appropriate and timely compensation. They shall allow for emergency and/or interim payments.
(5) Special care shall be taken to ensure that all eligible victims are
aware of this compensation and have assistance to apply. This
requires, *inter alia*, extensive dissemination of information on
the eligibility criteria and the procedure to be followed, as well
as application procedures using modern technologies such as the
Internet.
(6) In cases of cross-border victimization, the government where the
crime has occurred shall pay compensation to the foreign national
as payment of last resort.

ARTICLE 5. PROTECTION OF VICTIMS, WITNESSES, AND EXPERTS

(1) Appropriate measures shall be provided to protect the safety,
physical and psychological well-being, dignity, and privacy of victims, witnesses, and experts from potential retaliation or intimidation and, as appropriate, for their relatives and other persons close
to them.
(2) The measures envisaged in paragraph 1 of this article may include:
(a) establishing procedures for the physical protection of such persons, such as, to the extent necessary and feasible, relocating
them and permitting, where appropriate, nondisclosure or limi-
tations on the disclosure of information concerning the identity
and whereabouts of such persons;
(b) providing evidentiary rules to permit victims, witnesses, and
experts to give testimony in a manner that ensures the safety of
such persons, such as permitting testimony to be given through
the use of communications technology such as video or other
appropriate means;
(c) agreements or arrangements for the relocation of persons.

ARTICLE 6. RIGHT TO PARTICIPATION
AND REPRESENTATION

For harm suffered, victims shall be provided with access to the mechanisms of justice and redress in a manner which is expeditious, fair, inexpensive, and accessible, through:

(a) judicial and administrative mechanisms which will enable victims to obtain redress;
(b) informal mechanisms for the resolution of disputes, including mediation, arbitration, and customary justice processes or indigenous practices, where appropriate, to facilitate conciliation and redress for victims;
(c) timely information about their rights in seeking redress through all these mechanisms.
(1) Victims shall have access to informal, administrative and judicial processes responsive to the needs of victims. This shall be facilitated by:
(a) providing victims with participation and representation equal to that of the accused to have their interests in their safety, reparation, and justice respected and balanced fairly against interests of the accused or convicted offender in all judicial and administrative proceedings;
(b) giving the victim a fair hearing within a reasonable time in the determination of their entitlement to a remedy for the injury, loss, or damage suffered by them as a result of their victimization;
(c) the prompt return to victims of their property taken or recovered by the police or any other agency in the course of the investigation;
(d) providing to victims, where appropriate, the right of appeal against decisions of the prosecutorial authority not to prosecute in cases where they were victimized;
(e) providing proper assistance to victims throughout informal, administrative, investigative, and judicial processes;
(f) taking measures to minimize delays inconvenient to victims and to protect their privacy wherever appropriate;
(g) ensuring the safety of victims, as well as that of their families and witnesses on their behalf, from intimidation and retaliation;

(h) ensuring the enforcement of any order or decree granting awards to victims.

(2) Victims and witnesses shall be reimbursed for court expenses incurred as a result of their legitimate participation in criminal proceedings.

ARTICLE 7. RIGHT TO EFFECTIVE POLICIES TO PREVENT VICTIMIZATION

Strategies and programs shall be put in place to reduce victimization consistent with international guidelines and knowledge by, *inter alia*, developing:

(a) more effective detection, prosecution, sentencing, and corrections of perpetrators, consistent with internationally recognized norms;
(b) measures to reduce the risk of occurrence of crimes by tackling their multiple causes;
(c) strategies to reduce the opportunity for crime by improving protection for property and persons;
(d) collaboration between civil society and relevant governmental institutions, in areas such as schooling, social services, family, public health, and economic sectors;
(e) institutional frameworks to improve the planning, cost effectiveness, and sustainability of strategies;
(f) greater public participation in, and engagement with, strategies in both the short and the long term;
(g) international cooperation to exchange proven and promising practices and to seek transnational solutions.

ARTICLE 8. RIGHT TO FULL IMPLEMENTATION

(1) An *Office for Victims of Crime* shall be strengthened or established to ensure that funds are invested in the programs to implement the services in this Act.

(2) Standards and training shall be implemented by developing standards, norms, and codes of practice for all services in this Act, and providing training, education, and information to all persons working with victims to improve and sustain the necessary methods and attitudes. The standards and training shall include:
(a) standards, norms, and principles relating to victims;

(b) principles and ethical duties of personnel dealing with victims;

(c) crisis assessment skills and techniques, especially for making referrals, with an emphasis placed on the need for confidentiality;

(d) knowledge of the impact, consequences (including negative physical, mental, emotional, psychological, and financial effects), and trauma of crimes;

(e) special measures and techniques to assist victims and witnesses in the justice process (both formal and informal);

(f) cross-cultural and age-related linguistic, religious, social, and gender issues;

(g) appropriate communication skills;

(h) interviewing and assessment techniques that minimize any trauma to the victims while maximizing the quality of information received from the victim;

(i) skills to deal with victims and witnesses in a sensitive, understanding, constructive, and reassuring manner;

(j) methods to protect and present evidence and to question victims and witnesses;

(k) roles of, and methods used by, personnel working with victims and witnesses.

(3) *Monitoring* is essential to ensuring the full implementation. So appropriate measures shall be put in place to monitor the efficiency and effectiveness of policies and measures designed for the implementation of this statute. In particular, they shall undertake periodical reviews and evaluations of their legislation, regulations, and procedures, including through government surveys and independent research.

(a) A victim commissioner or ombudsperson shall be established to whom complaints from victims can be sent and who will recommend reforms to the legislation and practice to better meet the needs of victims of crime. The commissioner will investigate cases and act for individual victims to assist them in getting rights. The commissioner will recommend reforms based on these investigations, analysis of surveys, and research;

(b) The various agencies, organs, or bodies dealing with victims shall submit performance reports.

(4) *Surveys* shall be undertaken annually to measure rates of victimization, reporting to police, and costs and consequences of crime.

These shall include indicators of the extent to which each of the rights in this Act have resulted in service to victims. Additional surveys will examine the implementation of this Act in relation to vulnerable groups.

(5) One or more *Institutes for Research and Development* shall be created to undertake research to supplement the surveys and work of the Commissioner. To ensure independence, the funding will be based on 1 percent of the annual expenditures on corrections.

NOTES

INTRODUCTION

1. Marlene Young, "The Victims Movement: A Confluence of Forces," *National Organization for Victim Assistance*, www.trynova.org/victiminfo/readings/VictimsMovement.pdf (accessed April 3, 2010).

CHAPTER 1

1. United States, *President's Task Force on Victims of Crime Final Report* (Washington, DC: U.S. Government Printing Office, 1982), 3.

2. President's Task Force, *Final Report*, 3.

3. Helpguide, "Post-traumatic Stress Disorder," Helpguide website, www.helpguide.org (accessed March 20, 2010).

4. To help the reader, I have used the mid-point of the wide range, which signals that the presence of PTSD varies based on the nature of the victimization (as well as the survey method).

5. Dean G. Kilpatrick and Ron Acierno, "Mental Health Needs of Crime Victims: Epidemiology," *Journal of Traumatic Stress* 16, no. 2 (April 2003): 119–32.

6. Lawrence D. Klausner, *Son of Sam: Based on the Authorized Transcription of the Tapes, Official Documents and Diaries of David Berkowitz* (New York: McGraw-Hill, 1980).

7. Trisha Meili, *I Am the Central Park Jogger: A Story of Hope and Possibility* (New York: Scribner, 2003).

8. MADD, "Campaign to Eliminate Drunk Driving," Mothers Against Drunk Driving website, www.madd.org/Drunk-Driving.aspx (accessed February 19, 2010).

9. In the United States and the Netherlands, national victimization data are available for the past thirty years. Since 1972 in the United States, 80,000 persons aged twelve and over in 43,000 households have been interviewed twice a year about their victimizations from crime in the National Crime Victimization Survey. Since 1982 in England and Wales, more than 60,000 households have been interviewed every second year as part of the British Crime (Victimization) Survey, which became an annual survey in 2001. Since 1975, Canada has undertaken sporadic victimization surveys such as those conducted with 26,000 adults aged fifteen and over in 2004.

10. Eighteen percent is the estimate provided by Dean Kilpatrick, Heidi Resnick, Kenneth J. Ruggiero, Lauren Conoscenti, and Jenna McCauley, *Drug-Facilitated, Incapacitated, and Forcible Rape: A National Study* (Washington, DC: U.S. Department of Justice, National Institute of Justice, 2007), 2.

11. The 21 million applies to persons who are twelve years old or older. See U.S. Department of Justice, Bureau of Justice Statistics, http://bjs.ojp.usdoj.gov/ (accessed February 21, 2010) and National Center for Victims of Crime, "National Crime Victim Rights Week Resource Guide: Crime Victimization in the United States: Statistical Overview," www.ncvc .org/ncvc/AGP.Net/Components/documentViewer/Download.aspxnz?DocumentID=47449 (accessed February 21, 2010).

12. Jan van Dijk, John van Kesteren, and Paul Smit, *Criminal Victimisation in International Perspective: Key Findings from the 2004–2005 ICVS and EU ICS* (The Hague: Boom Legal Publishers, 2008).

13. Patricia Tjaden and Nancy Thoennes, *Full Report of the Prevalence, Incidence, and Consequences of Violence against Women* (Washington, DC: National Institute of Justice and the Centers for Disease Control and Prevention, 2000).

14. Kilpatrick et al., *Drug-Facilitated, Incapacitated, and Forcible Rape*, 2.

15. U.S. Department of Health and Human Services, "New Report Shows Child Maltreatment Decreased in 2008," Administration for Children and Families website, www .acf.hhs.gov/news/press/2010/child_maltreatment_2008.html (accessed April 4, 2010).

16. Tjaden and Thoennes, *Violence Against Women*.

17. National Center for Education Statistics and Bureau of Justice Statistics, *Indicators of School Crime and Safety* (Washington, DC: U.S. Departments of Education and Justice, 2010).

18. National Center for Education Statistics, *Indicators of School Crime*.

19. U.S. Department of Justice, "Homicide Trends in the U.S.," U.S. Bureau of Justice Statistics website, http://bjs.ojp.usdoj.gov/content/homicide/race.cfm (accessed February 19, 2010).

20. The chances of being killed in a car crash by a driver who is impaired is about the same for Canada (with 1,200 deaths per year) but much lower in England and Wales (with only 600 deaths per year). Death caused by impaired driving is less frequent than homicide in the United States and in England and Wales, but much more frequent than homicide in Canada. In the United States, half a million people who are victimized by drunk drivers are injured each year. See MADD Canada, "The Magnitude of the Alcohol/Drug-Related Crash Problem in Canada," Mothers Against Drunk Driving Canada website, http://

madd.ca/english/research/magnitudememo.html (accessed April 3, 2010); Laura Brasnett, "Drink-Driving: Prevalence and Attitudes in England and Wales 2002," Report 258 (London: Home Office Research Unit, 2003).

21. Graham Farrell and Ken Pease, *Repeat Victimization* (New York: Criminal Justice Press, 2001).

22. Ted Miller, Mark Cohen, and Brian Wiersema, *Victim Costs and Consequences: A New Look* (Washington, DC: National Institute of Justice, U.S. Department of Justice, 1996).

23. In terms of productivity alone, a 2004 World Bank study shows that one in five of the work days lost by women in established market economies is due to gender-based violence. See World Health Organization, *Economic Dimensions of Interpersonal Violence* (Geneva: World Health Organization, 2004).

24. Miller, Cohen, and Wiersema, *Victim Costs.*

25. These calculations do not include the estimated $25 billion for child welfare costs, or the $28 billion required for the police, courts, and corrections agencies to respond to the additional adult crime perpetrated by child abuse victims later in their lives. If these factors were taken into account, together they would push the total cost of crime to close to $104 billion annually. See Ching-Tung Wang and John Holton, "Total Estimated Cost of Child Abuse and Neglect in the United States," Prevent Child Abuse America website, www .preventchildabuse.org/about_us/media_releases/pcaa_pew_economic_impact_study_final .pdf (accessed April 4, 2010).

26. The calculations in figure 1.3 and the text were based on the logic and definitions in Miller, Cohen, and Wiersema, *Victim Costs.* However, the data were adapted to a recent year to allow for increases in costs and decreases in many types of victimization other than rape. Firstly, the losses per criminal victimization from table 2 in *Victim Costs and Consequences* in 1993 dollars were multiplied by 1.49 to put them in 2008 dollars allowing for average increases in costs consistent with inflation. Secondly, for figure 1.3, the numbers of victimizations in table 1 of *Victim Costs and Consequences* were adjusted to a recent year in the following ways: for NCVS assaults with injury were taken from table 1 for numbers of assaults and table 75 for the proportion injured from U.S. Department of Justice, BJS, "Criminal Victimization in the United States, 2007, Statistical Tables"; the numbers of child abuse cases, homicides, and DWI fatalities were taken from data on the page for the Overview of Crime and Victimization in the United States and for Drunk and Drugged Driving in the National Center for Crime Victims, "National Crime Victim Rights Week Resource Guide"; rape and sexual assault was taken from pages 2 and 22–23 in Kilpatrick et al., *Drug-Facilitated, Incapacitated and Forcible Rape.* Finally, for total estimates used in the text, the principal source of numbers of victimizations is the *NCVS,* 2007, Statistical Tables.

27. World Health Organization, *Economic Dimensions.*

28. Heather Strang, *Repair of Revenge: Victims and Restorative Justice* (Oxford: Clarendon Press, 2002).

29. Irvin Waller and Norm Okihiro, *Burglary: The Victim and the Public* (Toronto: University of Toronto Press, 1978); see also Mike Maguire and Claire Corbett, *The Effects of Crime and the Work of Victims Support Schemes* (Aldershot, UK: Gower, 1987); and Joanna Shapland, Jon Willmore, and Peter Duff, *Victims in the Criminal Justice System* (Aldershot, UK: Gower, 1985).

30. See Lisa Newmark, *Crime Victims' Needs and VOCA-Funded Services: Findings and Recommendations from Two National Studies* (Washington, DC: National Institute of Justice, 2006), 13–15.

31. International Association of Chiefs of Police, *Enhancing Law Enforcement Response to Victims: A 21st Century Strategy* (Alexandria, VA: International Association of Chiefs of Police, 2008), 11–12.

32. Kilpatrick and Acierno, "Mental Health Needs of Crime Victims."

33. Ellen Brickman, *Development of a National Study of Victim Needs and Assistance* (Washington, DC: National Institute of Justice, 2002), 148.

CHAPTER 2

1. Adedokun Adeyemi (law dean, Nigeria); Paulo Serigio Domingues (leading judge, Brazil); Sam Garkawe (law professor, Australia); Matti Joutsen (senior public servant, Finland); Raj Kumar (human rights dean, India); Karen McLaughlin (human trafficking task force, United States); Hidemichi Morosawa (university president, Japan); Irvin Waller (criminology professor, Canada); Marlene Young (president, WSV, United States); and the team from INTERVICT—Marc Groenhuijsen (judge and law professor), Jan van Dijk (victimization survey professor), Willem van Genugten (international law professor), Rianne Letschert (Ph.D. in immigration rights), and Frans Willem Winkel (psychology professor).

2. United States, *President's Task Force on Victims of Crime Final Report* (Washington, DC: U.S. Government Printing Office, 1982). Unfortunately, twenty years and thirty-three amendments to state constitutions later, the Senate could not agree on a wording that would have been adequate—likely because the lobby for offender rights was too rigid. A constitutional amendment might say that victims have a right to be present and heard on an equal basis with the accused (see chapter 8). Because they are in the Constitution, the rights of the accused override (or "trump") individual laws.

3. Steve Derene, executive director, National Association of VOCA Assistance Administrators, e-mail April 21, 2010.

4. U.S. Department of Justice, Office for Victims of Crime, *New Directions from the Field: Victims' Rights and Services for the 21st Century* (Washington, DC: U.S. Department of Justice, Office of Justice Programs, 1998).

5. General Assembly Resolution 40/34 of 29 November 1985, which adopted the Declaration of Basic Principles of Justice for Victims of Crime and Abuse of Power (1985).

6. United Nations General Assembly, *Declaration of Basic Principles of Justice for Victims of Crime and Abuse of Power*, 1985.

7. General Assembly Resolution 40/34 of 29 November 1985, which adopted the Declaration of Basic Principles of Justice for Victims of Crime and Abuse of Power.

8. Department of Justice Canada, "A Summary of Research into the Federal Victim Surcharge in New Brunswick and the Northwest Territories," Government of Canada, Justice Canada website, www.justice.gc.ca/eng/pi/rs/rep-rap/rd-rr/rr07_vic4/p3.html (accessed April 4, 2010).

9. On September 7, 1994, the International Bureau for Children's Rights (IBCR) was established in Montreal, Canada. Judge Andrée Ruffo of Canada and Dr. Bernard Kouchner of France (later the minister of health and foreign minister of France) created this groundbreaking agency. It was the first step of their international action plan to protect children around the world from physical and sexual abuse.

10. United Nations Office for Drugs and Crime, *Guide for Policy Makers on the Implementation of the Declaration of Basic Principles of Justice for Victims of Crime and Abuse of Power* (New York: United Nations, 1999).

11. United Nations Office for Drugs and Crime, *Handbook on Justice for Victims on the Use and Application of the Declaration of Basic Principles of Justice for Victims of Crime and Abuse of Power* (New York: United Nations, 1999).

12. Marc Groenhuijsen and Rianne Letschert, eds., *Compilation of International Victims' Rights Instruments* (Nijmegen, Netherlands: Wolf Legal Publishers, 2009).

13. Victim Support Europe, *Victims in Europe: Implementation of the EU Framework Decision on the Standing of Victims in the Criminal Proceedings in the Member States of the European Union* (Lisbon: Associação Portuguesa de Apoio à Vítima, 2010).

14. United Kingdom Home Office, "Code of Practice: A Consultation on the Final Drafts of the Code and the Guide for Victims" Home Office website, www.homeoffice.gov.uk/documents/cons-victims-code-2005/ (accessed March 27, 2010).

15. United Kingdom Ministry of Justice, "National Victims' Service," Ministry of Justice website, www.justice.gov.uk/news/speech270110a.htm (accessed March 27, 2010).

CHAPTER 3

1. National Research Council, *Fairness and Effectiveness in Policing: The Evidence*, ed. Wesley G. Skogan and Kathleen Frydl (Washington, DC: The National Academies Press, 2003).

2. U.S. Department of Justice, Bureau of Justice Statistics, *Criminal Victimization, 2008* (Washington, DC: Office of Justice Programs, 2009).

3. In Canada, however, the proportion of victims not reporting is increasing by about 5 percent every five years. In Canada in 2005, the proportion of nonreporting for property crime was down to 63 percent, though nonreporting rates for property crimes where a significant loss was incurred were closer to those of the United States. Statistics Canada, *Criminal Victimization in Canada, 2004*, Juristat 25, no. 7 (Ottawa, ON: Canadian Centre for Justice Statistics, 2005).

4. Jan van Dijk, John van Kesteren, and Paul Smit, *Criminal Victimisation in International Perspective: Key Findings from the 2004–2005 ICVS and EU ICS* (The Hague: Boom Legal Publishers, 2008).

5. Dean Kilpatrick, Heidi Resnick, Kenneth J. Ruggiero, Lauren Conoscenti, and Jenna McCauley, *Drug-Facilitated, Incapacitated, and Forcible Rape: A National Study* (Washington, DC: National Institute of Justice, 2007).

6. U.S. Department of Justice, "Offenses Cleared," Federal Bureau of Investigation, Criminal Justice Information Services website, www.fbi.gov/ucr/cius2008/offenses/clearances/index.html (accessed April 23, 2010).

7. Irvin Waller, *Less Law, More Order: The Truth about Reducing Crime* (Westport, CT: Praeger Imprint Series, 2006), 14.

8. The percentages in the figure are taken from table 101 in Cathy T. Maston, "Criminal Victimization in the United States, 2007 Statistical Tables," Bureau of Justice Statistics website, http://bjs.ojp.usdoj.gov/index.cfm?ty=pbdetail&iid=1743 (accessed April 6, 2010). The groupings are as follows—prevention includes: stop or prevent the incident, prevent further crimes by offender against victim, prevent crime by offender against anyone; recover property includes: recover property, collect insurance; duty includes: because it was a crime, duty to notify the police; and to punish offender includes: punish offender, catch or find offender; other reasons are omitted for ease of understanding.

9. Michigan Legislature, "William Van Regenmorter Crime Victims Rights Act and Constitutional Amendment," Michigan Legislature website, www.legislature.mi.gov/documents/Publications/CrimeVictims.pdf (accessed April 6, 2010).

10. Waller, *Less Law, More Order*, 90.

11. National Research Council, *Fairness and Effectiveness in Policing*.

12. National Sheriffs' Association, *First Response to Victims of Crime: A Guide Book for Law Enforcement Officers* (Washington, DC: U.S. Department of Justice, 2008).

13. Lisa Newmark, *Crime Victims' Needs and VOCA-Funded Services: Findings and Recommendations from Two National Studies* (Washington, DC: National Institute of Justice, 2006), 2.

14. International Association of Chiefs of Police, *Enhancing Law Enforcement Response to Victims: A 21st Century Strategy* (Alexandria, VA: International Association of Chiefs of Police, 2008).

15. National Research Council, *Fairness and Effectiveness in Policing*.

16. International Association of Chiefs of Police, *Enhancing Law Enforcement Response*, 13–15.

17. Holly Johnson and Myrna Dawson, *Violence against Women in Canada: Research and Policy Perspectives* (Toronto: Oxford University Press, 2010); and Rebecca Campbell, "Rape Survivors' Experiences with the Legal and Medical Systems: Do Rape Victim Advocates Make a Difference?" *Violence Against Women* 12 (2006): 30.

18. U.S. Department of Justice, Office for Victims of Crime, *New Directions from the Field: Victims' Rights and Services for the 21st Century* (Washington, DC: U.S. Department of Justice, Office of Justice Programs, 1998).

19. Evan Stark and Eve S. Buzawa, *Violence against Women in Families and Relationships*, vol. 1 (Santa Barbara, CA: Praeger, 2009), vii–xviii.

CHAPTER 4

1. United States, *President's Task Force on Victims of Crime Final Report* (Washington, DC: U.S. Government Printing Office, 1982).

2. National Association of Crime Compensation Boards, "Crime Victim Compensation Helps Victims," National Association of Crime Compensation Boards website, www.nacvcb.org/ (accessed March 20, 2010).

3. Rape, Abuse and Incest National Network, "Mandatory Reporting of Child Abuse," Rape, Abuse and Incest National Network website, www.rainn.org/public-policy/sexual -assault-issues/mandatory-reporting-child-abuse (accessed March 20, 2010).

4. The National Crime Victim Bar Association, "Helping Crime Victims Pursue Civil Justice," The National Crime Victim Bar Association website, www.victimbar.org (accessed April 7, 2010).

5. Safe Horizon, "Safe Horizon," Safe Horizon website, www.safehorizon.org/ (accessed March 20, 2010); and Helpguide, "Helpguide," Helpguide website, www.helpguide .org (accessed March 20, 2010).

6. Institute of Medicine, "Treatment of Posttraumatic Stress Disorder: An Assessment of the Evidence," National Academies Press, http://books.nap.edu/openbook.php?record_ id=11955&page=R1 (accessed April 7, 2010).

7. Ted Miller, Mark Cohen, and Brian Wiersema, *Victim Costs and Consequences: A New Look* (Washington, DC: National Institute of Justice, 1996), 9–13.

8. Lisa Newmark, *Crime Victims' Needs and VOCA-Funded Services: Findings and Recommendations from Two National Studies* (Washington, DC: National Institute of Justice, 2006), 5.

9. National Organization for Victim Assistance, *Victim Rights and Services: A Legislative Directory* (Washington, DC: National Organization for Victim Assistance, 1988).

10. Ellen Brickman, *Development of a National Study of Victim Needs and Assistance* (Washington, DC: National Institute of Justice, 2002).

11. Newmark, *Crime Victims' Needs*, 16.

12. Newmark, *Crime Victims' Needs*, 23–24.

13. Mike Maguire and Claire Corbett, *The Effects of Crime and the Work of Victims Support Schemes* (Aldershot, UK: Gower, 1987).

14. U.S. Department of Justice, Office on Violence Against Women, *2006 Biennial Report to Congress on the Effectiveness of Grant Programs Under the Violence against Women Act* (Washington, DC: U.S. Department of Justice, 2006); Office on Violence Against Women, *S.T.O.P. Program Services, Training, Officers, Prosecutors, Annual Report 2006* (Washington, DC: U.S. Department of Justice, 2006).

15. Eleanor Lyon, Shannon Lane, and Anne Menard, "Meeting Survivors' Needs: A Multi-state Study of Domestic Violence Shelter Experience," National Resource Center on Domestic Violence website, http://new.vawnet.org/ (accessed April 18, 2010).

16. Ten thousand beds relative to twenty thousand means that the daily shortfall is 50 percent. A daily rate of 20,000 is equivalent to 300,000 over a year or a factor of 15. So the shortfall is 10,000°365/15, or 243,000.

17. Statistics Canada, *Residents of Canada's Shelters for Abused Women, 2008* (Ottawa, ON: Government of Canada, 2009).

18. U.S. Department of Justice, Office on Violence Against Women, *S.T.O.P. Program*.

19. Dean Kilpatrick, Heidi Resnick, Kenneth J. Ruggiero, Lauren Conoscenti, and Jenna McCauley, *Drug-Facilitated, Incapacitated, and Forcible Rape: A National Study* (Washington, DC: U.S. Department of Justice, National Institute of Justice, 2007).

20. Rebecca Campbell, Debra Patterson, and Lauren Lichty, "The Effectiveness of Sexual Assault Nurse Examiner (SANE) Programs: A Review of Psychological, Medical, Legal, and Community Outcomes," *Trauma, Violence, and Abuse* 6, no. 4 (2005): 313–29.

Holly Johnson and Myrna Dawson, *Violence against Women in Canada: Research and Policy Perspectives* (Toronto: Oxford University Press, 2010).

21. National Children's Alliance, "Child Advocacy—Putting the needs of child abuse victims first," National Children's Alliance website, www.nationalchildrensalliance.org/ (accessed March 20, 2010).

22. National Research Council, *Elder Mistreatment: Abuse, Neglect, and Exploitation in an Aging America. Panel to Review Risk and Prevalence of Elder Abuse*, ed. Richard J. Bonnie and Robert B. Wallace (Washington, DC: National Academies Press, 2003); American Psychological Association, "Elder Abuse and Neglect: In Search of Solutions," American Psychological Association website, www.apa.org/pi/aging/resources/guides/elder-abuse.aspx (accessed March 20, 2010).

CHAPTER 5

1. National Center for Victims of Crime, "National Crime Victim Rights Week Resource Guide: Crime Victimization in the United States: Statistical Overview," National Center for Victims of Crime website, www.ncvc.org/ncvc/AGP.Net/Components/document Viewer/Download.aspxnz?DocumentID=47449 (accessed February 21, 2010).

2. U.S. Department of Justice, Bureau of Justice Statistics, "Criminal Victimization in the United States, 2007 Statistical Tables," Bureau of Justice Statistics website, http://bjs .ojp.usdoj.gov/content/pub/pdf/cvus07.pdf (accessed April 8, 2010); see table 82.

3. U.S. Department of Justice, "Criminal Victimization, 2007 Statistical Tables"; see tables 78, 83, and 89.

4. See for instance, U.S. Government Accountability Office, *Crime Victim Rights Act: Increasing Victim Awareness and Clarifying Applicability to the District of Columbia Will Improve Implementation of the Act* (Washington, DC: United States Government Accountability Office, 2009).

5. U.S. Department of Justice, Office for Victims of Crime, *Ordering Restitution to the Crime Victim* (Washington, DC: U.S. Department of Justice, Office of Justice Programs, 2002).

6. U.S. Department of Justice, Office for Victims of Crime, *New Directions from the Field: Victims' Rights and Services for the 21st Century* (Washington, DC: U.S. Department of Justice, Office of Justice Programs, 1998), 357.

7. U.S. Department of Justice, *Ordering Restitution.*

8. U.S. Department of Justice, *Ordering Restitution.*

9. U.S. Department of Justice, *Ordering Restitution*, 2.

10. U.S. Department of Justice, Office for Victims of Crime, *Victims of Crime Act Crime Victims Fund* (Washington, DC: U.S. Department of Justice, Office of Justice Programs, 2005).

11. Lisa Newmark, Judy Bonderman, Barbara Smith, and E. Blaine Liner, *The National Evaluation of State Victims of Crime Act Assistance and Compensation Programs: Trends and Strategies for the Future* (Full Report) (Washington, DC: National Institute of Justice, 2006).

12. Pennsylvania Commission on Crime and Delinquency, "Assessing the Use of Pennsylvania's Victims Compensation Assistance Program," National Criminal Justice Service website, www.ncjrs.gov/App/Publications/abstract.aspx?ID=245555 (accessed March, 2008).

13. Roy McMurtry, "Report on Financial Assistance for Victims of Crime in Ontario," Ontario Ministry of the Attorney General website, www.attorneygeneral.jus.gov.on.ca/english/about/pubs/mcmurtry/mcmurtry_report.pdf (accessed April 24, 2010).

14. National Crime Victim Bar Association, *Civil Justice for Victims of Crime* (Washington, DC: National Center for Victims of Crime, 2007).

15. National Crime Victim Bar Association, *Civil Justice*.

16. Federal Bureau of Investigation, "Offenses Cleared," U.S. Department of Justice, Criminal Justice Information Services Division website, www.fbi.gov/ucr/cius2008/offenses/clearances/index.html (accessed March 21, 2010).

17. Heather Strang and Lawrence Sherman, "Restorative Justice to Reduce Victimization," in *Preventing Crime: What Works for Children, Offenders, Victims, and Places*, ed. Brandon Welsh and David P. Farrington, 147–60 (Dordrecht, Netherlands: Springer, 2006).

CHAPTER 6

1. United States, *President's Task Force on Victims of Crime Final Report* (Washington, DC: U.S. Government Printing Office, 1982), 114.

2. United States, *President's Task Force*.

3. United States, *President's Task Force*, 9.

4. United States, *President's Task Force*.

5. United States, *President's Task Force*.

6. See NVCAP, "State VRAs," www.nvcap.org/ (accessed April 10, 2010).

7. NVCAP, "Making Illinois' Victims' Rights Enforceable," National Victims Constitutional Amendment Project website, www.nvcap.org/ (accessed April 10, 2010).

8. NVCAP, "Making Illinois' Victims' Rights Enforceable."

9. The amendment required a two-thirds majority each from the Senate and the House of Representatives. It would then have required the approval of three-quarters of state legislatures.

10. U.S. Government Accountability Office, *Crime Victim Rights Act: Increasing Victim Awareness and Clarifying Applicability to the District of Columbia Will Improve Implementation of the Act* (Washington, DC: U.S. Government Accountability Office, 2009).

11. California Secretary of State, "Votes For and Against," California Secretary of State website, www.sos.ca.gov/elections/sov/2008_general/7_votes_for_against.pdf (accessed January 11, 2010).

12. California Secretary of State, "Text of Proposed Laws," California Secretary of State website, http://voterguide.sos.ca.gov/past/2008/general/text-proposed-laws/text-of-proposed-laws.pdf#prop9 (accessed January 11, 2010).

13. California Secretary of State, "Text of Proposed Laws."

14. NVCAP, "Making Illinois' Victims' Rights Enforceable."

15. International Criminal Court, "Basic Legal Texts," ICC website, www.icc-cpi.int/Menus/ICC/Legal+Texts+and+Tools/ (accessed March 24, 2010).

16. International Criminal Court, "Reparation for Victims," ICC website, www.icc-cpi.int/Menus/ICC/Structure+of+the+Court/Victims/Reparation/Reparation+for+victims.htm (accessed August 31, 2010).

17. National Crime Victim Bar Association, *Civil Justice for Victims of Crime* (Washington, DC: National Center for Victims of Crime, 2007), see section on "Considerations for Pursuing Civil Justice."

CHAPTER 7

1. World Health Organization, *World Report on Violence and Health* (Geneva: World Health Organization, 2002).
2. Mothers Against Drunk Driving, "Campaign to Eliminate Drunk Driving," MADD website, www.madd.org/Drunk-Driving.aspx (accessed April 7, 2010).
3. Bureau of Justice Statistics, "Sourcebook of Criminal Justice Statistics Online," Sourcebook of Criminal Justice Statistics website, www.albany.edu/sourcebook/wk1/t228.wk1 (accessed April 7, 2010).
4. Home Office, *Crime in England and Wales, 2008/09, Findings from the British Crime Survey and Police Recorded Crime* (London: Home Office, 2009); see table 5a.
5. U.S. Department of Justice, "Gun Violence Prevention," National Institute of Justice website, www.ojp.usdoj.gov/nij/topics/crime/gun-violence/prevention/welcome.htm (accessed March 28, 2010).
6. Notably, the decreases exceeded the regional trends by 15 percent in New Haven, Portland, and Winston-Salem, and by 30 percent in Indianapolis. See Jan Roehl, Dennis P. Rosenbaum, Sandra K. Costello, James R. Coldren, Jr., Amie M. Schuck, Laura Kunard, and David R. Forde, *Strategic Approaches to Community Safety Initiative (SACSI) in 10 U.S. Cities: The Building Blocks for Project Safe Neighborhoods* (Washington, DC: National Institute of Justice, 2006), 72–73.
7. Edmund F. McGarrell, Natalie Kroovand, et al., *Project Safe Neighborhoods—a National Program to Reduce Gun Crime: Final Project* (Washington, DC: National Institute of Justice, 2009), vii.
8. Wesley G. Skogan, Susan M. Hartnett, Natalie Bump, and Jill Dubois, *Evaluation of CeaseFire-Chicago* (Washington, DC: National Institute of Justice, 2008); see executive summary at Institute for Policy Research, "CeaseFire Evaluation Report," Northwestern University website, www.northwestern.edu/ipr/publications/ceasefire.html (accessed March 28, 2010).
9. WHO, *World Report*.
10. Laura Dugan, Daniel S. Nagin, and Richard Rosenfeld, "Do Domestic Violence Services Save Lives?" *NIJ Journal* 250 (2003).
11. Holly Johnson and Myrna Dawson, *Violence against Women in Canada: Research and Policy Perspectives* (Toronto: Oxford University Press, 2010).
12. U.S. Department of Justice, Office on Violence Against Women, *S.T.O.P. Program Services, Training, Officers, Prosecutors, Annual Report 2006* (Washington, DC: U.S. Department of Justice, Office on Violence Against Women, 2006).
13. Dean Kilpatrick, Heidi Resnick, Kenneth J. Ruggiero, Lauren Conoscenti, and Jenna McCauley, *Drug-Facilitated, Incapacitated, and Forcible Rape: A National Study* (Washington, DC: U.S. Department of Justice, National Institute of Justice, 2007).

14. Centre for Prevention Science, "Strategies for Healthy Youth Relationships," Centre for Prevention Science website, http://youthrelationships.org/ (accessed April 2, 2010).

15. White Ribbon Campaign, "The White Ribbon Campaign," WRC website, www .whiteribbon.ca/ (accessed April 2, 2010).

16. Johnson and Dawson, *Violence against Women.*

17. Violence Interpretation and Prevention Center, "Green Dot Strategy," University of Kentucky website, www.uky.edu/StudentAffairs/VIPCenter/greendot.html (accessed April 2, 2010); and University of Ottawa, "Right to Respect," University of Ottawa website, www .respect.uottawa.ca/en/ (accessed April 2, 2010).

18. Centers for Disease Control and Prevention, "Child Maltreatment," CDC website, www.cdc.gov/ViolencePrevention/childmaltreatment/index.html (accessed March 25, 2010).

19. Ronald J. Prinz, Matthew R. Sanders, Cheri J. Shapiro, Daniel J. Whitaker, and John R. Lutzker, "Population-Based Prevention of Child Maltreatment: The U.S. Triple P System Population Trial," *Prevention Science* 10 (2009): 1–12.

20. Institute for the Prevention of Crime, "Making Cities Safer: Action Briefs for Municipal Stakeholders, 2009," University of Ottawa website, www.sciencessociales.uottawa .ca/ipc/eng/MCS_actionbriefs.asp (accessed March 25, 2010).

CHAPTER 8

1. U.S. Department of Justice, Office for Victims of Crime, *New Directions from the Field: Victims' Rights and Services for the 21st Century* (Washington, DC: U.S. Department of Justice, Office of Justice Programs, 1998).

2. U.S. Government Accountability Office, *Crime Victim Rights Act: Increasing Victim Awareness and Clarifying Applicability to the District of Columbia Will Improve Implementation of the Act* (Washington, DC: U.S. Government Accountability Office, 2009).

3. Ted Miller, Mark Cohen, and Brian Wiersema, *Victim Costs and Consequences: A New Look* (Washington, DC: National Institute of Justice, U.S. Department of Justice, 1996).

APPENDIX

1. This model law was inspired by the draft convention produced in 2005—see International Victimology Institute Tilburg, *Compilation of International Victims' Rights Instruments*, ed. Marc Groenhuijsen and Rianne Letschert (Nijmegen, Netherlands: Wolf Legal Publishers, 2009); International Victimology Institute Tilburg, "Towards Implementation of the UN Declaration on Basic Principles of Justice for Victims of Crime and Abuse of Power—Preparing a Draft Convention on the Rights of Victims of Crime, Abuse of Power and Terrorism," *Report on Expert Group Meeting* (Tilburg: University of Tilburg, 2005). Some sections from the convention have been eliminated as they are not applicable to a national law. Some sections in the model law are identical to those drafted by the experts. Though I was one of the experts, the conclusions from this book have resulted in some refinements to particular sections.

PRINCIPAL SOURCES

Beloof, Douglas, Paul Cassell, and Steve Twist. *Victims in Criminal Procedure*. Durham, NC: Carolina Academic Press, 2006.

Brickman, Ellen. *Development of a National Study of Victim Needs and Assistance*. Washington, DC: National Institute of Justice, 2002.

Campbell, Rebecca. "Rape Survivors' Experiences with the Legal and Medical Systems: Do Rape Victim Advocates Make a Difference?" *Violence Against Women* 12, no. 1 (2006): 30–35.

Campbell, Rebecca, Debra Patterson, and Lauren Lichty. "The Effectiveness of Sexual Assault Nurse Examiner (SANE) Programs: A Review of Psychological, Medical, Legal, and Community Outcomes." *Trauma, Violence, and Abuse* 6, no. 4 (2005): 313–29.

Canada. Department of Justice. "Canadian Statement of Basic Principles of Justice for Victims of Crime, 2003." Department of Justice Canada. www.justice.gc.ca/eng/pi/pcvi -cpcv/pub/03/princ.html (accessed April 4, 2010).

Canada. Standing Committee on Justice and Human Rights. *Victims' Rights—a Voice Not a Veto*. Ottawa, ON: Parliament of Canada, 2000.

Chan, Wing-Cheong, ed. *Support for Victims of Crime in Asia*. London: Routledge, 2008.

Council of Europe. *European Convention on the Compensation of Victims of Violent Crimes* (ETS no. 116, 24. XI). Strasbourg: Council of Europe, 1983. Ratified 1988.

European Council. *Framework Decision of 15 March 2001 on the Standing of Victims in Criminal Proceedings* (2001/220/JHA). Brussels: Commission of the European Communities, 2001.

Feder, Lynette, D. B. Wilson, and S. Austin. *Court-Mandated Interventions for Individuals Convicted of Domestic Violence*. Oslo: The Campbell Collaboration, 2008.

Federal Bureau of Investigation. "Offenses Cleared." U.S. Department of Justice, Criminal Justice Information Services Division, 2010. www.fbi.gov/ucr/cius2008/offenses/clearances/index.html (accessed March 21, 2010).

Fisher, Bonnie. "The Effects of Survey Question Wording on Rape Estimates: Estimates from a Quasi-Experimental Design." *Violence Against Women* 15, no. 2 (2009): 133–47.

Fisher, Bonnie, and John J. Sloan. *Campus Crime: Legal, Social and Policy Perspectives.* Springfield, IL: Charles C. Thomas, 2007.

Gaudreault, Arlène, and Irvin Waller. "Xe Symposium international de victimologie: Textes choisies du Symposium." Papers presented at the Association québécoise Plaidoyer-Victimes, Montréal, August 2001.

Groenhuijsen, Marc, and Rianne Letschert, eds. *Compilation of International Victims' Rights Instruments.* Nijmegen, Netherlands: Wolf Legal Publishers, 2009.

Helpguide. "Post-Traumatic Stress Disorder." Helpguide website. www.helpguide.org (accessed March 20, 2010).

Herman, Susan. *Parallel Justice for Victims of Crime.* Washington, DC: National Center for Victims of Crime, 2010.

Home Office. *Crime in England and Wales, 2008/09: Findings from the British Crime Survey and Police recorded crime.* London: Home Office, 2009.

Institute of Medicine. "Treatment of Posttraumatic Stress Disorder: An Assessment of the Evidence Committee on Treatment of Posttraumatic Stress Disorder." National Academies Press, 2007. http://books.nap.edu/openbook.php?record_id=11955&page=R1 (accessed April 7, 2010).

International Association of Chiefs of Police. *Enhancing Law Enforcement Response to Victims: A 21st Century Strategy.* Alexandria, VA: International Association of Chiefs of Police, 2008.

———. *Sexual Assault Guidelines: Supplemental Report Form and Investigative Strategies.* Alexandria, VA: International Association of Chiefs of Police, 2008.

———. *What Do Victims Want? Effective Strategies to Achieve Justice for Victims of Crime.* Alexandria, VA: International Association of Chiefs of Police, 2000.

International Victimology Institute Tilburg. "Towards Implementation of the UN Declaration on Basic Principles of Justice for Victims of Crime and Abuse of Power—Preparing a Draft Convention on the Rights of Victims of Crime, Abuse of Power and Terrorism." Report on Expert Group Meeting. Tilburg, Netherlands: University of Tilburg, 2006.

Johnson, Holly, and Myrna Dawson. *Violence against Women in Canada: Research and Policy Perspectives.* Toronto: Oxford University Press, 2010.

Karmen, Andrew. *Crime Victims: An Introduction to Victimology* 5th ed. Belmont, CA: Wadsworth/Thomson, 2004.

Karstedt, Susanne, Ian Loader, and Heather Strang, eds. *Emotions, Crime and Justice.* Oxford: Hart, 2010.

Kilpatrick, Dean, and Ron Acierno. "Mental Health Needs of Crime Victims: Epidemiology." *Journal of Traumatic Stress* 16, no. 2 (April 2003): 119–32.

Kilpatrick, Dean, Heidi Resnick, Kenneth J. Ruggiero, Lauren Conoscenti, and Jenna McCauley. *Drug-Facilitated, Incapacitated, and Forcible Rape: A National Study.* Washington, DC: National Institute of Justice, 2007.

Klausner, Lawrence D. *Son of Sam: Based on the Authorized Transcription of the Tapes, Official Documents and Diaries of David Berkowitz*. New York: McGraw-Hill, 1980.

Lyon, Eleanor, Shannon Lane, and Anne Menard. "Meeting Survivors' Needs: A Multi-State Study of Domestic Violence Shelter Experience." National Resource Center on Domestic Violence. http://new.vawnet.org/ (accessed April 18, 2010).

Maguire, Mike, and Claire Corbett. *The Effects of Crime and the Work of Victims Support Schemes*. Aldershot, UK: Gower, 1987.

McGarrell, Edmund F., Natalie Kroovand Hipple, Nicholas Corsaro, Timothy S. Bynum, Heather Perez, Carol A. Zimmermann, and Melissa Garmo. *Project Safe Neighborhoods—a National Program to Reduce Gun Crime: Final Project*. Washington, DC: National Institute of Justice, 2009.

McMurtry, Roy. "Report on Financial Assistance for Victims of Crime in Ontario." Ontario Ministry of the Attorney General, 2008. www.attorneygeneral.jus.gov.on.ca/english/about/pubs/mcmurtry/mcmurtry_report.pdf (accessed April 24, 2010).

Meili, Trisha. *I Am the Central Park Jogger: A Story of Hope and Possibility*. New York: Scribner, 2003.

Miller, Susan L., and LeeAnn Iovanni. "Domestic Violence Policy in the United States: Contemporary Issues." In *Gender Violence: Interdisciplinary Perspectives*, edited by Laura L. O'Toole, Margy L. Kiter Edwards, and Jessica R. Schiffman, 287–96. New York: New York University Press, 2007.

Miller, Ted, Mark Cohen, and Brian Wiersema. *Victim Costs and Consequences: A New Look*. Washington, DC: National Institute of Justice, 1996.

Minnesota Department of Health. *Costs of Sexual Violence in Minnesota*. Minneapolis: Minnesota Department of Health, 2007.

Mothers Against Drunk Driving Canada. "The Magnitude of the Alcohol/Drug-Related Crash Problem in Canada." MADD Canada. http://madd.ca/english/research/magnitude memo.html (accessed April 3, 2010).

National Center for Education Statistics and Bureau of Justice Statistics. *Indicators of School Crime and Safety*. Washington, DC: U.S. Departments of Education and Justice, 2010.

National Center for Victims of Crime. "National Crime Victim Rights Week Resource Guide: Crime Victimization in the United States: Statistical Overview." National Center for Victims of Crime. www.ncvc.org/ncvc/AGP.Net/Components/documentViewer/Download.aspxnz?DocumentID=47449 (accessed February 21, 2010).

National Crime Victim Bar Association. *Civil Justice for Victims of Crime*. Washington, DC: National Center for Victims of Crime, 2007.

National Research Council. *Fairness and Effectiveness in Policing: The Evidence*. Edited by Wesley G. Skogan and Kathleen Frydl. Washington, DC: National Academies Press, 2003.

National Research Council, Division of Behavioral and Social Sciences and Education. *Committee on Understanding Crime Trends Report*. Edited by Arthur S. Goldberger and Richard Rosenfeld. Washington, DC: National Academy of Sciences, 2008.

National Sheriffs' Association. *First Response to Victims of Crime: A Guide Book for Law Enforcement Officers*. Washington, DC: U.S. Department of Justice, 2008.

National Victim Constitutional Amendment Passage. "Making Illinois' Victims' Rights Enforceable." National Victims Constitutional Amendment Project. www.nvcap.org/ (accessed April 3, 2010).

Newmark, Lisa. *Crime Victims' Needs and VOCA-Funded Services: Findings and Recommendations from Two National Studies*. Washington, DC: National Institute of Justice, 2006.

Newmark, Lisa, Judy Bonderman, Barbara Smith, and E. Blaine Liner. *The National Evaluation of State Victims of Crime Act Assistance and Compensation Programs: Trends and Strategies for the Future* (Full Report). Washington, DC: National Institute of Justice, 2006.

Ombudsman of Ontario. *Adding Insult to Injury. Investigation into the Treatment of Victims by the Criminal Injuries Compensation Board*. Toronto: Ombudsman of Ontario, 2007.

Pennsylvania Commission on Crime and Delinquency. "Assessing the Use of Pennsylvania's Victims Compensation Assistance Program." National Criminal Justice Service. www.ncjrs.gov/App/Publications/abstract.aspx?ID=245555 (accessed March 20, 2008).

Prinz, Ronald J., Matthew R. Sanders, Cheri J. Shapiro, Daniel J. Whitaker, and John R. Lutzker. "Population-Based Prevention of Child Maltreatment: The U.S. Triple P System Population Trial." *Prevention Science* 10 (2009): 1–12.

Roehl, Jan, Dennis P. Rosenbaum, Sandra K. Costello, James R. "Chip" Coldren, Jr., Amie M. Schuck, Laura Kunard, and David R. Forde. *Strategic Approaches to Community Safety Initiative (SACSI) in 10 U.S. Cities: The Building Blocks for Project Safe Neighborhoods*. Washington, DC: National Institute of Justice, 2006.

Rosenberg, Mark L., Alexander Butchart, James Mercy, Vasant Narasimhan, Hugh Waters, and Maureen S. Marshall. "Interpersonal Violence." In *Disease Control Priorities in Developing Countries*, 2nd ed., edited by Dean T. Jamison, Joel G. Breman, Anthony R. Measham, George Alleyne, Mariam Claeson, David B. Evans, Prabhat Jha, Anne Mills, and Philip Musgrove, 755–70. New York: Oxford University Press, 2006.

Sauvé, Julie. "Victim Services in Canada: Results from the Victim Services Survey 2007/2008." Justice Canada website, Victims of Crime Research Digest. www.justice.gc.ca/eng/pi/rs/rep-rap/rd-rr/rr07_vic4/p3.html (accessed March 26–30, 2010).

Seymour, Anne, and Steve Derene. "An Oral History of the Crime Victim Assistance Field." University of Akron. http://vroh.uakron.edu/index.php (accessed April 3, 2010).

Seymour, Anne, Morna Murray, Jane Sigmon, and Melissa Hook. *National Victim Assistance Academy*. Washington, DC: U.S. Department of Justice, Office for Victims of Crime, 2000.

Shapland, Joanna, Jon Willmore, and Peter Duff. *Victims in the Criminal Justice System*. Aldershot, UK: Gower, 1985.

Sherman, Lawrence, and Heather Strang. "Empathy for the Devil: The Nature and Nurture of Revenge." In *Emotions, Crime and Justice*, edited by Susanne Karstedt, Ian Loader, and Healther Strang. Oxford: Hart, 2010.

Skogan, Wesley G., Susan M. Hartnett, Natalie Bump, and Jill Dubois. *Evaluation of CeaseFire-Chicago*. Washington, DC: National Institute of Justice, 2008.

Stark, Evan, and Eve S. Buzawa. *Violence against Women in Families and Relationships*, Vol. 1. Santa Barbara, CA: Praeger, 2009.

Statistics Canada. *Criminal Victimization in Canada, 2004. Juristat* 25, no. 7. Ottawa, ON: Canadian Centre for Justice Statistics, 2005.

———. *Residents of Canada's Shelters for Abused Women*, 2008. Ottawa, ON: Canadian Centre for Justice Statistics, 2009.

Strang, Heather. *Repair of Revenge: Victims and Restorative Justice*. Oxford: Clarendon Press, 2002.

Stretesky, Paul B., Tara O'Connor Shelly, Michael J. Hogan, and N. Prabha Unnithan. "Sense-Making and Secondary Victimization among Unsolved Homicide Co-victims." Unpublished manuscript, Colorado State University, Center for the Study of Crime and Justice.

Tjaden, Patricia, and Nancy Thoennes. *Full Report of the Prevalence, Incidence, and Consequences of Violence against Women*. Washington, DC: National Institute of Justice and the Centers for Disease Control and Prevention, 2000.

United Nations. General Assembly. *Resolution and Declaration of Basic Principles of Justice for Victims of Crime and Abuse of Power*. New York: United Nations, 1985.

United Nations. Office for Drugs and Crime. *Guide for Policy Makers on the Implementation of the Declaration of Basic Principles of Justice for Victims of Crime and Abuse of Power*. New York: United Nations, 1999.

———. *Guidelines on Justice for Child Victims and Witnesses*. New York: United Nations, 2005.

———. *Handbook on Justice for Victims on the Use and Application of the Declaration of Basic Principles of Justice for Victims of Crime and Abuse of Power*. New York: United Nations, 1999.

United Nations. Preparatory Commission for the International Criminal Court. *Report on the International Seminar on Victims' Access to the International Criminal Court*. New York: United Nations, 1999.

United States. *President's Task Force on Victims of Crime Final Report*. Washington, DC: U.S. Government Printing Office, 1982.

U.S. Department of Justice. *Attorney General's Task Force on Family Violence*. Washington, DC: U.S. Government Printing Office, 1984.

U.S. Department of Justice, Bureau of Justice Statistics. *Criminal Victimization, 2008*. Washington, D.C.: Office of Justice Programs, 2009.

———. "Criminal Victimization in the United States, 2007 Statistical Tables." Bureau of Justice Statistics. http://bjs.ojp.usdoj.gov/content/pub/pdf/cvus07.pdf (accessed April 8, 2010).

U.S. Department of Justice, Office for Victims of Crime. *International Crime Victim Compensation Directory*. Washington, DC: U.S. Department of Justice, 1999.

———. "Nationwide Analysis—Performance Reports." U.S. Department of Justice, Office of Justice Programs 2009. www.ojp.usdoj.gov/ovc/fund/vocanpr_va08.html (accessed April 7, 2010).

———. *New Directions from the Field: Victims' Rights and Services for the 21st Century*. Washington, DC: U.S. Department of Justice, Office of Justice Programs, 1998.

———. *Ordering Restitution to the Crime Victim*. Washington, DC: U.S. Department of Justice, Office of Justice Programs, 2002.

———. *Report to the Nation 2007–2008*. Washington, DC: U.S. Department of Justice, Office of Justice Programs, 2009.

———. *Restitution: Making It Work*. Washington, DC: U.S. Department of Justice, 2002.

U.S. Department of Justice, Office on Violence against Women. *2006 Biennial Report to Congress on the Effectiveness of Grant Programs under the Violence against Women Act*. Washington, DC: U.S. Department of Justice, Office on Violence Against Women, 2006.

———. *S.T.O.P. Program Services, Training, Officers, Prosecutors, Annual Report 2006*. Washington, DC: U.S. Department of Justice, Office on Violence Against Women, 2006.

U.S. Government Accountability Office. *Crime Victim Rights Act: Increasing Victim Awareness and Clarifying Applicability to the District of Columbia Will Improve Implementation of the Act*. Washington, DC: U.S. Government Accountability Office, 2009.

Van Dijk, Jan, Robert Manchin, John van Kesteren, and Gergely Hideg. *The Burden of Crime in the EU: A Comparative Analysis of the European Survey of Crime and Safety*. Brussels: Gallup Europe, 2007.

Van Dijk, Jan, John van Kesteren, and Paul Smit. *Criminal Victimisation in International Perspective: Key Findings from the 2004–2005 ICVS and EU ICS*. The Hague: Boom Legal Publishers, 2008.

Victim Rights Working Group. *Strategy Meeting on the Development of Structures and Procedures for Victims at the International Criminal Court, 6–7 December, 2002: Summary of Proceedings and Recommendations*. London: Victim Rights Working Group, 2003.

Victim Support Europe. *Victims in Europe: Implementation of the EU Framework Decision on the Standing of Victims in the Criminal Proceedings in the Member States of the European Union*. Lisbon: Associação Portuguesa de Apoio à Vítima, 2010.

Voth, David L. *Quality Victim Advocacy: A Field Guide*. Bluffton, OH: Workplay, 2010.

Waller, Irvin. *Less Law, More Order: The Truth about Reducing Crime*. Westport, CT: Praeger Imprint Series, 2006.

———. "Harnessing Criminology and Victimology Internationally." In *Lessons from International/Comparative Criminology/Criminal Justice*, edited by John Winterdyk and Liqun Cao, 233–48. Toronto: De Sitter, 2004.

Waller, Irvin, and Norm Okihiro. *Burglary: The Victim and the Public*. Toronto: University of Toronto Press, 1978.

Wang, Ching-Tung, and John Holton. "Total Estimated Cost of Child Abuse and Neglect in the United States." Prevent Child Abuse America. www.preventchildabuse.org/about_us/media_releases/pcaa_pew_economic_impact_study_final.pdf (accessed April 4, 2010).

Wemmers, Jo-Anne. *Introduction à la victimologie*. Montreal: Les Presses de l'Université de Montreal, 2003.

World Health Organization. *Economic Dimensions of Interpersonal Violence*. Geneva: World Health Organization, 2004.

———. *World Report on Violence and Health*. Geneva: World Health Organization, 2002.

INDEX

ABOUT THE AUTHOR

Irvin Waller is an influential author, professor of criminology, and vice president of the International Organization for Victim Assistance.

He has won awards in the United States and internationally for his work to develop and advocate for a *magna carta* for victims. This became a reality when the UN General Assembly resolved to adopt and implement the Declaration of Basic Principles of Justice for Victims of Crime and Abuse of Power. The *magna carta* has influenced the International Criminal Court and changed crime policy from Japan to Mexico. He was elected to the Board of the National Organization for Victim Assistance and was selected as one of the pioneers of the victim rights movement in the United States. He was reelected six consecutive times to the executive of the World Society of Victimology, including organizing its most successful symposium, serving as its president, and serving many times as its secretary-general.

He is a popular speaker and has advised the governments of more than forty countries on ways to prevent crime and respect victims. His work to stop victimization—the ultimate victim right—has won recognition across the world, particularly from his role as the founding executive director of the International Centre for Prevention of Crime, affiliated with the UN. His recent book *Less Law, More Order: The Truth about Reducing Crime* (available in five languages) is making legislators in North America, Europe, and Latin America rethink crime policy to prevent violence.